CAN RAIL SAVE THE CITY?

The Anglo-German Foundation for the Study of Industrial Society was established by an agreement between the British and German governments after a state visit to Britain by the late President Heinemann and incorporated by Royal Charter in 1973. Funds were initially provided by the German Government; since 1979, both governments have been contributing.

The Foundation aims to contribute to the knowledge and understanding of industrial society in the two countries and to promote contacts between them. It funds selected research projects and conferences on industrial, economic and social subjects designed to be of practical use to policymakers.

Anglo-German Foundation for the Study of Industrial Society
17 Bloomsbury Square
London WC1A 2LP
Telephone: 01 404 3137

The Joint Centre for Land Development Studies was founded in 1981 to bring together the common research interests of the University of Reading and the College of Estate Management in identifying and improving the land development process. The Centre's chief objective is to carry out land-based research by drawing on the knowledge and expertise of individuals both on the campus and from the professions involved in land management and development.

The Joint Centre for Land Development Studies
Whiteknights
Reading
Berkshire RG6 2AW
England
Telephone: Reading (0734) 861101 ext 67
Telex 848896 CEMRDG-G

Can Rail Save the City?

The Impacts of Rail Rapid Transit and
Pedestrianisation on British and German Cities

PETER HALL
*Professor of Geography,
University of Reading and
Professor of City and Regional Planning,
University of California
and*
CARMEN HASS-KLAU
Transportation Consultant

Gower

Published by

Gower Publishing Company Limited,
Gower House,
Croft Road,
Aldershot,
Hants GU11 3HR,
England.

Gower Publishing Company,
Old Post Road,
Brookfield,
Vermont 05036
U.S.A.

British Library Cataloguing in Publication Data

Hall, Peter, *1932-*
  Can rail save the city? : the impacts of rail rapid
transit and pedestrianisation on British and
German cities.
  1. Local transit——Great Britain   2. Local transit
——Germany (West)   3. Street-railroads——Great
Britain   4. Street-railroads——Germany (West)
  5. Subways——Great Britain   6. Subways——
Germany (West)
  I. Title   II. Hass-Klau, Carmen
  388.4'2'0941   HE4714

Printed in Great Britain

ISBN: 0 566 00947 1

Contents

Tables

Figures

Plates

Acknowledgements

The study on which this book is based was made possible by a grant from the Anglo-German Foundation to the Joint Centre for Land Development Studies, University of Reading. We are most grateful to the Trustees of the Foundation and in particular to its Director, Dr Wiener.

The research involved interviews, often long and probing, with busy officials in city administrations and public transport organisations in the thirteen case-study cities. We are extremely grateful to them all for giving so generously of their time and patience. We also received helpful assistance and advice from the various German statistical offices we consulted. We have special thanks to the following institutions and individuals in:

Bonn: Federal Ministry of Transport (Herrn Parnow); Bundesforschungsanstalt für Landeskunde und Raumordnung (Dr Türke).

Bremen: IHK; Einzelhandelsverband Nordsee Bremen e.V., the Stadtplanungsamt; the Verkehrsplanungsamt, Bremer Strassenbahn AG (Dr Meyer).

Dortmund: the Stadtplanungsamt, Einzelhandelsverband Westfalen-Mitte e.V.

Essen: the Stadtplanungsamt; IHK (Dr. Flitsch); Einzelhandelsverband; Essener VAG (Herrn Obst); Karlstadt AG (Dr. Kläsener).

Hannover: the Stadtplanungsamt (Herrn Lenk, Herrn Römer; U-Bahn Hannover (Herrn Scheelhaase); ÜSTRA (Dr. Fels), Herrn Professor Rippel, Einzelhandelsverband Niedersachsen e.V.

Köln: Hauptgemeinschaft des Deutschen Einzelhandels; the Stadtplanungsamt (Herrn Dupke and Herrn Friedrichs); IHK (Dr. Herrmanns).

München: the Stadtplanungsamt (Herrn Heidebach); the Verkehrsabteilung der Stadt München (Herrn Schwerdtfeger); IHK (Herrn Kürzinger), Landesverband Mittelfranken des Bayerischen Einzelhandels e.V. Bezirk Mittelfranken.

Nürnberg: the Stadtplanungsamt (Herrn Achnitz); IHK (Dr. Riesterer); Landesverband des Bayerischen Einzelhandels e.V.; Amt für Stadtforschung und Statistik (Herrn Schneider and Dr. Gütter); Verkehr AG Nürnberg (Dr. Siegloch and Herrn Wentzel).

In Great Britain we want to thank all the Passenger Transport Executives in the six case-study cities for their cooperation, especially in:

Glasgow: Strathclyde PTE (Mr Westwell, Director General, and Mrs Howatt).

Leeds: West Yorkshire PTE (Mr Cottham, Director-General).

Manchester: Greater Manchester PTE (Mr T. Young).

Newcastle: Tyne and Wear PTE (Mr Howard, Director-General).

Sheffield: South Yorkshire PTE (Mr Hellewell, Director-General; Mr Barlow).

We also obtained great assistance from officials in offices of the English County Councils, Strathclyde Regional Council and district councils, too numerous to list individually.

Furthermore we would like to thank the Chambers of Commerce in Glasgow, Leeds, Manchester, Newcastle and Sheffield; valuable contributions by Marks and Spencer, House of Fraser, John Lewis Partnership, Binns and Debenhams helped to complete this study.

Our particular thanks are due to Professor R. Monheim for his unstinting encouragement and help throughout the study of pedestrianisation. Ross Davies gave us useful advice on Newcastle's shopping developments.

Needless to say, despite all this help, the authors alone bear responsibility for any errors or omissions.

Mary Tull and Jacquie Lewis typed large sections of the manuscript with their customary efficiency and David Bishop, Co-Director of the Joint Centre, helped to complete the manuscript in its present state. Kathleen King provided her usual impeccable cartography. Patricia Davison copy-edited the final text and Dr Graham Crampton shared in the onerous job of checking the final proofs. Our thanks go to them all.

Finally we should like to thank Carmen Hass-Klau's colleagues in the public transport group of East Sussex County for their help and support.

Though the book was completed while one of us (Carmen Hass-Klau) was an employee of the East Sussex County Council, the views expressed in it are those of the individual authors, not of the Council.

Peter Hall
Carmen Hass-Klau

1 Introduction

In August 1984, British newspapers reported that the age of the tram had
dawned again in London. The last double-deck red tramcar, now remembered
only from old Edwardian music-hall songs, had made its farewell trip in
1952, a victim of age and obsolescence. Thirty-two years later, London
Regional Transport placed a contract for a brand-new light rail transit
system for the former docklands area of East London. The high-technology
driverless vehicles that would run on it, though not easily recognisable
as such, were nevertheless a late twentieth-century version of the old
tram.

One significant detail, tucked away in the news reports, was that the
new trams - though built in Britain - would be of German design. The
reason was that Britain had forgotten how to build trams. Between 1949
and 1961, every other major British city had also scrapped them. The
seaside resort of Blackpool was left as the only place in Britain,
outside tramway museums, where it was possible to see real trams in
motion. So the home market disappeared, and with it the industry.

That was a problem not only for the planners in London, but in a number
of other cities also. Manchester, where the trams went in 1949, was also
contemplating a new light rail system; so was Birmingham, where they last
ran in Coronation year 1953; so was Sheffield, which had been among the
last cities to see them go in 1960. And in all these cities, councillors
and transport specialists were casting envious and admiring looks at the
Federal Republic of Germany.

The reason why they were all having to contemplate buying German
technology - even Birmingham, with its proud tradition of vehicle
manufacture - was that the German cities had never scrapped their trams.
Instead, they had modernised and developed them. They had bought new
vehicles, introduced signal controls to speed them up and make them
safer, and finally put them underground in their central and inner areas.
The trams of the 1950s had become the Stadtbahn - literally City Rail -
systems of the 1980s.

The German cities had not stopped there. A few of them, like München
and Nürnberg, had actually completed fully fledged underground railway
systems. (München is a little larger than Birmingham, and Nürnberg is
fractionally bigger than Bradford.) In many of them, the
Deutsche Bundesbahn - German Rail - had opened completely new suburban
rail systems, called S-Bahn, with new trains and new stations; in some
places, such as Frankfurt and München, these systems burrowed in new

tunnels right under the central business district. And in parallel, earlier and more comprehensively than in Britain, the German authorities turned large parts of their central areas into vehicle-free pedestrian areas.

British visitors to Germany, whether casual visitors or members of official delegations, could not help noticing that the cities looked remarkably attractive. Indeed, most of them seemed to be positively bursting with life. The pedestrian streets were packed with people. Trade in the shops was booming. There seemed to be very few of the 'To Let' signs that festooned many British city centres. The new rail systems were full of passengers. Generally, German cities seemed to be free of the blight and depopulation that increasingly disfigured British cities.

An obvious question poses itself, with important implications for policy: exactly how successful has this huge programme of investment been? Has it justified itself in terms of operating results? And has it really had a major impact on the economic health of the cities? The question can be put in reverse. Britain, where extremely tough-minded economic assessment has been the rule of the day and where public investment has been far less generous, has up to now invested relatively little in new urban rail systems. Against more than a score of German cities with such systems, Britain has only two new underground lines in London - one of them created mainly out of existing track - plus two new links in Liverpool, the rehabilitation of old British Rail tracks and a Victorian underground system in Glasgow, and a Metro system (again largely on old tracks) in Newcastle. How far can the present decline of British cities be traced to this lack of investment in them?

Clearly, it will never be possible to give a precise answer to such questions. The connection between rail investment (indeed, any transport investment) and economic health is an indirect and obscure one. Attempts have been made to analyse such a connection for highway investment, but they can never be definitive. But it should at least be possible to assemble basic empirical evidence, and then to make an informed judgement.

This book is an attempt to make such a judgement. It is the result of a fourteen-month research project, financed by the Anglo-German Foundation, which set out to assess the impact of rail rapid transit (RRT) investment on urban structure in major cities in the Federal Republic and Great Britain, with special reference to the economic health of their central areas. To that end, we have taken a sample of cities, both from Britain and from the Federal Republic, which have invested heavily in RRT and we have compared them with a control group that have not.

The background to the study is a major shift in transportation planning policies that has occurred in both countries, and indeed in most countries of the advanced industrial world, during the late 1960s and the 1970s: a shift away from planning for the free use of the private car, and toward the promotion of public transport. The German Federal Republic took an early lead in this direction, and still provides the best set of examples in practice; other countries, such as Great Britain, have gone in the same direction but more slowly and with far less commitment of resources. In both countries, but again more comprehensively in Germany, this policy shift was especially evident in the bigger conurbations (in Germany: Hamburg, München, Rhein-Main Gebiet, Ruhrgebiet, Stuttgart; in Great Britain: Merseyside, Tyne and Wear, Strathclyde). Public transportation was seen as cheaper in terms of social costs, relatively pollution- and noise-free, and also space-saving. The new mood was well summed up by a comment from the mayor of München: 'With every million we spend on roads we will be closer to murdering our city' (Linder, Maurer, Resch 1975, p.216).

In both countries the shift was propelled by a change in the law. The German change in fiscal practice in 1967, whereby local authorities could draw part of the proceeds of petrol tax in order to improve their public transportation systems, and the British Transport Act of 1968, both permitted large government subsidies to be paid to local authorities to build or improve their public transport systems.

The result in both countries was a pronounced shift of emphasis away from urban highway construction and towards the promotion of public transport - though the commitment by government was more wholehearted in Germany than in Britain, and the resulting investment much greater. One result has been that transport planners have now developed a whole new set of technical terms, first in German, then in approximate English equivalents. Because these terms are important to an understanding of what has been done, and because some of them are ambiguous, we need to discuss them.

A brief guide to technical jargon

U-Bahn (Underground Railway)

This is the simplest and least ambiguous. It invariably refers to a newly constructed system, running in its entirety on its own right-of-way. Trains, typically carrying up to about 750 passengers, travel at headways which may go down to 90 seconds. This requires a sophisticated signalling system, invariably an automatic one. Such a system has a high carrying capacity of about 30,000 passengers per hour in a single direction, on a single line, at the peak hour. Station spacing is typically close: 1 km. or less in the central area, generally not more than 2 km. in the suburbs. Mainly for this reason, average speeds are not high (30-40 km./hr. 18-25 m.p.h.) and such systems usually do not extend more than about 20-25 km. (12-15 miles) from city centres; in other words, they are urban systems.

Oddly, a U-Bahn may not necessarily be underground. Following a model set by the extensions of London's tube railways in the 1930s, considerable stretches of the system - outside the congested central and inner areas - may run above ground. The tunnel stretches may be in shallow cut-and-cover section just below the street level, on the model set by early examples like London's Metropolitan and District lines or the Paris Métro, or alternatively in deep-bored tunnel on the model of the London tube. Trains may be of the same loading gauge as main-line railways, but are often smaller to save tunnelling costs; consequently, even if main-line trains could run on the same tracks, they cannot share the right-of-way. Finally, the supply of electric current may be different from that of main-line railways. Many U-Bahn systems use third- or fourth-rail systems for pick-up and return of current, because of restricted tunnel headroom; most main-line systems tend to use overhead pick-up.

Stadtbahn (Light Rail)

This is the term for a system using short cars of tramcar type, generally in two- or four-car formation, on tram tracks of lighter construction than is typical for U-Bahn systems. The capacity of these trains is lower than for U-Bahn, typically 500 a train. The system uses a much simpler signalling system, often depending on visual observation but with some signal support, especially in tunnel sections. The right-of-way is invariably segregated from other traffic, but may cross streets at grade, with or without signal control. In central and inner-city sections however the system runs in shallow cut-and-cover tunnel. The trains can achieve a headway of 90 seconds, comparable with U-Bahn trains. The total carrying capacity is however less than that of U-Bahn systems: about 20,000 per peak hour per track in a single direction, little more than that of the tram systems they replace (Table 1.1).

Because of these features, average speeds are low: 20-30 km./hr. (12-18 m.p.h.). This clearly restricts such systems to radii of about 15-20 km. (10-13 miles) from city centres; though in some areas (notably Rhein-Ruhr) they may travel over longer distances to connect two cities, few if any passengers travel the whole distance.

Trams

Nearly all German cities, even those that have invested heavily in new underground or light rail systems, have kept part of their old tram system and have modernised it, usually with extensive stretches of reserved right-of-way (Appendix B). Only two German cities with over 500,000 people, Berlin and Hamburg, have entirely scrapped their trams. Some smaller cities (e.g. Aachen, Trier, Fürth) have also done so. But

4

Plate 1.1 Tram and Light Rail in Dortmund

Dortmund still relied on surface and light rail at the time of our survey. The picture shows how they can be successfully integrated into a pedestrian city centre.

Plate 1.2 Light Rail in Köln-Bonn

The surface light rail line, converted from the old Rheinuferbahn, connecting Köln, Bonn and Bad Godesberg. The picture shows the station Landesbehördenhaus, the headquarters of the German political parties.

Plate 1.3 Light Rail in Hannover

Scene at Kröpcke, the main city-centre interchange in the capital of
Lower Saxony. The station is exclusively used by light rail trains,
which rise to surface level outside the central business district.

Plate 1.4 S-Bahn in Dortmund

A suburban train of German Rail (Deutsche Bundesbahn), which connects the
main Ruhr cities, at Dortmund Station. Elsewhere (Frankfurt, München),
such systems run in tunnels directly under the city-centre shopping area.

Table 1.1

Technical Characteristics of Trams, Light Rail and Rapid Rail Systems

	Tram[a]	Light rail[b]	Rapid rail U-Bahn	S-Bahn
Right of way: Shared/Not shared (Public transport: Individual transport)	Shared	Mainly not shared	Not shared	Not shared
Average Speed km/hr	10 - 20	20 - 30	30 - 40	45 - 60
Highest possible speed km/hr	50 - 70	60 - 80	-80	-120
Security system	Visual observation; some signal support	As trams but stronger signal support[c]	Automated signal system	Automated signal system
Efficiency (passengers per hour and direction - average value)	15,000	20,000	30,000	60,000
Passengers per train	250	500	750	1,500
Width of train (m.)	2.20-2.40	2.40-2.65	2.65-2.90	2.80-3.00
Length of train (m.)	70	70-100	130	200
Headway (seconds)	60	90	90	90
Minimum curvature (m.)	25	180	180	180
Platform height (m.)	- 0.40	- 0.95	0.90-1.10	0.38-1.10

a) Many tram systems have been converted to run on their own right-of-way.
b) May have at-grade crossings with streets.
c) Total signal support in tunnel sections.

Source: Bundesminister für Verkehr (1982) Kriterien der Bahnarten des öffentlichen Personennahverkehrs (internal memorandum).

in contrast nine cities in the 200-300,000 range have both modernised and
extended their systems.

S-Bahn (Suburban Rail)

This term is the most difficult of all, because though very widely used
in Germany it does not seem to be at all closely defined. The term,
which stands for Schnellbahn (Rapid Rail), first seems to have been used
in Berlin in 1930 to describe the electrification of the suburban rail
system of Berlin (Schreck, Meyer, Strumpf 1979, p.11). It refers to a
comprehensive upgrading of the suburban rail services of Deutsche
Bundesbahn (German Rail), including new trains running at fixed
intervals, remodelling of stations and the development of a strong
corporate image (including maps and a distinctive logo). It may or may
not include new stretches of track, including - in one or two instances
(Frankfurt, München) - new underground stretches under the city centre,
allowing suburban trains to serve the centre directly without transfer to
other modes of public transport. In 1984 there were five such systems in
the Federal Republic (Frankfurt, Hamburg, München, Rhein-Ruhr and
Stuttgart) and two more planned (Köln and Nürnberg). The West Berlin
system, which until 1984 was anomalously operated by the DDR's
Deutsche Reichsbahn, is a special case.

S-Bahn trains are faster than other modes, averaging 45-60 km./hr. (27-
37 m.p.h.). They are thus able to serve more extended areas up to 40 km.
(25 miles) and more from city centres. Working under automated signal
controls, with high-capacity trains (up to 1,500 passengers per train),
at headways as short as 90 seconds, they are able to achieve much higher
total passenger movements than other modes: up to 60,000 passengers per
peak hour per track.

The question naturally arises: how do the relatively few British
investments of recent years fit into this classification? The Victoria
and Jubilee tube lines in London are clearly U-Bahn systems. So is the
reconstructed Glasgow Underground. The Tyne Metro and the London
Docklands Light Rail are both Stadtbahnen, though both use abandoned rail
right-of-way, not former tramway.

Both Glasgow's Argyle Line and Liverpool's Loop-and-Link could properly
be regarded as S-Bahn systems: they are operated as distinct systems with
a separate identity, they involve new city centre links (newly
constructed in Liverpool, reopened in Glasgow), and they serve suburban
areas up to 25 km. (15 miles) from the city centre. They do not however
have completely new trains or the same degree of corporate identity as
their German equivalents.

Pedestrianisation

There is another definitional problem concerning the apparently simple
term pedestrianisation. The Germans habitually use the term for what

they have done so extensively: the closure of existing streets to
traffic, followed by environmental treatment in the form of street
furniture and paving. There need be no reconstruction of buildings, or
at the most piecemeal renewal. As we shall see, British cities have done
less pedestrianisation in this sense than have German cities. What they
have done, in many cases, is to construct completely new traffic-free
precincts in the centre of the city - sometimes open, more commonly
(since the mid-1960s) enclosed. These precincts may incorporate the
whole or parts of previous traffic streets, though they often tend to
destroy the previous street pattern. As a rule, they entail
comprehensive rebuilding of a substantial area, leaving little or none of
the original buildings.

The Germans have built some similar shopping centres, although smaller
in size, in most cities; they have also tended to build big department
stores which have some qualities similar to a completely enclosed British
pedestrian precinct. Generally, though, the typical German pedestrian
area is a pedestrianised (i.e. former vehicle) street while the typical
British pedestrian area is a precinct (open or enclosed). The British
consequently think of a pedestrianised area, whether or not it was
previously a vehicle street; the Germans think of the act of
pedestrianising a street. This gives rise to real difficulties of
comparison, and even of communication. In this study most of our direct
statistical comparisons will be for pedestrianisation in the strict
(German) sense; but we shall also discuss the development of pedestrian
precincts in British cities where these are relevant to the overall
comparison.

Rail transit: the German-British contrast

Earlier we have noticed the profound differences in investment in transit
between British and German cities, which provide the starting-point of
our study. These express themselves in the statistics. Between 1970 and
1978, the total length of U-Bahnen and Stadtbahnen (Light Rail) systems
in Germany increased from 191 to 278 km., with a projected increase to
340 km. by 1980 and 540 km. by 1985 (Difu 1980, p.131), a total increase
of 349 km. over a 15-year period. In addition there were some 4,000 km.
of S-Bahn. A comparable figure for Great Britain over the same period,
1970-85, would be some 67 km. of new construction and reconstruction. As
a result, by the early 1980s all major German conurbation cities, and
many of the largest free-standing cities, now had RRT systems focusing on
their city centres. In contrast the West Midlands and Greater Manchester
conurbations are now the largest European agglomerations without
underground RRT systems, and no British city - with the three exceptions
of Newcastle, the seaside town of Blackpool (where the ground-level
system is a legacy from the Victorian era), and the London Docklands
system under construction - has a light rail system.

The new German systems have been accompanied, in nearly all cases, by extensive pedestrianisation of the central business district. Most German cities had indeed pedestrianised some parts of their city centres before 1970 (and in some cases before 1939), but it was only in the last decade, as part of the extensive construction programmes which in many cases involved temporary street closures, that large and coherent central pedestrianised areas were developed. It is now generally true that the central business districts of German cities are almost completely vehicle-free areas. Again, British cities (with the notable exception of the early postwar reconstruction of Coventry) came later, but by the early 1980s almost all major British conurbation cities had fairly extensive pedestrian areas. It should however be noticed that some of the most ambitious British schemes - as in Birmingham, Coventry and Leeds - are in cities which have not invested in RRT on any scale, but continue to depend largely on conventional bus systems.

These differences are related to more generous and less variable government support for investment in the Federal Republic. The level of subsidy in Germany is somewhat higher, with 60 per cent of capital cost from the Federal Government and 20 per cent from the Länder government, as against 75 per cent from central government in Britain. And this support has been provided to twenty-one German cities for development of their rail or rapid rail systems (Table 2.6), against only three - Liverpool, Newcastle and Glasgow - in Britain. In addition, nine other smaller cities (Augsburg, Braunschweig, Darmstadt, Freiburg, Karlsruhe, Kassel, Krefeld, Mainz and Würzburg) have been given financial aid for the comprehensive modernisation of their tram systems.

An obvious question is whether these differences in policy, especially as between Great Britain and the Federal Republic, have had an impact on the patterns of economic activities and on the economic prosperity of central and inner cities. A number of studies in recent years have suggested that so far German inner city areas have suffered less population or employment loss, and have remained generally healthier in an economic sense, than their British or American counterparts (Hall and Hay 1980; Schwartz 1981; van den Berg et al 1982). Though German cities have begun to record population losses as a result of suburbanisation during the 1970s, this does not appear to have been accompanied so far by contraction of the economic base on the scale of that in some British cities (except in localised cases such as the Ruhrgebiet). It has been suggested that this may in part have occurred because of conscious planning policies on the part of German city authorities, designed to enhance the role of their central and inner city areas and to maintain their physical attractiveness. Among such measures, RRT investment and pedestrianisation might be assumed to have played a major role. But it is clear that RRT investment was mainly the result of political decisions taken in a time of economic expansion and buoyant public expenditure.

British city transportation planners and local politicians have clearly been impressed by what they have seen and heard of the German experience.

Rail plans, particularly light rail, are now being widely canvassed in many cities as an effective and economical answer to the twin problems of urban congestion and decline. Though only one such scheme - that for London's docklands - has actually won government approval and started construction (in August 1984), a number of metropolitan transport authorities - West Midlands, Greater Manchester, South Yorkshire - have schemes at various stages of preparation. In the United States, too, a whole series of cities have either completed light rail systems (San Diego) or are starting on them (Buffalo, Orlando, San Jose, Los Angeles). This, interestingly, comes at a time when the Germans themselves are increasingly questioning the justification for elaborate rail-based systems and are stressing the virtues of low-cost, mainly light-rail and tram solutions (Monheim 1984; Apel 1984, pp.310-311).

Objectives of the study

This then was the background to our study. Because there clearly are important policy-relevant questions to be asked, we aimed at an empirical study rather than at a major exercise in theory-building; our objective was to get a sense of the observed impacts of rail rapid transit and pedestrianisation, both _directly_ (in terms of numbers of public transport passengers or pedestrian flows) and _indirectly_ (in terms of measures like shopping turnover or rentals for shops and offices).

1. _Direct_ impacts embrace the performance of the system as against the norms set by the original forecasts and design objectives, related city plans and general public transport policies (for instance on subsidies). They include numbers and kinds of passengers, engineering and service levels, and financial performance. Particularly important, from the viewpoint of the direct effects, is the composition of the passengers in terms of journey purpose and previous mode of transport. Diversion of passengers from other modes (particularly the private car) would need to be distinguished carefully from generation of totally new journeys. However, these direct impacts were not our main concern; we wanted mainly to concentrate on the indirect impacts.

2. The _indirect_ effects are the impacts on economic activities and social patterns: in other words, the geography of the city. These formed the main emphasis of the evaluation, though they were necessarily more elusive to measure than were the direct effects. The focus was on the impact on employment and economic activity, by sector, in the central business district and in the surrounding inner city industrial-residential area. Estimates of economic change and related land use change - new construction, demolition, replacement, change of use - before and after the completion of RRT investment were obtained from both central and local sources, and interviews were conducted with local representatives of commerce and industry. Finally an attempt was made to gauge the measured results against the stated objectives of politicians and RRT planners, and against the cost of the schemes.

The study first aimed to test the _intended_ effects of RRT investment. The clear intention seems to have been to enhance the role of the city centre as the commercial core of an expanding city region - or, in the few British instances, to try to prevent the centre's decline in the face of out-migration of people and commercial activities. A first intention was to analyse the stated objectives and to ask how far in practice they were achieved.

The study however also aimed to test the hypothesis that in such areas, RRT investment may have had effects that were at least in part _unintended_. By conferring additional accessibility, it may have brought about rises in property rents and prices. Coupled with the fact that certain kinds of tertiary industries were showing rapid growth at this time - above all the so-called producer services such as banking, insurance, finance, advertising and the media - this may have led to a replacement of traditional activities by new ones having greater commercial power to generate and pay the enhanced land rents. It may also have benefitted the city centres at the expense of sub-centres in the metropolitan region. For this reason, the study should attempt to assess impacts also in these other centres.

The choice of cities

The choice of cities was obviously crucial to this end. We sought to analyse cities which showed critical differences in the key variables:

1. _Amount and type of RRT investment_. The sample must include cities with extensive U-Bahn investment, light rail investment and also no RRT investment at all. A problem here was that Britain has few cities with RRT investment whereas Germany has few cities without it. In practice, therefore, much of the study necessarily consisted of a comparison between a German 'RRT' approach and a British 'No-RRT' approach.

2. _Degree and type of pedestrianisation_. Variations were fewer here, since nearly every major city in both countries has pedestrianised some central areas (in Britain combined with bus access to pedestrian streets). In effect therefore we were comparing British cities with pedestrian areas and bus access as against German cities with pedestrianisation and RRT access.

3. _City size_. As far as possible, pairs of cities - two in each country, one with an RRT system and the other one without - were selected, similar in city size and population density. The relevant figure here is that for the entire urban agglomeration, not just the administratively bounded city.

4. _City structure_. Britain's major cities invariably form part of polycentric conurbations or metropolitan regions. With a few exceptions,

notably the Ruhrgebiet, Germany lacks such large urban agglomerations; its major cities tend to be free-standing. Therefore, no direct comparison is possible on this score. However, in order to achieve maximum possible comparability, two of the German case studies were chosen from the Ruhr area.

The resulting cities and urban agglomerations finally selected for comparison were thirteen in number: seven in the Federal Republic, six in Great Britain.

1. **Bremen.** One of the few major cities in the Federal Republic not to invest substantially in RRT; extensive conventional tram system, most on exclusive right-of-way; limited pedestrianisation coupled with 'four-cell' policy of restricted car access and public transport priority across city centre, later borrowed by other cities (Oxford, Cambridge, Göteborg).

2. **Dortmund.** The other major German city without RRT at the time of our study, except for recently completed S-Bahn link to Essen (part of Ruhr regional system); extensive pedestrianisation streets, some with trams, in city centre. (A Stadtbahn or light rail system opened in June 1984 after the conclusion of our study; further S-Bahn links are under construction.)

3. **Essen.** Chosen as comparison with Dortmund on ground of similarity in size and economic characteristics; major city of Ruhr industrial region, with light rail investment, regional S-Bahn and pedestrianisation (earliest in the world, about 1926; now very extensive, but further extensions planned).

4. **Hannover.** Major regional capital city, with most extensive light rail system in Germany, underground in city centre, plus large-scale pedestrianisation.

5. **Köln.** Early example of pedestrianisation (pre-1939), now very far-ranging; extensions and improvements planned; light rail in city centre.

6. **München.** Major regional capital city with very large-scale investment in new U-Bahn plus S-Bahn and extensive pedestrianisation of city centre; the 'showpiece' of rail investment and pedestrianisation in the Federal Republic.

7. **Nürnberg.** New U-Bahn partially completed during 1970s (the only city with under 500,000 population to receive a complete U-Bahn system); pedestrianised area among the largest in the Federal Republic.

8. **Glasgow.** Modernised underground system and suburban rail system (Blue Trains) introduced 1979-80; modest pedestrianisation in the city centre.

Plate 1.5   Tram and Pedestrianisation in Bremen

An example of the successful combination of a pedestrian street with access for public transport - here, trams.   In other cities (Mainz, Trier), buses have access.   The latter system is employed in some British cities (Oxford, Reading), but without good environmental treatment of these bus-only streets.

Plate 1.6   Minibus Service in Manchester, Connecting Rail Termini

This service, between Piccadilly and Victoria Stations, substitutes for the abandoned Picc-Vic link.

9. **Leeds.** No RRT system, though trolley bus system now under consideration as one of a number of options; early and extensive pedestrianisation in city centre.

10. **Liverpool.** New RRT system (S-Bahn type) introduced 1977; quite extensive central pedestrianisation; subsidised bus system; local economy subject to contraction with severe inner city problems.

11. **Manchester.** Major provincial centre, with strong commercial core serving as regional city for surrounding conurbation; planned RRT system (Picc-Vic) abandoned in early 1970s, so one of largest European agglomerations lacking RRT; plans for a light rail system.

12. **Newcastle upon Tyne.** New Metro system, on light rail principles and using converted BR track, opened in 1981 and completed in 1984, the most extensive in Britain; provincial capital of depressed region; limited pedestrianisation, but very large new shopping centre.

13. **Sheffield.** No rail investment, though experimental RRT (Cabtrack) considered and rejected in 1970s on cost and environmental grounds; extensive bus service; deliberate policy of heavily subsidised cheap fares and high service levels; light rail system under consideration.

Table 1.2
The Case Study Cities

	With RRT	Without (extensive) RRT
Great Britain	Glasgow	Leeds
	Liverpool	Manchester
	Newcastle	Sheffield
Germany	Essen	Bremen
	Hannover	Dortmund
	Köln	
	München	
	Nürnberg	

Research methodology

Our method was mainly to work through desk research, analysing available primary and secondary sources on employment, land use patterns, and commercial values. We supplemented this by visits to each of the cities, to obtain further information from planning offices, transportation departments and similar bodies. Because data were unavailable, we administered a brief questionnaire to business leaders on the effects of RRT investment.

Almost inevitably in a project of this kind, unforeseen problems arose in the collection of empirical material which at one point appeared to threaten its successful conclusion, and in the event compelled some modification of the original research objectives. The central difficulty was in obtaining empirical data on the indirect effects of RRT investment, in particular indices of shopping turnover and of shopping and office rentals. A particular problem was the lack of two basic statistical sources: the 1981 Population Census of the Federal Republic, which has been repeatedly postponed, and the 1981 Census of Retail Distribution in Britain which was cancelled.

Structure of the book

The structure of the remainder of this book is set by the objectives we set ourselves in the original proposal.

Chapter 2 sets out the background to the study in greater detail than was possible in this general introduction. It first shows how British and German cities developed down to the mid-1960s and how their internal structures, and their transportation systems, were different in some important ways. It then traces the history of transportation policy, with special reference to public transport, in the two countries down to the present time.

Chapter 3 develops a systematic general comparison of the thirteen cities in respect of population, economic activity, and transportation patterns. It is based on a statistical appendix (Appendix B).

Against this general background, Chapter 4 then returns to the particular. It looks at the evolution of public transport services in each of the cities, with a particular stress on the innovations of the 1970s, and with a sideways look at related policies such as traffic restraint and parking policies.

Chapter 5 runs in parallel; it sets out the history of city centre pedestrianisation in the two countries, looking both at origins and at some of the results. It thus acts as a bridge to the concluding chapters of the report, which focus on consequences.

Chapter 6 considers the impacts of pedestrianisation, in so far as these can be distinguished from the impacts of RRT investment.

Chapter 7 considers the impacts of investment in rail rapid transit. First it looks at direct effects in terms of numbers of passengers - both those transferring from other modes, and those newly generated - and also of their time spent in travelling.   Then it looks at indirect or secondary effects in terms of retail floorspace and turnover, office floorspace and employment, and rentals both for office and shop premises. It starts by summarising the results of previous related work, goes on to assemble available evidence, and then reports the results of the questionnaire survey.

Finally, Chapter 8 summarises the main conclusions of the report.   This chapter is designed to be read on its own, but rests on the evidence presented in earlier chapters of the report.

2 Public transport and planning policies

In this chapter, we set the background. First we describe how major British and German cities developed down to the mid-1960s, the point at which the new transportation policies began to evolve in both countries. Then we show for each country the form which the new policies took. We look in some detail at the administrative reorganisation of public transport in the major urban areas of both countries. We compare the arrangements for financing public transport as they evolved in each country. Finally, as a bridge to Chapter 3, we look specifically at the development of rail and light rail systems in British and German cities.

British and German cities pre-1945: physical development, transportation systems

The conventional wisdom is that in the first half of the twentieth century, English cities evolved in a way that was quite different from their counterparts on the mainland of Europe. A unique combination of factors - the poor environmental conditions in the old industrial cities, rising standards of affluence, the growth of the building society movement, low building costs and cheap land, the influence of the garden city and garden suburb movement, and the new transportation technologies of the electric train and the motor bus - allowed English cities to spread at progressively lower densities, permitting white-collar and even the more prosperous blue-collar workers to live at greater distances from their place of work than had ever been previously thought possible, in single-family suburban houses each with an individual garden. Though continental cities shared in some of these features, their combination was lacking; therefore, though electric tram services allowed them to spread out to some degree, they developed chiefly through apartment blocks at much higher densities than their English counterparts, thus remaining relatively compact. Scottish cities - so runs the conventional wisdom - followed the continental rather than the English model; perhaps because of lower living standards, perhaps because of a deep-set medieval tradition of tenement living, they remained compact cities of apartment blocks, in which only a small minority enjoyed the luxury of the single-family home.

In seeking to explain some of the critical differences in transport patterns and policies between British and German cities, our first instinct was to follow this conventional wisdom. Between 1890 and 1910 - a few years earlier in Germany than in Britain, on average - all European cities developed excellent tram systems, well adapted to the high densities and compact urban forms characteristic at that time. But during the 1920s and 1930s British cities, we hypothesised, spread out at lower densities. Because of this, they could no longer support tramcar systems, with their dependence on fixed capital investment in tracks and overhead cables. This was the main reason why, beginning in the 1930s in London and Manchester, one city after another first stopped extending its tram network, substituting buses on the outer suburban routes, and then planned to scrap the trams altogether. After World War Two, when extensive house building began again in the mid-1950s, the fate of the remaining British city tram systems was sealed. In Germany, however, the forces of outward spread were weaker, both before and immediately after World War Two; consequently, the tram system remained viable, and relatively short extensions to new apartment suburbs allowed the still-compact cities to function efficiently and economically.

This conventional wisdom is open to serious doubt. In Chapter 3, we shall produce figures for some of our case study cities which show that, before World War Two, the inner rings of typical large British cities were actually denser than their German equivalents; and these higher densities actually persisted into the middle rings consisting of the late nineteenth-century terrace housing and the early interwar council estates (Table 3.1). The fact is that though the average British city was developed - even in Victorian times - in the form of single-family housing, this provided an optical illusion; the densities thus obtained were high, ranging from extremely high in the inner ring to modestly high in the outer ring. Conversely, the German apartment blocks - the Mietskasernen of Berlin perhaps excepted - often resulted in quite modest densities, because of the fact that the individual apartments might be large - up to twice the size of a small English terrace house - and also because of the amount of communal yard space provided in the interior of each block. In seeking the explanation of the abandonment of the British tram systems, then, we cannot invoke low-density suburban sprawl. The process of abandonment actually began in the late 1920s and accelerated in the 1930s, at a time when Britain's cities were still compact - though, as we shall see below, the major losses came just after World War Two.

Neither in British nor in German cities were intra-urban rail systems particularly important for urban development - with the exceptions of the two great world cities. In London after 1860, some main-line railways developed commuter traffic, and traffic congestion led to the construction of the world's first underground railway (the Metropolitan Railway, 1863) and then the first deep-level tube (the City and South London Railway, 1890). Then, in the period between the two World Wars, the planners of London's railways - the Underground group (from 1933 part of London Transport) and the Southern Railway - deliberately forged new lines or electrification of existing lines into open country, thus producing suburban development on a huge scale. But there was no equivalent of this process elsewhere in Britain. Liverpool had its Mersey Railway, a modest suburban link between the city centre and the salubrious Wirral peninsula on the opposite bank of the river, opened in 1886 and electrified in 1903; it also electrified some other suburban lines in the 1930s. Manchester had two electrified lines, to Bury (1916) and to Altrincham (1931); Newcastle electrified its lines north of the river Tyne (1904); Glasgow's circular underground line, opened in 1896, was actually the second deep-level tube in the world. But, in general, these rail systems carried only a small minority of all central area commuters - in sharp contrast to London, where they carried the great majority.

Berlin's first suburban line opened to the public (having been originally constructed for military purposes) in 1872; it took the form of a ring around the city centre, connecting the eight main railway stations. Part was electrified in 1903 and the total system was electrified by 1929; it was designated as an S-Bahn system three years after (Schreck, Meyer, Strumpf 1979, p.98). Operated by the Deutsche Reichsbahn, the West Berlin section passed into the control of the DDR rail system after World War Two and deteriorated physically to the point of part-closure until its takeover by the West Berlin authorities in 1984. Berlin's so-called U-Bahn opened in 1902 (after a construction time of five and a half years). Most of the 11 km. ran on elevated tracks, and only 2.5 km. ran underground. By 1913, the U-Bahn system had a length of 38 km. which had doubled (to 76 km.) by 1930, when the train schedule was every 90 seconds. In addition there was a 720 km. S-Bahn system, giving a total rapid transit network of nearly 800 km. (Guhl 1975, pp.14-17).

The only other German city which had an urban rail system before World War Two was Hamburg. Its first 'underground' was opened ten years after Berlin (1912). Its structure, because of geographical circumstances, was rather different to the Berlin system. Hamburg constructed a ring system to cover a radius of 5 km. around the Alster basin, with a number of radial lines (initially three) running outward from it. Before the Second World War, Hamburg had nearly the same length in kilometres as Berlin (68.2 km.) (ibid., pp.21-22). Apart from these underground systems which were partly elevated and open lines, and were hardly ever in deep-bore tunnel, Hamburg also had an extensive S-Bahn system some 140 km. in length (ibid., pp.20-22).

Developments after World War Two

In the decade after World War Two, all Britain's major cities moved to scrap their tram systems. Some, such as London and Manchester, had begun to do so even before 1939, and had completed the process early (Manchester in 1949, Newcastle in 1950, London in 1952, Birmingham in 1953); others, such as Glasgow, Liverpool and Sheffield, did so more slowly and reluctantly: Liverpool in 1957, Sheffield in 1960, Glasgow in 1962.

The real reason for the end of the trams seems to have been deliberate policy, fortified by the hard accounting economics of municipal public transport systems. British tram undertakings had to undertake to maintain that part of the roadway in which they laid their tracks, which were built to higher standards than the German ones. Though most of them were municipal - so that the cost fell on the city anyway - from the viewpoint of the transport undertaking's balance sheet this made trams unfavourable as compared with buses. This fact might not however have proved definitive - for many British cities remained firmly wedded to their trams well into the 1950s - had it not been for two other factors. First, the powerful city engineer's departments had become converted to the view that in an age of rising car ownership, trams spelt unnecessary congestion - a view officially enshrined in the extremely influential central government manual, The Design and Layout of Roads in Built-Up Areas, published in 1946 (Ministry of War Transport 1946). Secondly, the emergent city planning departments, established as a result of the 1947 Town and Country Planning Act, tended to regard trams as an old-fashioned mode of transport which seemed inappropriate to the brave new world they were trying to create. This alliance, coupled with the prejudices of city councillors, seems to have been sufficient to seal the fate of the trams.

The British planning system would probably have proved fateful to the trams in another respect, even if they had not been scrapped as soon as they were. For after World War Two, as is well known, one of its principal objectives was to contain the further growth of the large conurbation cities and to direct any further growth to planned new and expanded towns which were generally too small to support effective fixed-rail systems. Generally, British cities after World War Two no longer had an opportunity to develop large-scale satellite suburbs at their own peripheries, as Manchester had before World War Two at Wythenshawe or Liverpool at Speke. There was no basis therefore for developing extensions of public transport systems - and, soon after 1950, the major British cities first stagnated in population and then began to decline.

In the Federal Republic, no such movement seems to have occurred. Tram systems were of course attacked and badly damaged during the air raids of 1943-5, but were soon restored as an essential basis to the reconstruction of the cities. With the economic recovery of the early 1950s, rolling-stock was rapidly renewed. When problems of traffic congestion began to arise in German cities - later than in Britain, because car ownership started from lower levels - the logical answer was not to scrap the trams, but to put them underground.

These decisions were not related at all clearly to those being taken at the same time by German city planners. In the critical period of reconstruction from 1948 to 1955, indeed, German planners were dominated by earlier concepts dating from the 1920s. The ideal city was seen to be spacious, leafy and with a clear internal structure ('aufgelockert und

Plate 2.1 Trams in Sheffield

A typical city-centre scene from the mid-1950s, a few years before final closure, showing the tram sharing the street with other traffic. In the suburbs, trams in Sheffield - as in other British cities - commonly had their own right-of-way.
(Picture: Mr Keeping)

Plate 2.2 Abandoned Tram Line in Glasgow

A typical example of the separation of car and tram traffic, already widely applied in the outer suburban sections of British tram systems in the 1930s.

gegliedert', Farenholtz et al, 1977, p.118). This structure was to include the separation of the different functions, such as living, working, recreation and transportation.

Understandable, at this time, was a certain admiration for American suburban structures and also the main American transportation mode - the car - which implied a freedom of movement much appreciated in Germany after twelve years of Nazi regulation. The destruction of many German cities offered a unique possibility to rebuild the street and road network - though, with a few exceptions, this consisted in widenings and junction improvements rather than the construction of completely new urban motorways. The number of cars increased steeply in these early years, from 515,600 in 1950 to over 4,066,000 in 1960 (Statistisches Bundesamt, 1951, 1961).

Nevertheless, in nearly all cases public transportation systems still provided the connections to the new urban areas built during the 1950s, because many of these areas consisted of redevelopments of existing areas destroyed during the war. In 1950, eighty tram undertakings with about 4,500 km. of tram lines were still serving the public in Germany; the network actually increased in the early 1950s, as extensions were made to new districts at the urban peripheries. By the early 1980s, in contrast, Germany had only 2,000 km. (BOStrab, 1983, p.3). After 1956, the number of passengers carried by public transportation ceased to increase. Yet it still carried the majority of the workforce in the large cities; 60-70 per cent, for example, in 1960 in the three cities of Hamburg, Düsseldorf and Essen (Hollatz, Tamms 1965, p.103).

In the 1960s the concepts of the previous decade were strongly attacked by planners and architects. The leafy and spacious suburbs were seen as a continuation of an antiurban trend which had originally started with the garden city movement. The ideas of urbanisation moved to other extremes. Urban structures of high density were planned and built. Not only Corbusier but also other architects of the school 'Das Neue Bauen', such as Gropius, Scharoun, May, etc., were rediscovered. High-rise housing estates, today strongly criticised, were built on the urban fringes while high-rise office blocks were developed either in the city centre or close by.

As already noted, at this time physical planning and transportation planning in the Federal Republic were poorly coordinated, so that the newly built housing areas were not well linked to city centres or other employment nodes. Further, the spatial division of different functions - living, working, and recreation - forced people to overcome the spatial distances by car. Before 1967 public transportation did not receive any funds from the Federal Government, and by 1965 had reached a low point in terms of efficiency and number of passengers (BOSTrab 1983, pp.2-3). Transportation planning at this time was merely road and street construction planning (Linder, Maurer, Resch 1975, p.5). Between 1950 and 1964, 41.4 billion DM were invested in road and bridge construction whereas only 660 million DM were spent on public transportation, representing only 1.6 per cent of the total investments in transportation of the Federal Government (Pöllmann 1982, p.2, Hass-Klau 1982, p.190).

The result of this policy, predictably, was that traffic expanded to fill the new road space; urban congestion progressively increased. In 1961, about fifty journalists were invited by radio and television stations to study the traffic situation in Germany's large cities which was seen to be the most urgent and most difficult question of local urban politics at the time. One quotation gives the flavour of the response:

> It was our first morning, we were stuck in an immense queue, wedged in at the notorious Stachus in München. In the afternoon our driver tried desperately to reach the Schlossplatz in Stuttgart. The picture was the same in the shadow of Köln's cathedral or in front of Frankfurt's Hauptwache. Everywhere there was an intense effort to meet at least some of the pressure from the constantly increasing number of cars - by widening streets (demolishing complete rows of houses), cuttings, new bridges, subways and viaducts, one-way streets, no-go areas (Bremen) pedestrian streets (Essen) elevated roads (Hannover) or urban motorways (a modest start in Düsseldorf). There is not one city in which large construction sites do not demonstrate their efforts .... (First 1962)

Three years after this, the traffic in city centres was described as being unpleasant and dangerous for pedestrians, while car drivers were faced every morning and evening with solid traffic jams. Transport in cities, as experts put it, 'was developing more and more into a public emergency' (Hollatz, Tamms 1965, p.25).

The shift in urban transport policies

In Britain, policies showed a major break in the mid-1960s. Immediately after World War Two some of the significant regional plans called for extensive reconstruction of public transport systems. But there were no funds for these schemes, and from the mid-1950s onwards both local and central planners were obsessed with the implications of the boom in car ownership, which rose from 2.3 million in 1950 to 5.5 million in 1960 and 11.5 million in 1970. The late 1950s saw at last a belated start on construction of an inter-city motorway network, some quarter-century after Germany: the first short stretch of motorway (Preston By-Pass) opened in December 1958, the first major inter-urban section (Watford-Rugby) in November 1959.

By the early 1960s, with work well advanced on completion of a basic 1,600 km. network, the attention of planners turned to urban motorways. Large-scale American-style transportation studies, conducted in most cases by American consultants, dealt almost exclusively - at least in the

early years - with the need to provide more highway capacity for the
rapidly increasing numbers of private motorists; the result was a series
of recommendations for construction of very extensive urban motorway
networks for all the major British urban areas (Starkie 1982). The
historic Buchanan report of November 1963 (Ministry of Transport 1963),
though it actually urged a balance between road spending and traffic
restraint in the interests of environmental standards, was widely
interpreted as a basis for extensive urban road-building; and, logically,
plans followed for the extensive multi-level reconstruction of large
parts of British cities, as in Piccadilly Circus or Covent Garden in
London.

Very rapidly, these plans brought about what David Starkie has called
the 'environmental backlash'. Plans both for large-scale reconstruction
- as at Covent Garden - and for urban motorway building aroused
passionate opposition. During the late 1960s and early 1970s, one city
after another abandoned large parts of its motorway-building plan
(Newcastle, Manchester, Cardiff) or even abandoned the plan altogether
(London). Logically, there was a shift to investment in new or improved
public transport systems as an alternative. This change was even
reflected in the later transportation studies. Thus the Merseyside Area
Land Use and Transportation Study (1966-69) advocated the construction of
the Link and Loop rail connections in central Liverpool, the Greater
Glasgow Transportation Study (1968) recommended rail electrification and
reopening, and the Tyneside Transportation Study of 1971 recommended
construction of the Tyne Metro. In London the Victoria Line (opened
1968-69) was the first new tube line in central London for sixty years.

Events in the Federal Republic moved virtually in parallel. In 1964,
the Federal Government responded to the increasingly evident traffic
congestion in the cities. It commissioned a group of experts to give
some advice on the transport situation in local authorities. In 1965,
their report - The Traffic Problems of Local Authorities in the Federal
Republic of Germany (Die kommunalen Verkehrsprobleme in der
Bundesrepublik Deutschland) was published (Hollatz, Tamms 1965). This
publication was the direct and indirect outcome of the British work
published two years earlier: the Buchanan Report, Traffic in Towns. It
has since been used as a guideline by local and central governments, and
most of its ideas and concepts are still relevant today. It saw a close
interaction between traffic and the development of the urban economic
structure. The improvement of new transportation systems had to be
related in all kinds of ways to urban improvements. This interaction,
between urban structure and transportation, was seen as a problem in that
cars had encouraged urban dispersal; development no longer occurred, as
it formerly did, along an axis or at one point. The connection between
working and residential areas had loosened over time; there had been a
strong trend to decentralisation of housing, in contrast to the
centralisation of place of work in the city centre.

It was useless, the report concluded, simply to continue to create more and more space for the motor car; instead, improvements in mass transportation would be needed. In the major cities, three kinds of improvement were recommended:

1. Some adjustment of the urban highway network because of the increased demand for personal transportation. A demand for urban motorways and expressways, with at least four lanes, should in part be met.

2. In parallel, the promotion of public transport systems.

3. Better traffic regulation and management.

The main difficulties with public transportation were seen in the conflict between the car and public transport systems, mainly trams. As cars and trams were using the same right of way, conflicts were inevitable. The main attributes of public transport - speed, punctuality, regularity and reliability - were seen as being threatened. Even at this time, the major aim was to influence commuters to give up their cars and to use public transport (Hollatz, Tamms, 1965, p.103), which meant enhancing the technical and economic efficiency of public transport. Apart from general improvement, different cities needed - according to their urban and economic structures - different transport systems. Cities with more than 300,000 inhabitants and certainly cities with more than 500,000 inhabitants should have, as used to be the case, trams; these should partly go underground in the city centre. Some cities, especially cities with more than 500,000, should decide to build light rail systems which could later be transformed into rapid rail systems. For weaker transportation flows, typical for suburban areas, buses would be best. Trams should have their own right of way separate from other transportation modes. Even by 1962, eleven cities had already decided to build or extend light rail systems which might subsequently be upgraded to U-Bahn (Köln, Essen, Düsseldorf, Frankfurt, Dortmund, Stuttgart, Hannover, Bremen, Duisburg and Bielefeld, (ibid., p.235). Furthermore, several cities also planned S-Bahn systems, such as Düsseldorf, München, Frankfurt, the Ruhr area, Stuttgart and Mannheim (ibid., p.238).

Roads, the report recommended, should be planned either to encircle the city centre or in the form of tangents. The individual transportation flow must be taken out of the city centre; the city centre should be free of car traffic and parking space, with an emphasis on pedestrianisation. At this time (1965/6), over sixty cities had already introduced pedestrianisation (Monheim 1980, p.63). Bremen had its well-known system whereby the city centre was divided into four transportation cells; while movements within each cell were possible, individual traffic could only enter/leave each cell on a ring road. Public transportation in connection with pedestrianisation was seen as important. Wherever possible, trams should be given their own right of way, under or above pedestrianised areas (Hollatz, Tamms 1965, p.118). Although the report emphasised the strong role of public transportation, it did so half-heartedly; thus public transportation was not generally given precedence over the motor car (ibid. p.125).

Despite the report, the Federal Government took two more years to act. It finally gave active support to public transport investments in 1967. Local authorities were subsidised with part of the petrol taxes - about one penny (3 Pfennige) per litre; from 1972 the subsidy was raised to one and a half pence. However 60 per cent of the subsidies were still given for road building and 40 per cent for public transport investments (Linder, Maurer, Resch 1975, p.58). Later this ratio changed to 50:50, then 45:55, and in 1984 it was again 50:50. How powerful the road lobby still was, even around 1970, can be seen from the Bill passed in 1971 for the completion and extension of trunk roads which included motorways (Ausbau der Bundesverkehrsstrassen in den Jahren 1971 bis 1985) (BMBau 1973, p.111). It was planned to have such a dense network of motorways that 85 per cent of the population could reach a motorway from their place of residence in at most 10 km. (Linder, Maurer, Resch 1975, p.58).

In 1973, the Bundesverkehrswegeplan (Federal Transport Plan) provided a guideline for every kind of transportation including public transportation (BMBau, 1973, pp.104-118). This year, which saw the start of the Social Democrat-Liberal coalition, represented a turning point not only in transportation but also in urban planning. Willy Brandt, Chancellor at this time, expressed in his major opening speech 'the priority of public transportation versus the private car' (Linder, Maurer, Resch 1975, p.60). It had thus taken the Federal Government eight years to recognise the importance of public transport, during which private motorisation had reached over 15 million cars (Statistisches Bundesamt 1974); and changes in the mode of transportation, which meant even more changes in the behaviour pattern, had already occurred. The car was seen as a symbol of success, whereas public transportation had the stigma of the mode for the unsuccessful. The change in policy happened after the first rapid rail system had opened in München (1972), and other cities had already started to build either light rail or rapid rail systems.

Urban planning had in fact already undergone a major policy shift two years earlier, with a Bill passed to promote the renewal of inner city areas (Städtebauförderungsgesetz 1971), whereby local authorities could receive subsidies by the Federal Government to carry out extensive renewal programmes. This change in urban planning was the result of a clear tendency towards a decline in population in the city centres and inner areas of the conurbations and an increase in population in the outer suburbs and the hinterland, as repeatedly emphasised in Federal Government Planning publications after 1968 (BMBau 1969, 1971, 1973). The conurbations still showed a population increase in 1970 but changes inside the settlement structures of the conurbations had already occurred. One of the reasons quoted as to why people moved out of inner city areas was the unfavourable housing and living conditions, which really meant traffic congestion, noise and air pollution (BMBau 1973, pp.25, 63). There was certainly also a lack of large, relatively cheap tenement flats, and some of these flats were in poor condition.

The major Federal Government annual statement on planning of 1972 (BMBau 1973), whose contents did not change substantially in the report two years later (BMBau 1975), could be interpreted as a clear example of the change in transportation policy. The 1972 report suggests that building more roads for motor cars, especially in the city centre, will not solve the problems of traffic congestion. Just the opposite is likely; new roads increase the number of cars. The report therefore called for a reduction in individual motorisation within the city. To this end, it suggested several promotion policies which, significantly, echo those made by the experts in 1965:

1. extension and new construction of underground systems

2. promotion of new transport technologies

3. exclusive right of way for trams and buses

4. funds to make public transportation economically attractive for the user

5. further building of park and ride systems

6. united transport authorities in all conurbations.

In connection with these policies, the report suggested a series of related planning actions:

1. extensive pedestrianisation in the city centre

2. increased parking charges for car drivers

3. reduction of parking space for long term users.

In 1975, expenditure on public transport was about five times higher than in 1967, and reached a high point between 1973 and 1982 (BMBau 1979, p.224; personal interview). However, the annual Federal planning report of 1978 (BMBau 1979) gives no attention to the possible effects of a further increase of expenditure on public transportation; indeed, public transportation is merely mentioned as means to increase accessibility in the city (ibid., p.212). The continuing trend is still the concentration of the tertiary sector in the major inner city areas, which continues to displace population from these areas. The spatial separation of housing and employment has continued, and as a result total commuter traffic has increased further. The 1978 report repeats the conclusion of the 1960s: one of the major reasons why people move out of inner city areas is the damaging effect of private motorisation which will, according to

28

forecasts, increase even more in the coming years. The conflict between transportation and traditional settlement structure will sharpen (ibid., p.214). There have been two transportation measures which have tried to counteract the trend to population decline in inner city areas. First, the promotion of public transportation as a precondition to relieve the inner city areas from private car traffic; and secondly, the concentration of private through traffic on to major roads, thus keeping minor roads relatively free or completely free of car traffic. The 1978 report emphasises these 'traffic free' policies, yet further major investment in public transportation is not mentioned.

The latest Federal Government annual report on planning, of 1982 (BMBau 1983) shows that the strong environmental trend of the last years has been reinforced. 7,000 km. of planned motorways are not being built because of the negative effects they could have on 'nature and landscape' (ibid., p.27). The emphasis now is on construction of bypasses for middle-sized and small cities. The interest in public transportation has changed completely away from the conurbations towards a different kind of promotion policy for public transportation in rural areas (ibid., p.29). The report also mentions that public transport investment in the conurbations will continue, but because of increasing financial problems of local authorities and the Federal Government itself, this investment is supposed to be made much more carefully (e.g. on the basis of cost-benefit analysis).

In 1982, political power in the Federal Republic passed from the Social Democrats under Helmut Schmidt to the Christian Democrats under Helmut Kohl. Interestingly, there has been no change in the political commitment of the government to public transport investment, nor is any change expected (personal interview, Verkehrsministerium). Independently of the political change, the Federal Department of Transport in agreement with the corresponding Länder Ministries has developed a kind of standardised cost-benefit form to evaluate rapid rail or light rail investments of above 50 million DM, which has been used by cities since 1983. In addition there is further research to evaluate projects in a wider sense, including non-economic aspects. There has been some opposition to the use of the new technique from individual cities. At present the Federal Government and the Länder have agreed to test the method until about 1985. Although the Federal Department of Transport does not yet use the results to determine whether or not to give financial support to a project, some kind of unified evaluation certainly needs to be established.

The reorganisation of public transport in the conurbations

In Britain, the 1968 Transport Act also provided for public transport in the major conurbations to be unified. Passenger Transport Authorities were to be set up, initially in the West Midlands, Merseyside and South East Lancashire-North East Cheshire (Greater Manchester) and Tyneside

areas, with local authority representation. These **ad hoc** authorities were
necessary because at that date no metropolitan unit of government existed
for entire conurbation areas. In 1969, the Transport (London) Act
transferred authority for London Transport to the Greater London Council.
Finally, the Local Government Act of 1972, which established the six
metropolitan counties in England and Wales, provided that each should
constitute a Passenger Transport Authority. At this point, therefore,
the four original PTAs were joined by two others, for West and South
Yorkshire. Parallel 1973 legislation for Scotland established the
Strathclyde Regional Council as responsible for the Greater Glasgow
Passenger Transport Authority, which had been created in 1972 prior to
local government reorganisation. The government's present proposals to
abolish the metropolitan counties would mean that the English PTAs would
again revert to the status of **ad hoc** authorities; and the Greater London
Council has already lost responsibility for London Transport.

In the Federal Republic, interestingly, a similar process took place
from about 1965. As a result, today nearly all large conurbations have a
unified transport authority but not all smaller conurbations have yet
formed such bodies. The Federal Republic of Germany has twenty-four
defined conurbations, of which only six have over one million. The
smallest conurbations (Freiburg, Siegen, Bremerhaven) have between
160,000 and 180,000 inhabitants, which according to British standards
would not count as conurbations. In these smaller conurbations - which
really include all major cities in Germany - each local authority is
responsible for its own transportation system. Apart from this, there is
the Deutsche Bundesbahn (German Rail) which runs suburban trains and
buses and Deutsche Bundespost (German Post) which has its own bus system
in rural areas. These two organisations were united in 1982. To increase
the complexity further, there are also private companies operating in
many local authorities. The resulting complexity provides some
inconvenience for the passengers, such as different tickets, different
timetables etc., though this is not nearly as serious as in the British
conurbations (Hass-Klau 1982, pp.191-192).

Hamburg was the first city totally to reorganise its transportation
structure. In 1965 the city formed a transport authority - called
Verkehrsverbund - with the aim of setting up between all the transport
enterprises (public and private) a unified fare system, coordinated
timetables, a systematic and coordinated transportation network (which
meant for example that a bus was not allowed to serve the same area as an
underground line or another bus if it was uneconomical. This also
applied to private bus lines). There were at the time nine
transportation enterprises in Hamburg including German Rail and German
Post, and the boats and ferries - all of which had to agree to the same
principle (ibid., p.192).

With some delay, other conurbations followed Hamburg's example. In
1970, **Hannover's** city and its hinterland formed the second
Verkehrsverbund. (Strictly speaking, the organisation - called

Grossraumverkehr (Regional Transport) - differs slightly in its organisational structure from the typical Verkehrsverbund.) **München** established a united transport authority in 1972 which today includes four different enterprises and thirty-eight private companies. Many of the regional bus services joined years later, mostly after 1980 (MVV 1982b, p.16, MVV 1983, pp.14, 15). **Frankfurt** Verkehrsverbund came into operation in 1978 including only two transportation enterprises (City of Frankfurt and German Rail). Forty-three enterprises are still operating independently in the hinterland of Frankfurt but the long-run aim is to unite them all into one transport authority. The largest transport authority is the **Rhein-Ruhr** which was formed in 1980, including over twenty enterprises. There is also the Vekehrsverbund **Stuttgart** which was established in 1978. Unified transport authorities will be formed during the mid-1980s in the Rhein-Neckar area, in Rhein-Sieg (Köln-Bonn) and Nürnberg. There is also strong opposition to the formation of new unified transport authorities, especially in those cases where several cities are involved and some of them have effective low-cost public transport systems. A unified system will spread the debts somewhat more equally over all cities. According to personal interviews, a unified transport system in Nürnberg will not now be realised.

Financial support for public transport

This shift to public transport was massively assisted in both countries by changes in the legal basis of central government support for public transport. In Britain, until 1968, the government supported road building by providing 100 per cent of funding for trunk roads and motorways - basically through inter-city routes, which however sometimes passed through urban areas - and 75 per cent for approved local authority roads. In that year, the Transport Act provided for the first time that similar 75 per cent support could be given for approved capital investment projects in public transport. It was this that made possible the few rail systems that were built or reconstructed in Glasgow, Tyneside and Merseyside during the 1970s. Nevertheless, it was a relatively small shift in the total pattern of public investment in transportation - the great bulk of which still went on to road building and maintenance. Even during the late 1970s, when these schemes were being carried through, capital investment in public transport was actually declining - from £255 million in 1975/6 to £188 million in 1979/80 (at constant 1980 prices), as against corresponding figures of £540 million and £342 million on local roads, or £728 million and £467 million on trunk road construction and maintenance.

In the Federal Republic, the Federal Government forecast in 1963 that expenditure for public transportation would average about 37.5 billion DM for the next 25-30 years. Over the same time period investments of about 90 billion DM were forecast for urban roads, and another 106 billion DM for trunk roads and motorways which are financed completely by the Federal Government and the Länder (Girnau 1983, p.8). Table 2.1 shows the forecast total new investments.

During the first ten years it was planned to spend about 15 billion DM on local public transport to which local authorities themselves would contribute, and the remainder of 3 billion DM on suburban rail investment (S-Bahn) which was given to the German Bundesbahn (mainly paid by the Federal Government, Länder and in small part by local authorities - see Table 2.2). In reality, the new investments for public transportation were not as high as forecast over the fifteen-year period between 1967 and 1981. Only 15.3 billion DM were spent on construction of rapid rail and light rail, about the amount which had been forecast for ten years. However, the 7.6 billion DM spent on S-Bahn investments were about twice as high as forecast. Completely at variance with the forecast were also the road building programmes which cost about eight times the forecast costs (195 billion DM). Table 2.2 shows the actual expenditure in rail transport between 1967 and 1981.

The Deutsche Städtetag has calculated the average costs per km. - including stops - to be:

- for rapid rail 35-45 million DM with 78 per cent tunnelling;
- for light rail 20-25 million DM with 23 per cent tunnelling; and
- for trams 2-4 million DM, all in 1973 prices (Kalwitzki 1981, p.35).

Table 2.1

Forecast Investments in Transportation, Federal Republic of Germany, 1963

Investment and Source	Costs in billion DM	
	Cost, first 10 years	Total costs 25-30 years
Total investments in transport facilities to which local authorities contribute:	56.92	140.8
Through roads) urban roads	28.77	78.3) 90.0
Residential roads)	3.68	11.7)
Parking facilities	6.45	13.3
Public transport	18.02	37.5
Additional road investments paid **solely** by the Federal Government and Länder	42.40	106.0

Source: Girnau 1983, p.8

Table 2.2

New Transportation Investments, Federal Republic of Germany, 1967-1981

Paid by	Rapid rail and light rail million DM	%	S-Bahn million DM	%	Total million DM	%
Federal Government	7,800	51	5,100	67	12,900	56
Länder	2,800	18	1,900	25	4,700	21
Local Authority	4,700	31	600	8	5,300	23
Total	15,300	100	7,600	100	22,900	100

Figures do not include investments in bus garages, repair shops, etc.

Source: Girnau 1983, p.9.

Another calculation of light rail costs, by the Deutsche Städtetag, gives 40 million per km. with 70 per cent tunnelling at 1976 prices (Difu 1980, p.130).

As can be seen from Table 2.2, between 1967 and 1981 the Federal Government paid on average 56 per cent of total annual investments in rail transport. Officially the Federal Government is empowered to pay up to 60 per cent of investments in:

- S-Bahn
- rapid rail or light rail
- construction of bus garages
- park and ride systems.

In general each Land may pay up to 25 per cent and the local authority pays the remainder of 15 per cent. However, Table 2.2 clearly indicates that between 1967 and 1981 local authorities paid much more than 15 per cent (23 per cent). As only rail transport is financed so heavily by the Federal Government, most cities of reasonable size (around 500,000 and more) decided to invest in this transportation mode. It is always argued that bus transportation does not receive comparable investment (to rail transport) from the Federal Government. However, the considerable investments in road building programmes directly and indirectly favoured bus operations. The number of buses has increased considerably between

1960 and 1970, and again at the beginning of the 1970s. Furthermore, a future increase is likely with the reduction of old tram lines (Difu 1980, pp.124-125).

In the stringent conditions of the 1980s, Federal support for public transport investment is being somewhat reduced (Table 2.3). Unless the Land or local governments pick up the bill, this is almost certain to mean some reduction in total investment and a more stringent scrutiny of projects. As already noticed, the Federal Government is introducing a form of cost-benefit analysis for new public transport investments.

Table 2.3

Programme of Investments in Public Transport by the Federal Government of Germany, 1983-1987

1983	:	1,289,000 DM (plus special 600,000 DM supplement)
1984	:	1,240,000 DM
1985	:	1,226,000 DM
1986	:	1,226,000 DM
1987	:	1,226,000 DM

Note: These sums are derived from the revenue from tax on petrol, at 1984 prices.

Source: Federal Ministry of Transport, internal information.

Although in general operating costs are paid by local authorities, subsidies to support concessionary fares are paid by both the Federal Government and the Länder. These vary between 15 and 30 per cent of the total costs. In the more stringent conditions of the 1980s, these generous subsidies may be cut back, which will mean higher operating costs for the cities. In the meantime, controversy continues between the Länder and Federal Government about their respective contributions to concessionary fare support. Even if the Federal Government succeeds in easing its financial burden at the expense of the Länder, each Land in turn will try to reduce its burden at the expense of the cities.

Total operating subsidies in German cities have tended to vary between 30 per cent and 50 per cent of total costs. Thus in München the subsidy fell from 56.7 per cent of costs in 1974 to as low as 38.9 per cent in 1980, rising slightly afterwards (MVV 1982a, p.12; 1984, p.9, own calculations).

Table 2.4

Public Transportation Costs, Income and Subsidies in Köln (1963-1982) and München (1972-1982), (Million DM)

Year	Costs	Income	Subsidies	Subsidies as percentage of costs
Köln				
1963	101	72	29	28.6
1967	124	92	32	25.6
1971	148	92	57	38.2
1973	174	119	56	32.1
1975	205	127	78	37.9
1977	227	144	83	36.5
1979	242	163	79	32.6
1981	275	187	88	32.0
1982	286	191	95	33.3
München				
1972*	278	129	149	53.6
1973	493	213	275	55.8
1974	559	236	317	56.7
1975	578	246	327	56.6
1976	595	291	299	50.3
1977	604	296	277	45.9
1978	624	301	286	45.8
1979	658	317	305	46.4
1980	705	395	274	38.9
1981	757	412	306	40.4
1982	791	413	337	42.6

* From 28 May 1972.

Source: KVB, internal information; MVV 1981, 1984; own calculations.

   The Verkehrsverbund München received from the Federal Government and the Land Bayern (concessionary fares) and the city of München in the last ten years about 48.3 per cent of costs in subsidies. This amount is in line with subsidy figures in Bremen (44.1 per cent in 1982), Hannover (lower than 50 per cent), and the Rhein-Ruhr Area (47.4 per cent in 1981). However, the Verkehrsverbund Stuttgart showed a total subsidy level of 56.2 per cent in 1982 (internal information).

Comparing the British and German subsidy situation one can see in the following table by Crampton that the British rate fund contribution to public transportation measured in £ per capita does not vary a great deal from the German situation.

Table 2.5

Rate Fund Contributions to Passenger Transport, £/per Capita

Metropolitan County	1982/83 £	Verkehrsverbund or City	1982 DM	£a)
Greater Manchester	21.6	Rhein-Ruhr	136.3	34.0
Merseyside	37.6	München	140.8	35.2
South Yorkshire	49.9	Stuttgart	126.1	31.5
West Yorkshire	24.7	Frankfurtb)	164.1	41.0
West Midlands	15.6			
Tyne & Wear	30.5			

a) one £ = about 4 DM
b) inhabitants in the transport area 2,460,307.

Source: Crampton 1982, p.3; own calculations

Development of rail transit after 1965

The era of new underground lines in the Federal Republic of Germany started with the city in which such a system already existed, namely **Hamburg.** Plans for an extension of the existing U-Bahn system were made as early as 1955. In 1963, a whole new line was opened (Jungfernstieg to Wandsbek Garden City, the U2). Another new line was started in 1961 and opened in 1972 in the same year as München's underground system opened. In 1972, the U-Bahn system of Hamburg had a track length of 90 km. with planned extensions to 150 km. (track length) (Guhl 1975, pp.67-69).

Around 1962 rapid rail systems and light rail systems were planned and initiated in nearly all cities which had about 500,000 inhabitants or more. There are however several exceptions. **Bremen** has planned - and is still planning - a light rail system, but - as explained in Chapter 4 - has only been able to achieve 10 km. of track, none of it in the city centre. **Dortmund** still relied mainly on trams and buses during the period of our study, though in June 1984 it opened about 10 km. of new light rail in the city centre. Its connection to the Rhein-Ruhr S-Bahn will increase future accessibility for the city centre and inner city areas, as explained in detail in Chapter 4.

Duisburg and **Düsseldorf** are intermediate cases: although they do not yet have a light rail system, they possess what is called a 'Schnellstrassenbahn' (fast tram) which in reality has nearly the same effect as a light rail line. Both cities are also part of the Rhein-Ruhr transportation authority, and further stretches of the authority's light rail system will open during the mid-1980s.

Essen had the first light rail line in the Ruhr area. In 1982, it had built 10 km. of the 28km. originally planned light rail network (track length).

There are also a few cities around 400,000 inhabitants or even less which have at least some lines built as light rail lines, such as Bonn. The **Bonn** system is however part of the connecting traffic axis Köln - Bonn - Bad Godesberg. Further **Mannheim** and **Ludwigshafen**, the twin cities on opposite sides of the Rhein, have an existing light rail network which mainly connects the two cities. There are future plans to extend the lines (Guhl 1975, p.87). In 1983, only 10.8 km. were already built.

Bielefeld, with a population of only just over 300,000, is the smallest free-standing city in the Federal Republic which has a light rail system. 5.1 km. already exist and a further 41 km. are planned.

The best-known rapid rail and light rail systems, which were newly developed in their entirety after the Second World War, are found in **München** (U-Bahn system of 37.5 km. track length), **Frankfurt** (mixture of light rail and U-Bahn, track length 41.3 km.), **Hannover** (light rail, track length 60.7 km.), **Stuttgart** (light rail, track length 39.5 km.) and **Köln** (light rail, track length 41.6 km.).

Nürnberg is exceptional, because it only just reached the 'critical' level of 500,000 inhabitants in 1970, but also because it built a U-Bahn system against the advice of transportation experts who suggested a light rail system. In 1972 part of the underground line was opened, from the largest of the city's satellite towns in the direction of the city centre (3.5 km.). The connection to the city centre was finished in 1978. A further extension to Fürth's main station is planned to open in 1985, exactly 150 years after the first German railway ran for the first time along at least part of the same alignment. There are two further lines planned, and the complete system will have, if ever finished, a total track length of 42 km.

Overall, therefore, over twenty German cities have invested in new or reconstructed rail systems since the mid-1960s (Table 2.6). The great majority of these are light rail systems based on the upgrading of existing tram systems.

In comparison, the British investment in rail systems has been minimal; it consists of the 4.2 km. **Liverpool** Loop and Link system, the 56 km. **Tyne and Wear** Metro (only 12.8 km. of which is new construction) and the reconstructed 10.5 km. **Glasgow** Underground and 7.5 km. Argyle Line, together with the 16.9 km. Victoria Line, Heathrow extension (3 km.) and Jubilee Line (5.6 km. of new construction) in **London.** Major British conurbations of over two million population, such as the West Midlands and Greater Manchester, are still without rail transit systems. In comparison the German record, if transferred to Britain, would have brought such systems to cities like Edinburgh, Leeds, Bradford, Sheffield and Bristol.

The central question therefore remains: was the German policy of generous rail investment, extending as it did to relatively small middle-sized cities, justified either in terms of its direct operating results or in terms of its indirect impact on urban life? To this question we turn in the chapters that follow.

Table 2.6

Existing and Planned U-Bahn Systems and
Light Rail Systems in the Federal Republic of Germany
including Berlin (West)

Town	System	Length[c] in km. Existing	Under construction	Planned	First line
Berlin	U.B	101	8.2	200*	1902
Hamburg	U.B	89.5	6.5	120	1912
München	U.B	37.5	14.5	90	1972
Nürnberg	U.B	15.0	4.8	42.1	1972
Bielefeld	L.R	5.1	3	41	1971
Bremen	L.R	10.0	-	39	1968
Frankfurt	L.R	41.3	10.5	50.8	1968
Hannover	L.R	60.7[a]	6.5	98	1975
Köln	L.R	41.6	5.0	continuation of changing the tram to L.R	1968
Bonn	L.R	25.5	3.1	?	1975
Ludwigshafen	L.R	9.0	2.8	23.4	1969
Mannheim	L.R	1.8	-	?	1971
Stuttgart	L.R	39.5	4.0	100	1962
Wuppertal	R.R[b]	13.3	-	0	1901[b]
Stadtbahn Rhein-Ruhr**		53.9	42.5	139	1977

* For whole of Berlin
** Light Rail System includes the cities of:

Bochum	3.3 km.
Dortmund	13.0 km.
Düsseldorf	1.6 km.
Essen	10.1 km.
Gelsenkirchen	0 km.
Herne	0 km.
Mülheim/R	5.5 km.

a) VÖV (Verband Öffentlicher Verkehrsbetriebe) 1983
b) Schwebebahn (Monorail)
c) Track length

Source: Anon, 1983 Position as at 31 December 1982, and internal information.

3 The thirteen cities: a comparative overview

This is the first of three chapters that seek to compare the thirteen cities chosen for study - seven in the Federal Republic, six in Britain - in terms of their urban structures, public transport systems, and city-centre pedestrianisation schemes. The three chapters are based on the detailed statistical appendix for each of the cities, which appears as Appendix B; the reader in search of further detail should find it there.

This chapter is in the nature of a general overview, and therefore sets the scene for the other two. It starts with a brief historical excursion which looks at densities, by rings, for certain of the cities from the pre-World War Two period onwards. Then it goes on to give some comparative basic figures about urban structures: areas, populations, employment, city centre activities. It then presents the basic statistical facts about the cities' public transport systems, which are however discussed in much more detail in Chapter 4. Then it similarly gives basic data about city-centre pedestrianisation, which is treated in detail in Chapter 5.

Urban structure

In Chapter 2 we have already observed that, contrary to the conventional wisdom, British cities before World War Two were not developed at lower densities than their German equivalent. Table 3.1 presents the detailed evidence for a selection of the case study cities. It shows that in 1931 the inner ring of British cities - between 1 and 3 kilometres from the centre, that is the ring just outside the Central Business District - actually tended to have higher densities than its German equivalent; and this was even more true in 1951, when bombing had greatly reduced densities in German cities while the great reconstruction of British cities had not yet begun. It was only during this reconstruction, that is principally during the 1960s, that the inner rings of British cities were drastically thinned out. Also notable from Table 3.1 is that even in the 3-6 kilometre ring - characteristically representing development between 1900 and 1930 - densities in the British cities were higher, representing the relatively high density of early twentieth-century terrace housing and early interwar local authority cottage estates. And these relatively high densities even persist into the 6-9 kilometre ring, developed in the 1930s.

Table 3.1

Density Table for Selected British and German Cities

Cities	Radius	0-1	km			Radius	1-3	km		
	1931	1951	1961	1971	1981	1931	1951	1961	1971	1981
Manchester	-	24.5	16.6	11.0	a)	202.5	151.5	121.9	66.1	a)
Liverpool	-	-	50.7	29.5	a)	287.8	215.2	186.9	100.2	a)
Newcastle	-	63.2	46.8	32.6	a)	-	112.8	89.6	61.4	a)
Sheffield	-	-	76.7	65.2	a)	98.5	78.5	64.3	58.3	a)
	1939	1950	1961	1970	1982	1939	1950	1961	1970	1982
Bremen	130.6	75.7	79.2	74.7	56.0	97.6	71.4	95.5	121.1	108.3
Dortmund	-	-	-	65.1	54.8	-	43.4	62.8	59.6	49.9
Hannover	249.6	98.9	134.4	114.8	89.2	120.4	103.6	149.9	114.9	96.2
Köln[b]	-	89.0	117.0	103.0	97.0	-	85.0	113.0	107.0	98.6
München[c]	208.5	164.3	174.9	146.0	117.0	218.3	145.9	182.3	166.2	148.3

a) British 1981 figures not available due to boundary changes.

b) 1982 figure is for 31.12.1981.

c) Figures are for 1933

41

Table 3.1 con't

Density Table for Selected British and German Cities

Cities	Radius 3-6 km					Radius 6-9 km				
	1931	1951	1961	1971	1981	1931	1951	1961	1971	1981
Manchester	81.4	74.2	68.3	61.4	a)	36.7	40.7	40.8	40.3	a)
Liverpool	126.5	96.8	91.1	77.7	a)	24.6	35.5	40.3	42.1	a)
Newcastle	-	77.6	70.4	59.1	a)	No wards included				
Sheffield	63.6	59.9	45.4	42.3	a)	8.8	15.5	17.8	20.5	a)
	1939	1950	1961	1970	1982	1939	1950	1961	1970	1982
Bremen	22.3	29.7	40.1	37.2	35.6	6.1	7.5	14.2	25.7	21.7
Dortmund	-	14.7	19.3	25.7	24.2	No districts included				
Hannover	22.6	33.7	33.9	34.5	35.3	6.3	10.6	19.1	20.2	19.5
Köln[b]	-	41.6	55.0	55.6	52.4	-	7.4	10.7	15.4	19.9
München[c]	34.3	44.1	55.7	64.1	61.0	5.2	14.8	21.3	31.3	35.0

a) British 1981 figures not available due to boundary changes.

b) 1982 figure is for 31.12.1981

c) Figures are for 1933

Sources: Census, 1931, 1951, 1981, Scotland, Vols I & II; Census 1931,
1971, 1981, England & Wales, County Reports
Statistiche Landesämter
Own calculations

Against this historical background we can turn to compare the thirteen cities in the decade 1970-1980. Basic data about areas and populations are set out in Table 3.2. It is immediately evident that we are dealing with medium-sized cities; in terms of their 1981 populations they range from a maximum of 1,292,000 (München) down to a minimum of 273,000 (Newcastle). This represents a deliberate choice; in both countries the largest cities (London, Berlin West, Hamburg) were excluded, primarily on the ground that because of their size all had invested in rail rapid transit systems - in the case of London and Berlin, very extensive systems - well before the 1960s. The essence of the comparison is thus to consider cities in the population size range between approximately a quarter of a million and one and a quarter million, which in both countries constitute the typical regional capital cities. Traditionally, such cities did not invest in rail rapid transit; and this is still generally true for Britain.

The cities do not vary markedly in area but do show some variations in average density, from 42/ha. (München) down to only 12.5/ha. (Leeds). However, Leeds and its near neighbour Sheffield are special in being very over-bounded, with large areas of rural land, as a result of the English local government reorganisation of the 1970s. Bremen is the only other case with an average density of under 20/ha. Otherwise the density range is narrower, with six of the thirteen cities falling in the range between 21 and 32/ha. As already noticed in Chapter 2, contrary to expectation British cities tended to have somewhat higher historic population densities than their German counterparts; though the wholesale renewal of the 1960s produced a big reduction in populations, with resultant densities that closely resembled those in the reconstructed German cities, it is notable that after München two of the British cities - Liverpool and Manchester - have the highest overall densities. Generally, however, in both countries the densities tend to be in the middle range; they would not appear to offer the ideal conditions for rail rapid transit.

Table 3.2 also shows, where available, figures for the total population of the regions surrounding the thirteen cities. These are based on the definitions as officially used in the country concerned; they are not available for all cities. Because of this fact, they tend to vary rather strikingly from city to city. In the case of the English cities, they are the areas of the Metropolitan Counties, which coincide with those of the official Passenger Transport Executives. Thus, while the cities of Manchester and Liverpool have approximately equal areas and similar populations, the Greater Manchester PTE covers an area almost double that of the Merseyside PTE and has a population nearly 50 per cent greater. The Glasgow regional figure is that for the Strathclyde region, which is rather more generously defined than the English metropolitan counties. In general, while the British PTE (in England, Metropolitan County) populations were declining in the 1970s, their German equivalents were still tending to increase.

Table 3.2

The Thirteen Cities: Areas, Population and Densities

	Area ha. (1981)	City Population 1970	City Population 1981	Change 1970-81	Density /ha. (1981)	Area ha. (1981)	Region Population 1970	Region Population 1981	Change 1970-81
Bremen	32,672	593,182	555,118	-6.4	17.0	370,329	1,004,119	1,021,299	+1.1
Dortmund	28,017	646,954	608,908	-5.9	21.6	-	-	-	-
Essen	21,024	698,434	653,319	-6.5	32.7	-	-	-	-
Hannover a)	20,400	522,603	554,575	+6.1	27.0	228,900	1,068,400	1,073,459	-1.0
Köln	40,512	994,705	971,403	-2.3	26.0	412,012	1,829,344	2,027,891	+10.9
München	31,039	1,293,590	1,291,828	-0.1	42.0	198,350	2,112,410	2,305,444	+9.1
Nürnberg	18,576	480,407	483,472	+0.6	25.8	293,530	1,022,752	1,163,56	+13.8
Glasgow	19,757	977,500	755,429	-22.7	38.8	1,353,698	2,564,550	2,375,410	-0.9
Leeds	56,215	738,931	704,885	-4.6	12.5	203,912	2,067,642	2,037,165	-1.5
Liverpool	11,291	599,453	503,722	-16.0	45.2	65,202	1,642,963	1,503,120	-8.5
Manchester	11,621	543,650	437,663	-19.5	46.0	128,674	2,721,815	2,575,407	-5.4
Newcastle	11,187	300,729	272,914	-9.2	24.8	54,006	1,209,959	1,135,492	-6.1
Sheffield	36,756	520,327	530,843	+2.0	14.4	156,049	1,313,957	1,292,029	-1.7

a) Boundary changes 1971-81; affect comparison.

Source: Appendix B

Table 3.3

The Thirteen Cities Compared: Economic Structure

	Total employ-employ-ment 1971	Insured employees[a]						
		1974	1982	Change 1974-1982 in %	1982 Composition			
					Mfrg	Dis-trib.	Trans port in %	Other services
Bremen	315,585	262,704	242,106	-3.8	30.3	18.1	13.4	26.3
Dortmund	276,775	239,847	216,925	-9.6	27.7	16.4	5.4	24.2
Essen	303,973	249,271	225,692	-9.5	25.2	17.7	5.5	27.6
Hannover	401,055	313,275	295,234	-5.8	30.6	15.1	7.7	28.3
Köln	528,710	408,856	415,478	+1.6	30.7	16.5	6.9	30.8
München	784,000	648,217	651,122	+0.5	29.7	15.8	6.3	32.1
Nürnberg	314,064	276,443	263,871	-4.5	38.0	18.9	7.7	27.8

	Total Employment		Change 1971-1981 in %	1981 Composition			
	1971	1981		Mfrg	Dis-trib.	Trans port	Other services
Glasgow[b]	426,590	362,310	b)	23.2	19.0	8.5	39.7
Leeds[b]	255,700	317,640	b)	27.5	21.3	6.2	33.2
Liverpool	325,200	258,770	-20.4	21.5	18.0	13.0	40.3
Manchester	335,540	295,090	-12.1	23.0	19.1	9.7	40.6
Newcastle[b]	152,710	168,750	b)	19.6	17.6	7.9	45.2
Sheffield[b]	266,300	253,860	b)	35.5	18.7	5.6	32.1

a) Excludes many non-manual workers and employees in mining; not directly
   comparable with total employment, either in Germany or Britain.
b) Major boundary changes affect comparison.

Source: Appendix B

Table 3.3 shows the economic structure of the thirteen cities. The German examples have very similar employment structures, with between 25 and 30 per cent of their insured employees in manufacturing, between 15 and 18 per cent in distributive trade, between 5 and 10 per cent in transport and communications, and 25 and 30 per cent in other services. (Bremen is unusual; as a port it has a much higher proportion in transport and communication and a correspondingly lower proportion in other services.) The British cities show lower proportions in manufacturing, and higher proportions in both distribution and transport, than their German equivalents.

Table 3.4 focuses on the central business districts (CBDs) of the thirteen cities - the main concern of this study. These are fairly similar in area, ranging between 93 and 399 hectares; they have relatively low residential populations, ranging from 4,000 to 23,000 in 1970. All the German examples showed sharp population losses from 1970 to 1981; no comparison is possible for the English cities because of extensive intervening changes in the ward boundaries which are used to define the CBDs. 1970 employment in the CBDs ranged from 35,000 in the relatively compact Essen CBD to as high as 83,000 in the CBD of Hannover. In every case, the great bulk of this employment - ranging from 74 per cent in Hannover to as high as 92 per cent in Essen - was in the tertiary sector. The figure for Essen reflects the fact that the central business district is very tightly bounded, excluding nearby manufacturing plants.

Table 3.4 also shows the extent of pedestrianisation in each centre and the associated parking provision. The length of the pedestrian area ranges from a low of only 700 m. in Bremen to as much as 5,000 m. in Nürnberg. On average the pedestrian area in the British cities is slightly smaller than that in their German counterparts (1,620 m. - including bus - only streets - against 2,286 m.). Parking provision is also very similar in both the German and the British cities, ranging from 10,000 spaces in Nürnberg to a very high figure of 39,500 in Köln; no other city has more than 20,000 spaces. This would seem to suggest that all the thirteen cities have followed similar policies with regard to pedestrianisation and car parking; it is only in the extent of their rail rapid transit provision that they differ. However, the _total_ effect of the policies is that the German city centres have a much higher overall accessibility, in terms of rapid transit and parking provision combined, than their British counterparts. It is also interesting that Nürnberg and München, with the most extensive pedestrianisation schemes, have the lowest parking provision of any centre for which figures are available.

Table 3.5 presents further city centre data, relating to retail floorspace (with the exception of Leeds, for which we could obtain no data). It compares this with equivalent floorspace in the entire city, and then attempts to give a standardised figure for CBD floorspace in relation to the entire population for the region, or hinterland, served by the CBD. (German figures here are for City Regions as officially

defined; British figures for Metropolitan Counties.) Evidently, with
some exceptions, the figures are closely comparable, indicating that the
cities are of very similar status as regional shopping centres. Hannover
and Bremen seem to be over-supplied with shopping floorspace, whereas
Sheffield appears to be under-supplied. It is significant that, of the
British cities, Sheffield is not a regional shopping centre.

Table 3.4

The Thirteen Cities Compared: Central Business Districts

	Area (ha.)	Population 1970	1981	Change 1970- 1981 %	Employment 1970/71 Total	% Tert- iary	Pedes- trian area (m.)	Parking spaces
Bremen	312	21,950	15,953	-27.3	74,135	87.6	700	19,400
Dortmund	178	11,576	9,751	-15.8	56,716	81.9	1,405	15,700
Essen	93	4,602	3,712	-19.3	34,498	92.4	2,000	18,750
Hannover	222	15,006	11,523	-23.2	82,807	74.0	3,500	19,150
Köln	243	22,499	21,471	-14.7	77,097	86.6	3,000+	39,500
München	208	25,161	20,471	-18.6	76,342	84.3	2,000+	13,250
Nürnberg	286	22,434	17,255	-23.1	62,189	83.3	5,000	10,000
Glasgow	182	6,931	11,300	+63.0	110,970	77.4	895	13,855
Leeds	395	12,927	a)	a)	a)	a)	1,677	19,760
Liverpool	380	7,321	a)	a)	91,900	81.4	2,000	24,100
Manchester	317	3,740	a)	a)	122,870	75.4	2,150	16,299
Newcastle	399	2,774	a)	a)	66,840	80.6	1,300	12,860
Sheffield	261	16,760	a)	a)	46,400	a)	1,700	19,000

a) Figure not available.

Source: Appendix B

Table 3.5

Selected Case Study Cities: Gross Retail Shopping Floorspace

Cities/Region	Pop. (1981)	Total floorspace a) sq. m.	Floorspace city centre a) sq. m.	City centre floorspace per 10,000 pop. in the region
Bremen	555,118	1,261,386	303,472	2,971
Region Bremen	1,021,299	-		
Dortmund	603,847	1,252,000	378,300	-
Essen	653,319	1,211,934	301,100	-
Hannover	554,575	1,107,000	398,000	3,708
Region Hannover	1,073,459	-		
Köln	971,403	1,990,200	397,100	1,950
Region Köln	2,027,891	-		
München	1,291,828	2,248,100	416,600	1,807
Region München	2,305,444	-		
Nürnberg	483,472	1,089,300	302,600	2,601
Region Nürnberg	1,163,556	-		
Glasgow b)	755,429	1,176,658	478,284	2,014
Strathclyde Region	2,375,410	-		
Manchester c)	437,663	1,234,000	717,000	2,784
Greater Manchester	2,575,407	-		
Newcastle	272,914	-	316,000	2,783
Tyne & Wear	1,135,492	1,149,657		
Sheffield d)	530,843	785,700	216,000	1,672
South Yorkshire	1,292,029	-		

a) Figures for German cities are from the Handels- und Gaststättenzählung 31.3.1979, 'Geschäftsflächen' für Einzelhandel.
b) Floorspace figures for the city of Glasgow are from 1982, and for the city centre from 1980, city centre of Glasgow = Ward 11. The CBD is defined according to the Census of 1971 = 382,300 ha.
c) The city centre is defined according to the the Local Plan, area of the city centre: 403 hectares.
d) Size of CBDs of British cities do not correspond with definition in Appendix B.

Sources: Census 1981; information about gross floorspace in Britain from Districts or County Councils of the case study cities; (from estimates 1981-1983) Handels-und Gaststättenzählung 31.3.1979; Statistische Ämter of the case study cities in Germany.

Table 3.6

The Thirteen Cities: Transportation Statistics

| | Modal Split[a] | | | | Rail S-Bahn km. | Rapid Transit U-Bahn km. | LRT km. | Tram km. | Car owners/ 000 pop. | Parking spaces in CBD |
	Entire city Public	Priv- ate	CBD only Public	Priv- ate						
Bremen	33	67	54	46	-		10	57	358	19,400
Dortmund	32	68	38	62	c)		12	98	361	15,700
Essen	27	73	-	-	c)		10	71	382	18,750
Hannover	33	67	-	-	-		93	63	316	19,150
Köln	35	65	47	53	-		35[d]	122[d]	394	39,500
München	45	50	70	30	412	38	-	101	366	13,250
Nürnberg	40	50[e]	48	47[f]	-	18	-	43	346	10,000
Glasgow	28	72	60	40	8	10	-	-	142	13,855
Leeds	42	58	-	-	-	-	-	-	-	19,760
Liverpool	44	56	64	36	4	-	-	-	a)	24,100
Manchester	22	78	50	50	-	-	-	-	250	16,299
Newcastle[b]	34	66	62	38	-	-	56	-	194	12,860
Sheffield	41	59	58	42	-	-	-	-	230	19,000

a) Dates as in Appendix B; for Britain, 1971
b) Tyne and Wear County
c) Details found under S-Bahn system Rhein-Ruhr
d) About 5 per cent use bicycles in the CBD
e) 10 per cent use bicyles in the city of Nürnberg
f) difficult to define - see Appendix B

Source: Appendix B, Hall 1980.

Table 3.6 shows the most important details about the variations in the cities' transportation systems. In the city overall, the public:private modal split varies between 45:55 in München (and 44:56 in Liverpool) to 22:78 in Manchester. These figures seem to bear little relationship to the level of car ownership, which is generally much higher in the German cities and is very low in some of the British ones. (The very similar modal split figures for München and Liverpool conceal the fact that München had 366 cars per thousand population, Liverpool 166.) There seems to be some prima facie evidence here that by investing generously in public transport, German cities have maintained higher levels of public transport usage than would be expected given their high car ownership levels.

This emerges even more strikingly from the corresponding figures for journeys to and from the city centres. Several German cities achieve a better than 50:50 ratio in favour of public transport, and the most extreme - Hannover and München - manage 65-70:35-30, figures similar to that of Liverpool (64:36) with its much lower car ownership. One interesting point does however emerge: that of the two German cities that invested relatively little in rail rapid transit, Bremen and Dortmund, the first achieved a city-centre modal split relatively favourable to public transport, the other did not. It should be noticed that most of the figures in this Table relate to the late 1970s, when by no means all of the rail investments in the German cities were complete.

The most striking feature of Table 3.6 is of course the evidence of extensive rail investment in German cities and the relative lack of it in British cities. (Here the figures are the latest available, generally dating from 1982/3.) All the German cities have either underground or light rail systems (though that of Dortmund was minimal at the time of our survey); München also has a very extensive S-Bahn system. The equivalent British networks are either very small or non-existent.

We can sum up by saying that the case studies deal with cities of broadly similar size, population, and economic structure. They have similarly-sized CBDs which they have pedestrianised in broadly similar ways (the Germans rather more comprehensively than the British) and they make broadly similar provision for the private car. Where they do differ, very strikingly, is in their rail investment. In the next chapter we look at the transportation histories of the thirteen cities in more detail, with special emphasis on this difference.

4 The thirteen cities: public transport systems

Having compared the thirteen case study cities in terms of their socio-economic and morphological features, we now turn to a systematic comparison of the evolution of their public transport systems. Because these systems are so individual to each of the urban areas, we find it more logical first to present each in turn, and then only at the end to attempt a summary comparison. Further, in some of the German cities and all the British cities the logical unit of analysis is the entire urban agglomeration. Essen and Dortmund, two of our German case studies, are thus here treated together as part of the Verkehrsverbund Rhein-Ruhr.

Bremen

Bremen's first tram line opened in 1876 and was electrified in 1890, the first in Germany; from 1924, buses were introduced. In 1950, the system had eleven tram lines, eighteen bus lines and one trolley-bus line, with a total track length of 241.8 km. (Bremen Stadt, Der Senator für das Bauwesen 1982, p.4); the average number of trips per inhabitant, 249 a year in 1950, had sunk to 187 trips a year by 1982 (Bremen Strassenbahn AG 1959, 1983).

In 1971 the legislature and government of Bremen decided to build a rapid rail system (underground and S-Bahn system) on the basis of over-optimistic population and employment forecasts (Grabe 1967, p.38). In 1975, the decision of 1971 was changed because weaknesses had appeared in the forecasts. The new policy framework, covering the ten-year period 1975-85, changed the U-Bahn proposal into one for a Stadtbahn (light rail system). This could be progressively developed from the existing tram system and as a rule would continue to run on the surface; it can merely be put underground or elevated where absolutely necessary, though it would be impossible to start this operation in the city centre before 1985 (Bremische Bürgerschaft 1975, p.3). Plans for an S-Bahn system were also abandoned at this time.

At present therefore Bremen has only a minimal light rail system. In 1968 a short stretch was opened to the newly built housing estate of Osterholz as an extension of an old tram line; five years later, the same line got another extension at the other end to Arsen (Meyer 1973, p.551). Another 3 km. were built in 1976, also on the outskirts of Bremen, to give a total light rail length of some 10 km. Although this is very short in comparison with other German cities, about 50 per cent of all tram lines have a reserved right of way through physical separation or special road markings.

Bremen has become internationally celebrated for its city-centre traffic restraint policies. These began just before Christmas in 1960. The city centre was divided into four parts (transport cells) in which drivers of private cars can enter or leave a cell by a ring road but cannot drive between these four cells. The main aims were:

1. to stop through traffic in the city centre;

2. also to stop what is called in German 'vagabond' traffic which is looking for parking space and moves from one parking lot to another;

3. to give priority to public transportation.

There is no doubt that these regulations affected the subsequent decisions on construction of light rail lines. They were so effective that it was decided not to start construction in the city centre; instead, as noted above, the first stretches of new light rail lines were started on the outskirts (Bremen VG, planning office: interviews). Bremen thus avoided the problem faced by most other German cities, which started their construction programmes in the city centre, and then found when money became tight that they still had to complete the works.

As well as lacking extensive light rail, Bremen almost completely lacks an S-Bahn network. Though ambitious plans were made, around the same time as for the light rail system, the only line of any significance is the connection between Bremen main station and Bremen Vegesack, northwest of the city, which was electrified and opened in 1967. The trains run every thirty minutes with an average speed of 53 km./h. (Schreck, Meyer, Strumpf 1979, p.112), but lack the feel of a modern S-Bahn line.

In October 1980, the City and the Deutsche Bundesbahn set up a Transport Association which made it possible to extend a regular-interval and ticketing commuter train service to the whole region; a uniform fare and ticketing structure was introduced for municipal and rail operations.

Dortmund and Essen (The Rhein-Ruhr Area)

The Rhein-Ruhr Transportation Area is the largest of its kind in Europe. Its network of 12,000 km. (route length) corresponds to a distance from Düsseldorf to New York and back (VRR 1981, p.13). However its 5,025 sq. km. size is second to München. The Rhein-Ruhr area has a population of 7,262,000 and a workforce of 2,608,000 (VRR 1982b, p.4). The Rhein-Ruhr Transportation Area includes 55 cities - of which four had in 1981 over 500,000 inhabitants - and seven counties (VRR 1981, p.13). The Transportation Authority, called the VRR (Verkehrsverbund Rhein-Ruhr), was established in 1980. With one standard ticket one can use either the S-Bahn, suburban trains, the trams, buses, light rail lines, the elevated monorail line in Wuppertal, or the trolley buses in Solingen. The tram network is nearly 850 km. long, the light rail about 30 km., the S-Bahn 744 km. and the buses 7,774 km. (VRR 1982b, p.4 and internal information). Solingen has a trolley bus system of 46.7 km. (route length) (VRR 1983b, p.9).

S-Bahn

Around 1920, the first ideas were developed to create a fast suburban service in the Rhein-Ruhr area. In 1932 the German State Railways (Deutsche Reichsbahn) introduced the 'Ruhr Fast Traffic' - Ruhr-Schnellverkehr - which after the Second World War became part of the suburban service of the German Bundesbahn (Schreck, Meyer, Strumpf 1979, p.103).

    The first modern S-Bahn line was the S6 which partly opened in 1967, and the whole line, from Düsseldorf to Essen and south of Düsseldorf to Langenfeld, about 20 km. north of Köln, opened in 1968. In 1972 a further new S-Bahn station was opened to serve the western suburban areas of Düsseldorf (VRR 1983b, p.10). The S3 running from Oberhausen to Essen and Hattingen began service in 1974, at the same time as the S1, which connected Düsseldorf with Duisburg, Essen and Bochum. (VRR 1977, p.3). The S7 leading from Düsseldorf airport, mainly along the tracks of the S1 to Düsseldorf main station, began service in 1975. The south-eastern part of this line, running to Solingen-Ohlings, opened five years later. In 1980 the total S-Bahn network was 152.9 km. plus 125.7 km. of suburban trains (track length) (VRR, 1981, p.30). In 1983 the S1 was extended to Dortmund main station via the University of Dortmund, thus connecting the five largest cities in the Ruhr area.

    The eastern part of the Ruhr will have an effective new S-Bahn network only in 1986, with the opening of the S2. This line is planned to run from Dortmund West (Mengede) to the main station of Dortmund. With this connection the inner city areas of Dortmund will be reached easily. The future line S4 will serve Herne, west of Dortmund, Castrop-Rauxel, and will run from there to southern parts of the inner city area of Dortmund. The terminus stop will be east of Dortmund (Unna). The S4 was partly opened in spring 1984. With these two lines and some minor light rail lines, Dortmund and the eastern part of the Ruhr will have a 60 km. long network.

    The last major S-Bahn line in the Ruhr area, the S8, will be an east-west connection. The construction of the S8 started in 1978 and will connect the cities of Neuss, Düsseldorf, Wuppertal and Hagen. Its total length will be 82 km. The S8 will partly use existing tracks and will partly need new tracks; the finishing date is supposed to be 1990 (VRR 1982c, pp.6, 7 and 12).

Most S-Bahn trains run either every 20 minutes or every 30 minutes. The average speed is 52 km./h. (Meyer, Schreck, Strumpf 1979, p.103). In 1982 there were 6,700 parking spaces available for cars at 186 S-Bahn stations. A parking space costs about £4 a month (VRR. 1982a, p.14).

Light Rail

In 1974 the Land Government of Nordrhein-Westfalen took a crucial decision to develop a light rail system for the entire Ruhr area. It accepted the conclusions of a 1970 expert report (Der Minister f.W.,M.u.V.d.N.-W. 1970) by passing legislation to support and finance both an inter-city light rail system and a regional S-Bahn network (Gesetz zur Landesentwicklung 1974). This parallels the work of a newly created body, Rhein-Ruhr Light Rail Association (Stadtbahn-Gesellschaft Rhein-Ruhr mbH), (Der Minister f.W.,M.u.V.d.N.-W. 1976/77, p.6), founded in 1970. This aims to co-ordinate the light rail systems in the different cities according to uniform technical standards to give an eventual total planned network of 300 km., longer than London's underground today (ibid., p.6).

Here there was a major technical hurdle. The trams in the centre of the Rhein-Ruhr district - the cities of Bochum, Gelsenkirchen, Mülheim and Essen - run on 1 m. gauge tracks, narrower than the standard rail gauge of 1.433 m. (4'8 1/2") which will be used for the future light rail system. There is also a difference in the height of the platform between light rail cars and tram cars. Interchange from tram and light rail is more complicated and costly in the Ruhr cities than e.g. in Hannover where tram tracks have the same width as light rail tracks. And the conversion of tram to light rail involves costly change of gauge.

The Rhein-Ruhr area at the time of our survey had three cities with operational short light rapid rail 'systems' totalling 27.5 km. (VRR 1982b, p.4). **Düsseldorf's** first light rail line which opened in 1981 has only two stops and runs 1.6 km. underground; further stretches were under construction in 1984. **Bochum's** light rail line is also short, only 3.3 km. Its line was opened in 1979. A further line, the U35, is already under construction and will go into service in 1986 (VRR 1981, p.7). **Dortmund** opened a 10 km. long network in the city centre in June 1984.

Essen's first line, from the city centre to Mülheim, opened in 1977; a second, running from the south west through the centre to the university, opened in 1981. The two together give a length of 10 km. within the city; Essen and Mülheim together have a network of 15.6 km., the longest in the Ruhr area. The city also has a late nineteenth-century tram network, fairly modest in size compared with other German cities, and built on a narrow (1 m.) gauge; it began to modernise it in 1953. At the end of the 50s, the first ideas for an underground light rail system were

discussed, and in 1967 the first tram tunnel was opened in the city
centre. The light rail system shares the tram tunnels, which thus have
two different track gauges.

By 1990 the network of light rail lines in Essen should have a length
of 28 km. However, in 1976 the Essen city council decided to build only
20 km. for the present (Essener VAG 1977, p.19), of which about 12 km.
will be light rail and 8 km. on the surface crossing other traffic at
grade. Of this planned network, a further stretch will be running in
1985/86.

Table 4.1

Planned Development of Light Rail in Essen, 1984-1990

Phase	Main station	Mode	Time in minutes	Saving in minutes
-B2E	to Margarethen-höhe (4 km.)	Tram	16	
		Bus	17	5-6
		LR	11	
-B3E	Main station to	Tram	7	4
	Berliner Platz	LR	3	
-B4E	Saalbau to	Tram	12	
	Bredeney	LR	9	3
-B5E	Freistein to	Tram	5	
and	Porscheplatz	LR	2	3
-B6E	Haupteingang to	Tram	7	
	Porscheplatz	LR	4	3
	Westendstr to	Tram	9	
	Porscheplatz	LR	6	3
-B7E	Main station to	Tram	30	
	GE-Horst Sparkasse	LR	21	9
		Total savings:		30-31

Source: Essener Verkehrs-AG 1977, pp.26, 30, 36, 48, 56/57.

As in all cities which have light rail, one of the main advantages is
seen in the time savings. It has been calculated that the average speed
of the light rail cars is 32 km./h., for the tram 19.7 km./h. and for the
bus 20.5 km./h. (Essener VAG 1977, p.7). Table 4.1 shows the time

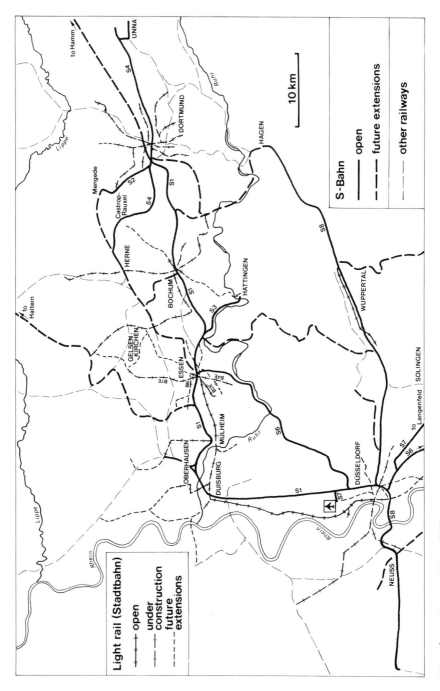

Fig. 4.1 Rhein-Ruhr: RRT

savings expected on the seven new light rail lines in comparison with the tram or bus systems they will replace.

Hannover

A unified transport authority for Hannover was formed in 1970; called Grossraumverkehr (Regional Transport), it provides transportation for the city of Hannover and its administrative hinterland (Landkreis), with a size of about 2,300 sq. km. and a population of more than one million, about 500,000 of them in the city of Hannover (Appendix B). The Grossraumverkehr is a Verkehrsverbund but there are some administrative and financial differences as compared with other German cities (USTRA 1983a, p.54). The main participants are the German Federal Railway (DB), Regional Transportation Authority Hannover (RVH), Hannoversche Verkehrsbetriebe AG (called USTRA), and two private transport organisations (Grossraumverkehr Hannover 1981, p.10). Until 1969, the tram system - the largest tram network of all German cities of comparable size (Guhl 1975, p.13) - was operated by a private company but the poor services resulted in a takeover by the public (Scheelhaase 1980, p.23).

The policy decision to build a light rail network (originally called underground tram), was made in 1965 (USTRA, 1983a, p.5). It was believed that unless this was done, it was only a matter of time before the traffic in the city centre came to a complete standstill during the rush hours (ibid., p.54). The light rail system would go completely underground in the city centre, with trains under automatic control; in suburban areas tracks would run on ground level with their own right of way. The main reasons for choosing light rail were that:

1. the building costs were much lower than for a 'heavy' rapid rail system (underground system). Only about 25 per cent of the tracks needed to run underground.

2. the construction of a complete underground system would have taken two or three times as long. This has proved right, as can be seen by comparing the extent of the Hannover system with that of the Nürnberg underground system.

3. the light rail system would be more effective in the critical aim of improving the traffic situation in the city centre as quickly as possible (Scheelhaase 1980, p.25).

As with all light rail systems built in the Federal Republic of Germany, the system could be changed into a full underground system if a policy decision were made in the long run future.

It is planned to have a network of three radial lines, called A, B and C, in service by 1989. A further line D is planned at an indeterminate

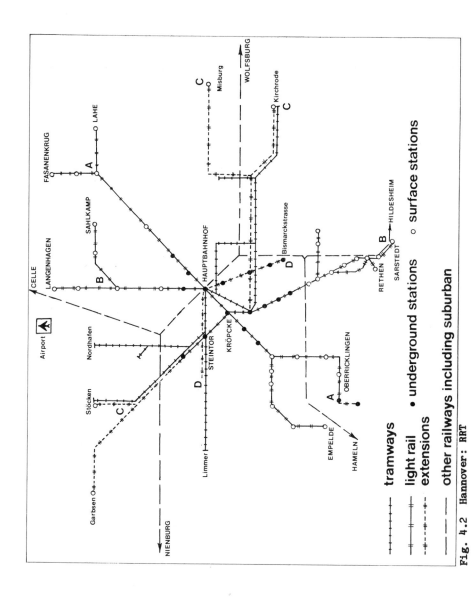

Fig. 4.2 Hannover: RRT

date in the future (USTRA 1983a, p.55). For the first three lines, the main interchanges are the city centre station Kröpcke and the central railway station (ibid., p.56). In contrast to Essen, the tram system runs on standard gauge tracks; however, the new light rail cars are heavier and need stronger electrical overhead wires. The first line - Line A, 23.04 km. long including a 3.9 km. tunnel under the city centre from south-west to north-east - opened in stages from 1976 to 1979; thence, the system was progressively extended to 1984 (ibid., p.54; Hannover Landeshauptstadt 1982, p.4; interview with U-Bahn Bauamt). The last city centre station, Steintor, opened at the end of March 1984. As a result, all city centre stations can be reached by pedestrians in a maximum of five minutes (USTRA 1983a, p.56).

According to a survey carried out in urban areas around light rail stops in 1978, the light rail system in Hannover has the full support of the population. 91 per cent of respondents thought that the light rail system was a good investment, and 81 per cent believed that further investment in the light rail system should be a first priority in the city's transportation planning (USTRA 1982a, p.34).

In contrast to most other large conurbations, Hannover's S-Bahn system is not yet fully developed; indeed, it is now questionable whether it ever will be. All suburban trains share the same track with inter-city traffic and rather too often the same tracks are also used by freight (Menke 1982, p.5). Some of the east-west lines are overloaded, especially during the peak hours, and the service suffers from the rule that gives inter-city traffic priority over suburban traffic; one train in ten is six or more minutes late (Forschungsinstitut der Friedrich -Ebert-Stiftung 1981, p.42). There is also no regular-interval service as in many other conurbations.

Köln

Köln's immediate post-war transportation plans gave the city a new road system. The narrow city-centre roads were kept unchanged, but several large six-lane ring and arterial roads were to be built. In addition, a new location for the main railway station was considered because of its closeness to the largest cathedral in Europe and also because of its limited access by two Rhein bridges (all passenger traffic is handled by the Hohenzollern bridge, while freight traffic uses the South bridge). Today, the station is still in its old location; the Hohenzollern bridge has to handle all passenger traffic and Köln is still the bottleneck in Germany's railway network, handling up to 900 trains a day (Köln Stadt 1980, p.1).

As in Britain, there were voices in favour of abandoning the old-fashioned tram system and replacing it with buses. But traffic research showed that the tram was the best mode for one of the largest German cities, such as Köln is (Schwarz 1950, p.37). Earlier than in most other

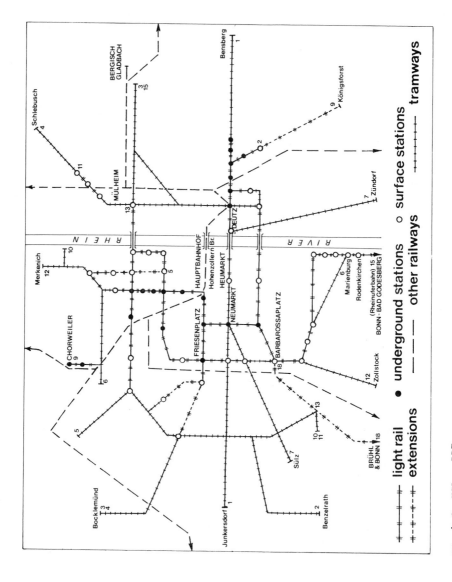

Fig 4.3 Köln: RRT

German cities, therefore, in 1962 a decision was made to build an underground system based on the existing tram network and connected to it (Dübbel, 1983, p.4). At that time, neither the Federal Government nor the Land Government of Nordrhein-Westfalen were prepared to give financial help; only after one year of construction did the Land Government give support, leaving the city to pay 50 per cent of the total costs (Köln Stadt 1983).

The first 1.3 km., from the main railway station to Friesenplatz, opened in 1968. Thence, short extensions were opened almost annually, giving the city a total track length of 41.6 km. of new light rail by 1983 (Dübbel 1983, p.6; Bollhöfer 1983, p.10). Additionally, more than 90 km. of track length has exclusive right-of-way, leaving only about 30 km. of track shared with cars and other traffic (Braitsch 1983, p.31, Dübbel 1983, p.6; plus own calculations). In addition, there is a 44 km. long light rail line from Köln-Mülheim to Bonn-Bad Godesberg, converted from the former Rheinuferbahn at a total cost of 150 million DM; the 10.1 km. section in the city of Köln, opened in 1978, cost 43.8 million DM (3.7 million DM per kilometres). This system, still under the management of the Köln-Bonn railway company (KBE), has had considerable success in increasing the number of passengers, with average increases between 1977 and 1982 of between 114 and 241 per cent (Meyer 1983, p.12). Because of this success, the KBE plans to rebuild the 31.9 km. Vorgebirgsbahn from Köln to Bonn, and work started in Bonn in 1982.

In May 1979, the city began to rethink its light rail plans, resulting in a major shift in policy (Köln Stadt 1982, p.26). Tunnel construction had proved expensive because of the underlying geology; the average cost for light rail line tunnel was 50 million DM per kilometre including stops (ibid., p.34). Further, the light rail system did not necessarily offer a superior or an economical service. The city has analysed that in 1980 more than 40 per cent of the city's population had to walk more than 500 metres to a tram or light rail stop, while about 20 per cent had no connection at all (ibid., p.5). While most lines were fully utilised, the line to the southern suburbs operated at well below capacity; the number of users was as low as on bus routes (ibid., p.8). In 1982, the Köln city government decided to abandon the objective of a complete light rail system and instead to develop a so-called Mischbetrieb (mixed system), including light rail in tunnel, in elevated form and at ground level, as well as the traditional tram system which will be extended (ibid., pp.3, 4). The city centre will still have surface tram lines; several planned underground connections have been given up (ibid., p.33); existing tram lines will be altered only if there is a substantial time saving to passengers.

München

München has probably the most impressive public transportation system in
the Federal Republic of Germany. The construction of the two new
transportation systems, the suburban and underground trains (S- and U-
Bahn) started about 45 years ago. In 1937 the Council of München decided
to build a west-east and a north-south orientated rail system. The
Reichsbahn Management (Reichsbahndirektion) started one year later with
tunnelling the Lindwurm Strasse (south of the main station). Further
construction work was stopped in 1941 because of the Second World War; at
this time only 600 meters of tunnelling was built (Guhl 1975, p.67).

In 1963 the city council agreed to a general transportation plan which
included a suburban rail (S-Bahn) and an underground (U-Bahn) and tram
system. The suburban rail was intended to connect the suburban areas with
the city and the underground system was intended to serve passenger flow
in the city of München. Connections between the two systems were to be
provided not only inside the city centre but also outside. The basic
concept was one tunnelled alignment in the city centre in an east-west
direction which was to be crossed by three (at first four) underground
lines in a north-south direction (Guhl 1975, pp.67-71).

Construction of these lines started in 1965 and the first passengers
were carried in 1972, for the opening of the Olympic Games. The
connection between S- and U-Bahn trains was also finished in 1972, and in
the same year a regional transportation authority was established. In
1981 the public transportation system had a total track length of 543 km.
and a route length of 2,900 km. (MVV 1982a, p.50).

The S-Bahn lines serve an area of 5,300 sq. km. in and around München,
in which about 2.3 million people live in 170 separate local authorities.
München has a network of seven S-Bahn lines to the west and five to the
east, all leading to a 4.2 km.-long west-east tunnel under the centre of
the city (Guhl 1975, p.45). The total track length of the network is
about 410 km., reaching 40 km. into the hinterland. Part of the S-Bahn
network is served by S-Bahn trains only (420 DB model), but especially
the outer stretches have to share the alignment with intercity trains.
(The S-Bahn has priority in most cases but there are still short
stretches where the intercity trains have priority.) The aim is to get
the S-Bahn their own alignments on the busiest routes (MVV 1982a, p.15).

The opening of the S-Bahn occurred at the same year as the opening of
the underground (1972); only the line to the north-east, to Ismaning,
remained to be opened one year later. A new line in the south
(Wolfratshausen), the S7, which used to be a route for suburban trains,
was opened in 1981 (ibid., p.23). Normally trains run every 20 minutes;
there are however some lines which run during the offpeak hours every 40
minutes. The average travel speed is 49 km./h., on some lines 27 km./h.
The number of daily passengers using the S-Bahn was 430,000 in 1973 and

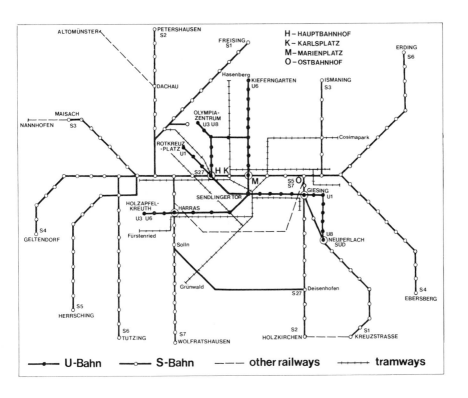

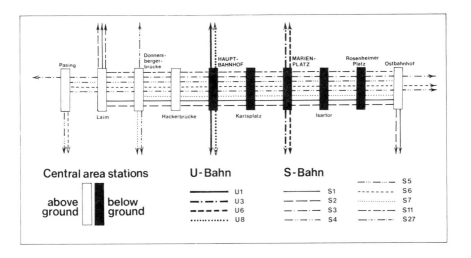

Fig. 4.4 München: RRT

600,000 in 1982 (MVV 1982b, p.5). There were further plans to increase
the S-Bahn lines; the most important one was to be the one from Ismaning
to the airport (23 km.). It is forecast that about 40 per cent of all
airport passengers will use the new line.   There are also still
traditional suburban trains (Wendezüge) which run south of München.   As
the capacity of the S-Bahn alignments is already exhausted, these trains
have to use the old suburban station (Starnberger Bahnhof) (Schreck,
Meyer, Strumpf 1979, pp.106-107).

There is also a strong emphasis on building free park and ride systems
for cars, mainly at the outer S-Bahn stations, but also at outer
underground stations.   In 1982 there were about 8,100 spaces available at
the S-Bahn stations and 1,000 at the U-Bahn stations, which are still
not enough (MVV 1982b, p.14).   There is also an increase in providing
bicycle racks at the park and ride places.   In 1982 there were about
13,000 places for bicycles available.   A count in 1981 revealed that
18,000 bicycles were parked in these places (MVV 1982b, p.15).

The first U-Bahn system had a track length of 16 km. of which 11 km.
were tunnelled (Guhl 1975, p.70).   In the following years, the three
underground lines were extended considerably.   In 1975, the system
increased by another 2.5 km., and in 1980 by a further 15.5 km. (MVV
1982a, p.50). In 1981 the total U-Bahn system had a route length of 40.2
km. and a track length of 31.5 km. In 1983 further extensions have been
opened.   The lines U3 and U6 reached Holzapfelkreuth, where the 1983
International Flower Show took place, and the U1 is a new short line from
München main station to Rotkreuzplatz.   The track length reached 37.5 km.

Apart from the underground system, München still relies on its old
trams with 101 km. of track (1981) (MVV 1982a, p.50). 75 per cent of the
trams have their own right of way and their average speed is up to 25
km./h., only 10 km. less than the underground trains (MVV 1981, pp.6, 7).

Nürnberg

The Nürnberg transportation region includes the cities of Nürnberg,
Fürth, Erlangen, Schwabach, Stein, Zirndorf and a few other local
authorities (Nürnberg Stadt 1983, p.74).   The region is polycentric; all
cities are in close proximity to each other, while Nürnberg and Fürth
(which has about 100,000 inhabitants) are one built-up area.   The region
has an area of about 330 sq. km. and a population of about 777,000 (VAG,
1983).   It does not yet have a Verkehrsverbund like München or the Rhein-
Ruhr cities; there have been plans and discussions on this question over
recent years, but agreement is not yet certain.

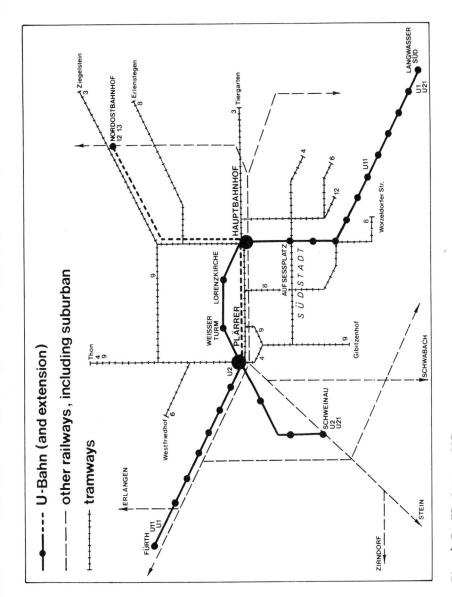

Fig. 4.5 Nürnberg: RRT

Nürnberg is famous for having the first railway in Germany; it ran to Fürth, and was opened in 1835. When tram lines were laid, around 1881, one led to Fürth; it was also the first one to be electrified (Nürnberg Stadt 1982, p.41).

Plans for a new underground system were made in the early 1960s, and in 1965 the decision was made by the local authority to build a 'real' underground system instead of the planned light rail system (Nürnberg Stadt 1972, p.10). About one year later it was decided to adopt the design of München's underground trains. The first stretch of the underground opened in 1972. In 1984, 18 km. of underground were in traffic. The total network originally planned was to be some 42 km. in length, but some reduction now seems likely. Apart from the underground, there are still seven tram routes, 43 km. in extent, in Nürnberg; in neighbouring Fürth, trams were withdrawn in 1981 (V+T 1983, p.143). The Nürnberg transport authority also has a large network of buses, with some sixty routes and a length of 346 km. The biggest daily trip movements are within Nürnberg and Fürth with 700,000 daily trips out of a total of 1.5 million trips in the region (Nürnberg Stadt 1972, p.4).

The original plans for the underground network consisted of three lines (U1, U2, U3). The first part of the U1 was started in the south-east of Nürnberg from the satellite town of Langwasser (40,000 inhabitants). The first stretch (3.7 km.) was opened in 1972; the city centre was reached in 1978. By 1985 it is planned to reach Fürth's main rail station. The last station of the U1 will be beyond this point. The U2 runs from the south-west, close to the city centre, to the north-east. The first section opened in January 1984 (Plärrer-Schweinau). The 25 stations are on average 0.7 km. apart; the headway is 150 seconds (Wentzel 1982, pp.4, 7). Today discussion centres on the completion of the U1 (which is nearly complete) and of the U2 - though even the extension of the latter to the airport is questioned. Probably therefore the total network will be reduced from the original planned 42 km. to about 25 km.

In contrast to München's underground system the two interchanges in Nürnberg are not in the city centre, though they are close to it; the second interchange will also serve the S-Bahn system. Some parts of the U1 are not tunnelled; there is a 1,000 m. long bridge on the stretch to Fürth, and the first stretch of the underground from Langwasser was built without tunnelling. The average speed is about 32 km./h., the top speed is 80 km./h.

Nürnberg also has a very good suburban train system which will be partially developed into an S-Bahn system. The first improvement was in 1983; however, on some lines there will be no time savings since some of the old suburban trains omitted some stops while the S-Bahn stops everywhere. Nürnberg will actually be one of the last major German city to receive an S-Bahn system. The opening of the first 17 km. stretch is scheduled for 1987.

66

Glasgow

Up to the 1950s Glasgow had one of the world's finest tram systems (GGPTE, 1980, p.10). The first trams, in 1870, were privately run (McKay 1976, p.173), but the city became the first in Britain to take over the operation, in 1892; it operated at a profit, and in 1899 it electrified the entire system (ibid., pp.176, 177, 181). By 1914 the tramway network had a length of 315 km., with some additional 69 km. planned (ibid, p.183) - a system even more extensive than Hannover's 292 km. (in 1901), albeit for a city with about twice the population. Glasgow was also later than most British cities in scrapping its trams, starting in 1952 and not finishing until 1962 (Joyce 1962, pp.60, 104).

The first planning report for Glasgow, published in 1945, suggested feeder bus services linking with suburban railway stations and a direct connection between Buchanan Street underground and the Queen Street main line station (GGPTE 1980, p.10). The Clyde Valley Regional Plan, published one year later, followed up similar ideas. It mooted an interchange between British Rail at Partick and the underground, then at Merkland Street. Later reports (by Fitzpayne in 1948 and by Inglis in 1951) emphasised the inefficiency of different public services competing with each other and put forward the idea of common ticketing between trains and buses; in 1954 the Halcrow Report proposed an extension of the underground (ibid., p.10). None of these ideas was acted upon, since the 1950s were a period of minimal capital investment in public transport in Britain.

The Greater Glasgow Transportation Study, published in 1968, proposed - as well as a large programme of urban motorways and expressways - also to improve public transport including the re-opening and electrification of numerous railway lines (ibid., p.12). In 1972 the Greater Glasgow Passenger Transport Authority and Executive were set up (ibid., p.12). In 1972-73 the GGPTE applied to the Government for a 75 per cent infrastructure grant for the Argyle Line project and the modernisation of the underground; this was granted in 1974 (ibid., p.12).

The Glasgow underground was first opened in 1896 as a twin-tunnel cable operated system. It consists of a circle which runs through the city's central business district in the east and through inner residential areas on the south and west. Its 10.5 km. length connected the shipyards of Govan with the city centre and the west end mansions (Acton 1979, p.19). At its peak the underground, which was electrified in 1935, carried 35 million passengers each year; but by 1976 patronage had dropped to just over 10 million (ibid., p.19).

The underground was closed for modernisation in 1977 and reopened three years later. The modernised system can run three-car trains. Each car has 36 seats and another 54 standing spaces. The headway is 3.5 minutes. Trains run every four minutes at peak hours, every six minutes between

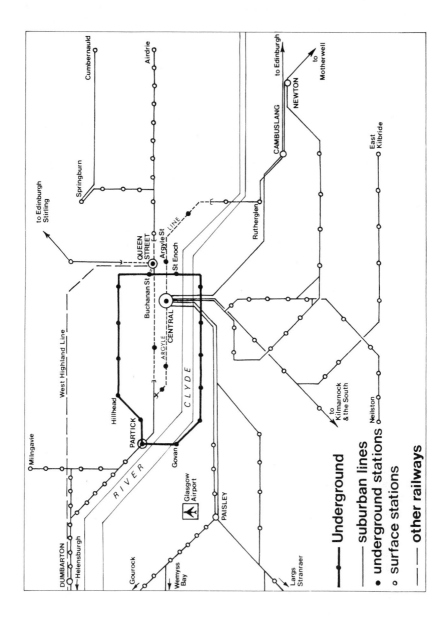

Fig. 4.6 Glasgow: RRT

peaks and every eight minutes in the evenings. Trains run only on weekdays. A top speed of 54 km./h. can be reached. All stations were rebuilt or improved as part of the modernisation, with new connections to BR suburban services at Partick in the west and at Buchanan St./Queen St. in the east.

Glasgow, like most large British cities, has a large suburban railway network. Most of it was electrified during the 1960s. The northern group of suburban lines had its main city centre terminal station at Queen Street and the southern group at Central Station. A central low-level line, connecting Partick north of the Clyde with Rutherglen south east of the river, was closed in 1964 (Martin & Voorhees Associates 1982, p.7). With the reopening of this line in 1979, now known as the Argyle Line, a connecting link between the northern and southern lines was established again. The main part of this link is a 7.5 km. long tunnel running from east to west under the city centre (Acton 1979, p.18). Most stations were newly built or improved, and some new rolling-stock was introduced (ibid., p.7).

Because the modernisation of the Glasgow system did not involve new rail construction, it was cheap compared with a new system. The modernisation of the underground cost £59 million, reconstruction and equipment of the Argyle line £36 million (ibid., p.75).

West Yorkshire

Of all of Britain's major urban areas, West Yorkshire is the most polycentric in form: it consists of two major cities (Leeds and Bradford), two middle-sized towns (Halifax and Huddersfield) and three smaller towns (Keighley, Dewsbury and Wakefield), each of which at one time had its own municipal transport system. All developed electric tram systems around 1900, though in rather different ways: Bradford, hemmed in by hills, substantially completed its system by 1904 while Leeds, free to expand on flatter ground, continued to expand its system as late as 1949 (Jones 1984, p.36). In 1911 the Leeds and Bradford systems simultaneously pioneered the introduction of the trolley-bus on to British city streets; Leeds scrapped its system as early as 1928, but Bradford kept its as late as the 1970s. Leeds, which had begun to develop its satellite housing estate at Middleton from 1920 onwards, opened the Middleton Light Railway in 1925; it ran on its own reserved track on the outer section, but plans for the innermost section, almost to the edge of the central business district, were abandoned in 1926 (ibid., pp.75, 97). But in the 1930s the city developed very extensive stretches of reserved-track tramways in the outer suburbs (Joyce 1962, p.57), and planned to extend these into the city centre via tram subways (Jones 1984, p.124).

From the early 1930s onwards, these municipal tramway systems were
engaged in tough competition with bus companies, many of them run by
subsidiaries of the railways; yet Leeds continued to forge ambitious
plans for new express services to outlying housing estates, and
compaigned for operating subsidies, scrapping trams only where they
suffered operating difficulties (ibid., pp.115, 120, 124, 129). After
World War Two the tramway systems were suffering from serious accumulated
lack of maintenance, and the nationalisation of municipal electricity
undertakings had a serious effect on finances (ibid., p.156). In fact,
though Bradford's last tram ran in 1950 (ibid., p.160), Leeds was one of
the last British cities to retain trams: it actually extended the system
in 1949, making the Middleton Light Rail into a circular route through
the southern suburbs; it ordered new trams down to 1954, and scrapped its
last tram as late as 1960 (Joyce 1962, pp.34, 36, 57).

The bus system that replaced the trams remained under municipal control
until 1974, when they were united as part of the West Yorkshire Passenger
Transport Executive as a result of the creation of the West Yorkshire
Metropolitan County Council. Ironically, by the early 1980s the PTE was
planning a large-scale reintroduction of trolley-buses in both Bradford,
where they had run until 1972, and in Leeds, where they had been scrapped
as early as 1928 (Jones 1984, p.105; anon. 1984c, p.179).

Liverpool (Merseyside)

Starting about 1850, Merseyside built up the most comprehensive local
rail system outside London. In 1886 the Mersey Railway was opened,
providing passenger service under the river Mersey from James Street
station in Liverpool to Green Lane in Birkenhead (MPTE 1978, n.p.) Two
years later the branch to Birkenhead Park was opened and in 1891 the line
was extended from Green Lane to Rock Ferry; a year later, the line was
extended under central Liverpool from James Street to a low-level
Liverpool Central station, there providing connection with trains from
the high-level station to Manchester.

At its peak, in 1890, the Mersey Railway carried 10 million passengers.
Thence however the numbers began to fall because of the problems of
ventilation on a steam-hauled system. In 1903 the system was electrified
- the first such electrification in the world, preceding the process in
London (ibid.).

A short time after, a separate electrification scheme followed: that of
the lines radiating from Liverpool Exchange station, at the northern side
of the central business district, to Southport (1904), Aintree (1906) and
Ormskirk (1913). However, there was no physical connection between this
system and the Mersey Railway or Central Station systems - or between
either of these and the suburban and main-line trains from Liverpool's
most important station, Lime Street.

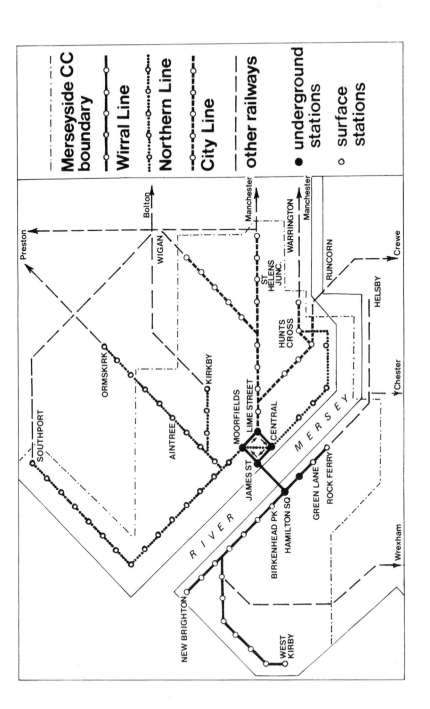

Fig. 4.7 Merseyside: RRT

Legend:
- Merseyside CC boundary
- Wirral Line
- Northern Line
- City Line
- other railways
- ● underground stations
- ○ surface stations

In 1962 therefore British Rail proposed to link these different systems. The Mersey Railway would be extended in a one-way loop under the city centre with stations on the site of Exchange Station, at Lime Street and at Central. The Exchange services would be connected with the Central services by a new underground link; both Exchange (renamed Moorfields) and Central High Level would become underground stations. The Merseyside Area Land Use Transport Study (MALTS), which appeared in 1966-69, endorsed these proposals and called for their implementation as a priority. It also recommended reorganisation of bus services and their integration with the new train services.

These proposals came nearer realisation when in 1968, under the Transport Act of that year, passenger transport services in Merseyside were combined under the management of the Merseyside Passenger Transport Authority (MPTA) and Executive (MPTE). The same year, the Merseyside Railway Extension Act authorised the first stage of the improvements, with a government grant of 75 per cent provided under the new arrangements in the 1968 Transport Act.

In 1974, when control of MPTA passed to the newly created Merseyside County Council, work had already started on the Loop and Link lines. The new system was opened in May 1977 (MPTE 1978, p.15). It consists of three lines. The Wirral Line is the old Mersey Railway whose branches unite at Hamilton Square station on the Birkenhead side to run under the river and thence via the one-way loop under central Liverpool. The Northern Line collects branches from Southport, Ormskirk and Kirkby to run via the new loop from Moorfields to Central and thence as far as Hunts Cross near the giant Ford Halewood plant at the southern edge of Liverpool. The City Line consists of a number of suburban services running into the Lime Street main-line station. Connections are made between the Wirral Line and Northern Line at Moorfields and Central, and between the Wirral Line and City Line at Lime Street (MPTE 1983, p.15). A physical link between the City Line and Northern Line at Lime Street is under investigation.

The trains, which are run for MPTE by British Rail, achieve an average speed of 50-70 km./hr. (30-45 m.p.h.) and run at headways down to 120 seconds on the Wirral Line and 150 seconds on the Northern Line. Most of the 71 stations within the Merseyside County Council area have been improved or will be improved in a programme which runs through the mid-1980s (ibid., p.27). Park-and-ride car parks are provided at most suburban stations, and there are bus interchanges at selected stations. Season and off-peak tickets are valid for all bus, rail and ferry services.

Despite the radical change in services which the new lines have brought about, most travel on the MPTE system is still by bus and will remain so; in 1981/2, 73 per cent of all passenger miles were made by bus on MPTE and associated services. This reflects the fact that the bulk of journeys are short-distance ones. The Liverpool central business district is relatively small, with 91,900 workers in 1971; longer-distance suburb-to-centre commuting is relatively unimportant.

Greater Manchester

Manchester, the principal commercial centre of North-West England, has suffered since the beginning of the railway age from the lack of a direct connection between its major main-line and suburban railway stations. Originally, there were no less than four of these: Piccadilly, Central, Exchange and Victoria. But as a result of rationalisation, Central and Exchange were closed in 1969 and traffic was concentrated on the remaining two stations. Suburban trains from Victoria serve the northern part of Manchester, and Piccadilly railway station the southern part of the conurbation. The two stations are about 2 kilometres (1 mile) apart on opposite sides of the central business district. The walk between the two (about 20 minutes) is too long to be convenient.

Plans to provide a better rail access to the city centre were first developed in the early railway age. The first proposal, in 1839, included a tunnel connection between Victoria and Piccadilly; the second, in 1866, a viaduct connection. Further proposals were put forward - for a rapid transit system in 1914, for tube links across the central area in 1928 - but none materialised because of financial and political difficulties (Joyce 1982, pp.59-60, 97-99; Young, Berry 1984, p.2).

A new round of proposals for the conurbation started in 1965. The contractors Taylor Woodrow planned a Safege monorail between Middleton in the northern suburbs, Wythenshawe in the south and Manchester Airport (Young, Berry 1984, p.2). Subsequently De Leuw Chadwick Oh Eocha and Partners recommended in the Manchester Rapid Transit Study (1967/68) a system of conventional rapid transit lines which would run initially on the Wythenshawe-Middleton route, later to be extended to include Bury, Oldham, Hyde, Romiley, Swinton, Eccles and Sale (ibid., p.2). However neither proposal was successful, and a new transport study (SELNEC 1973) proposed a tunnel link between Piccadilly and Victoria which could unify the British Rail suburban rail services in the northern and southern suburbs. The entire long-term strategy of the study included four elements:

1. Bus priority measures to make buses sufficiently reliable that passengers would continue to use them;

2. The Picc-Vic tunnel and the improvement and integration of trains and bus services;

3. A future East-West railway network;

4. A light rail system serving those parts of the conurbation without improved railways (GMC 1975, p.6; SELNEC 1973, pp.63, 75, 86).

The Picc-Vic link, which would have been an integral part of British Rail - based on the Hamburg concept - was to be 4.4 km. (2.75 miles) long and was to run from Ardwick Junction (south of Piccadilly) to Queens Road Junction (north of Victoria), the actual tunnel length just over 3.5 km. (2 miles) (GMC 1975, p.9). There were to be five new central stations (Piccadilly, Whitworth, Central, Royal Exchange and Victoria). The headway would have allowed trains every 90 seconds (ibid., pp.9-10). Apart from the new tunnel construction several other rail improvements were planned including the reinstatement and re-electrification of the route from Bury to Victoria coupled with the electrification of the Bolton-Radcliffe link, a total of 40 km. (25 miles), allowing through running to the existing electrified suburban services to the Stockport and Styal lines in the south (Young, Berry 1984, p.3).

In November 1974 the cost for the tunnel link was estimated to be £55,870,000 or about £16 million per km., a figure comparable with costs of similar schemes in Germany during the 1970s which ranged from £7.5 million to £20 million/km. (Scheelhaase 1980, p.205). The total costs of the Manchester project were estimated at £118,315,000, spread over nine years (GMC 1975, pp.55, 56).

The main problem with the project was that the Department of Transport insisted on evaluating the costs and benefits of the tunnel divorced from the rest of the proposed system, which did not give a true picture. Even so, the GMC still managed to calculate the rate of return on the tunnel to be 12.1 per cent. Consequently, though parliamentary powers had been obtained and the project had reached contract stage, in 1973 the necessary finance was denied by the central government (Leatherbarrow 1984, p.279).

There were still hopes at this stage that the project might be revived, but in 1977 the Conservative majority on the newly elected Greater Manchester Council abandoned the Picc-Vic project. The new Council proposed to link the north and south networks between Deansgate and Salford Station (Castlefield Curve) which although much cheaper (about £10 million) skirted the edge of the central business district and so would have done little to improve accessibility to central offices and shops (Young, Berry 1984, p.3).

Since 1982, the GMC has however been considering a new proposal - though this in turn is threatened by the proposed abolition of the Metropolitan County in 1986. This proposal stems from a joint working party set up comprising British Rail, the Greater Manchester Council and the GMPTE in 1982. Its main feature is a surface light rail line which would cross the city centre, connecting Piccadilly with Victoria and Deansgate, and providing interchange with British Rail at all these three stations. Outside the central area the light rail system would take over existing BR tracks to Bury, Rochdale via Oldham, Hadfield and Glossop, Marple and Rose Hill, Altrincham, and (over the abandoned tracks from the former Central station) to East Didsbury (ibid., p.11). There would also be outer suburban interchanges with the BR system at Altrincham, Marple and Rochdale. Several other alternatives were examined and costed (Table 4.2).

Table 4.2

Manchester: Rapid Transit Alternatives: Costing
(at November 1982 prices)

Mode	Works	Rolling stock	Total
	£m.	£m.	£m.
Conventional rail, Cross Centre Tunnel[a]	136.4	19.5	155.9
LRT Surface	47.9	37.6	85.5
LRT Tunnel (Mosley St. Route)	65.9	37.6	103.5
LRT Tunnel (Cross St. Route)	72.8	37.2	110.0
Busway[b] [d]	92.0	16.0[c]	108.0[d]
Guided Busway(s)	110.5	17.0[c]	127.5[c]

a) excluding Didsbury route

b) minimum cost busway - requires speed restrictions and reduced safety margins

c) vehicle life approximately half life of rail vehicles

d) excludes conversion of Romiley-Marple

Source: Young, Berry 1984, p.10.

Newcastle (Tyne & Wear)

Like most British conurbations, Tyneside made few major capital investments in public transport in the two decades from 1945 to 1965. Newcastle, which had an extensive tram system - much of it on its own reserved rights-of-way - scrapped its last line in 1950 (Joyce 1962, p.98). Newcastle and South Shields introduced trolley buses, but these too were completely replaced by motor buses after 1966 (Tyne & Wear County Council 1979b p.156). By the late 1960s, neglect of public transport and increase in car ownership meant a reduction in bus fleets and in the suburban rail service (ibid., p.156).

A railway passenger service had operated since Victorian times, principally using lines built for coal movements. The North Eastern Railway had electrified part of the North Tyne Loop suburban line as early as 1904. The resulting electric rail network was quite extensive, serving Whitley Bay via North Shields and Benton, Walker and Wallsend; the line from Newcastle to South Shields via Jarrow was electrified in 1938. A large passenger network remained intact until the 1960s; but after 1961 several railway lines and stations were closed, and the electrified network was replaced by slower diesel trains in 1967 (ibid., p.156).

Following the Transport Act of 1968, the Tyneside Passenger Transport Authority (TPTA) and Executive (TPTE) were set up in 1969. The resulting area had 1,200 buses, carrying 850,000 passengers per day; suburban railway trips only contributed five per cent of local movements (Tyne & Wear PTE 1984, p.3). The PTA became responsible for overall policy and finance including fare charges, with the PTE determining the pattern of routes and service levels; services were provided directly by the PTE and also through agreements with BR, private operators and the National Bus Company (NBC). One of the main tasks was to integrate bus services. The PTE services are concentrated in Newcastle, South Shields and Sunderland, whereas NBC subsidiaries provide services for the remaining area including Gateshead (Tyne & Wear County Council 1979b, p.160). Five local rail services were still in operation, three of which were supported by the PTE as part of the integrated network.

In 1971 a transportation plan for the whole area - the Transport Plan for the 1980s, published in 1971 - tested several alternative road and public transport strategies including conventional rail and bus improvements and busways, and emerged with a recommendation for a balanced programme of highway and public transport improvement. The principal public transport element was a new Metro system based on the British Rail suburban tracks north and south of the Tyne, which would be connected by a direct linking rail tunnel under Newcastle and Gateshead. The North Tyne Loop study, published in the same year, confirmed this recommendation. Government grants were made available in 1973, and the design of the Metro followed in 1974 (Howard 1980, p.11).

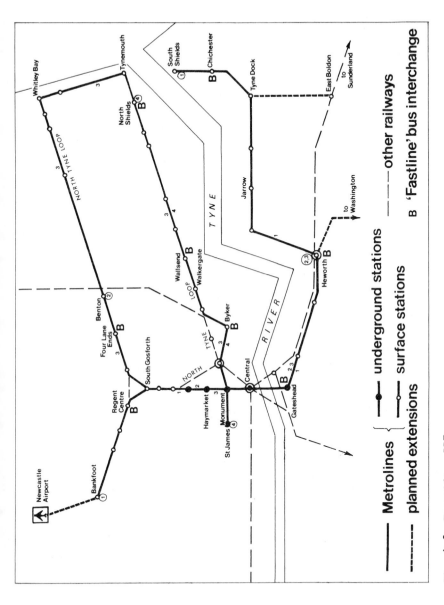

Fig. 4.8 Tyneside: RRT

Metrolines
planned extensions

underground stations
surface stations

other railways
'Fastline' bus interchange — B

Newcastle Airport
Bankfoot
Regent Centre B
South Gosforth
Four Lane Ends B
Benton
Whitley Bay
Tynemouth
North Shields B
NORTH TYNE LOOP
Wallsend B
Walkergate
Byker B
St James
Haymarket
Monument
Central
Gateshead B
Heworth B
to Washington
Jarrow
Tyne Dock B
Chichester
South Shields
East Boldon
to Sunderland
NORTH TYNE LOOP
TYNE
RIVER

77

In 1974, local government reorganisation resulted in the creation of the new Tyne & Wear County Council, which agreed fully to the construction of the Metro. One year earlier, in fact, Parliament had passed the Tyneside Metropolitan Railway Act, authorising the PTE to purchase the necessary land in order to carry out the required construction work. Furthermore, agreements had to be made between the PTE and British Rail regarding the ownership and operation of the Metro (Tyne & Wear PTE 1984, p.4).

The resulting light rail system is 56 km. long, of which 43 km. are converted British Rail tracks and 13 km. had to be newly built. Even by comparison with the German cities in this study, this is a rather extensive network (Hannover has 93 km., Köln 42 km.). The system consists of surface ex-British Rail lines running mainly east-west on both the north and the south banks of the Tyne, linked by a new connection which tunnels under the centres of Newcastle and Gateshead and runs between the two on a new bridge across the Tyne (ibid., p.5). Part of the system is still shared with BR, which runs two freight trains a day between Benton Junction and Bankfoot (ibid., p.6). The system consists of four so-called Metrolines and is integrated with the bus service at several interchanges. Apart from the conventional buses, 'Fastline' (limited stop) services with coach-type buses have been introduced to provide fast links between the outer areas, off the Metro, and the major centres (ibid., p.12).

The first stretch of the Metro was opened in 1980, running from Haymarket, one of the city centre stations in Newcastle, to Tynemouth. (Tyne & Wear County Council, and Tyne and Wear PTE 1981). In November 1981, the Metro was extended from Haymarket south to Heworth. Exactly one year later the St James-Tynemouth section opened, and in March 1984 the last part to South Shields was finally ready (Tyne & Wear C.C. 1984 Commemoration).

The complete LRT system has 90 articulated cars, each car providing a peak-hour capacity of over 200 people (Tyne & Wear PTE 1984, p.9). In general, two-car trains run every 10 minutes; between South Gosforth and Heworth this is increased to every 3 minutes and between North Shields and St James to every 5 minutes (Tyne & Wear C.C. 1984, Commemoration). Tyne & Wear is one of the few conurbations in Britain which has an integrated fare system which, however, does not extend fully to BR. (In the German Verkehrsverbund systems, in contrast, DB is included.) There are 900 park-and-ride spaces.

The original cost estimate for the Metro system was £65.5 million at 1971 prices. This was the figure on which the central government awarded a 75 per cent grant adjusted for inflation. In 1976 the figure had risen to £170 million, and in 1983 it was estimated that the total cost would be £274 million (Tyne & Wear PTE 1984, p.11). (Most of this increase was due to inflation; in constant costs, it was only 5 per cent.) Running costs in 1982-3 were 8.5 pence per passenger mile, lower than buses (8.8) or British Rail (9.8); for 1984/85 they were expected to fall to 8.0 pence. Only 46 per cent of the total costs in 1983-4 were wages - a sharp contrast with bus undertakings, where wages count for over 60 per cent. Howard points out that 'the overall level of revenue support for the integrated network is 29 per cent'. (ibid., p.15).

The Metro was designed to be extended and several such projections have been suggested, including one from Heworth to Washington New Town, from Bankfoot to the Airport, and from Tyne Dock southwards through Whiteleas estate to East Boldon on the Newcastle-Sunderland BR line (ibid., p.15,). The airport extension would run slightly outside the area of the Tyne and Wear County Council. In view of the projected demise of the Council in 1986, these plans remain uncertain.

Sheffield (South Yorkshire)

Sheffield had one of the best-developed tram systems in Britain. Its first horse trams appeared in 1873; twenty years later Sheffield Corporation took over the privately owned transport system, electrifying it in 1896. The city was still building new lines as late as the 1930s. Rotherham and Doncaster also had tram networks, but partly replaced them in the 1930s by trolley buses (SYPTE 1983b, p.4); the county's fourth urban area, Barnsley, was the only one where the system was run by a private company, which concentrated on buses after 1930. In contrast, Sheffield was one of the last cities in Britain to give up trams (Joyce 1962), withdrawing its last tram only in 1960 (ibid., p.103, SYPTE 1983b, p.4).

In 1973 the Government's Transport and Road Research Laboratory (TRRL), in conjunction with the city of Sheffield, published a study from the consultants Robert Matthew, Johnson-Marshall and Partners. This was a technological feasibility study for a rapid transit line (called mini-tram), which suggested Sheffield as the site for a demonstration project. The system would have run on elevated guideways about 5.1 m. in height. The estimated costs were relatively cheap in comparison with a conventional rapid rail transit system (McKean 1974, p.964). The proposal was for a mere 2.4 km. city-centre system, running from Moorfoot (a redevelopment area on the edge of the centre) to The Moor (a major shopping area) to Fargate and High Street (City Centre) and then via the main bus station to the Midland rail station. Each driverless electronic vehicle could take 12-30 passengers. The hourly capacity of the system was 5,000 people. It was planned to start construction in 1978 and to open in 1981 (ibid., p.971).

However, as with many other transport plans in Britain the system was never built. In 1976 the Sheffield/Rotherham Land Use Transportation Study was published. It re-evaluated minitram in detail but rejected it. Instead it recommended that alignments should be safeguarded for a segregated passenger transport system (SPTS). This protection was approved by the South Yorkshire County Council in 1979.

Since 1982 a working group has been formed, consisting of officers of the Passenger Transport Executive, County Council and City Council in the area of transportation and planning. After considering several options, including articulated trolley buses both on a conventional busway and a guided busway, it has concluded that the long-term solution for Sheffield would be a light rail system. So far two main transport corridors are proposed for the light rail system, to Mosborough in the south and to Hillsborough in the north. Infrastructure costs for a light rail option would be higher than for other options, but the preliminary financial analysis shows that a segregated light rail system would have lower operating costs than any new bus-based system and substantially lower operating costs than existing bus services. To provide a more accurate estimate of costs and benefits, a more detailed feasibility study has been started to show whether a cross-city light rail line, from Hillsborough to Mosborough, would be justified.

The South Yorkshire Passenger Transport Executive was established in 1974 on the creation of the Metropolitan County of South Yorkshire (SYPTE 1978, Foreword). Since 1974 the number of passengers has increased by 8 per cent; South Yorkshire is the only PTE in Britain which has not lost any passengers in this period (SYPTE 1983b, p.17; Goodwin, Bailey et al., 1983, p.14) This success has been achieved through an above-average rate of subsidy (in the mid-1980s about 75 per cent of operating costs) which is high even by German standards. Thus, despite the inability so far to implement any light rail proposal, Sheffield is an outstanding example of a high-density, heavily subsidised urban bus opeation which provides an interesting comparison with those British and German cities that have invested in rail.

Summing up

The obvious conclusion is that German cities have invested generously in rapid rail while British cities have not. That is not a function of the cities we have chosen for our case studies. Three of the six British examples are in fact the only provincial British cities that have invested at all in new rail systems since World War Two. The three British cities that have not invested are only examples; we might have chosen many others, the West Midlands for instance, or Bristol, or Edinburgh.

The second conclusion is that the form of investment has been heavily conditioned by the previously existing situation. German cities have invested heavily in light rail because they could develop it out of existing tram systems. In this respect our sample is somewhat under-representative of light rail cities and over-representative of U-Bahn cities. British cities have had no such choice, though in many cases they still have old tram right-of-way that could be used for light rail, some of it of quite high quality (for instance, the old Middleton Light Railway track in Leeds). Thirdly, however, British Rail has abandoned more track mileage than Deutsche Bundesbahn, so that there is more possibility of conversion to light rail, as in Tyneside - or, indeed, to other modes such as busways, as was suggested by consultants for the city of Nottingham (Freeman Fox 1975).

The fourth conclusion is that where British cities have developed systems comparable to the German ones, as in the Glasgow Argyle Line and Merseyrail systems, they have tended to do so on a somewhat economical basis. The Argyle Line did not refurbish its stations extensively (apart from the new interchanges at Partick and Queen Street) and kept the old trains; Merseyrail kept some of its old trains though it has replaced others. The Tyne Metro and the Glasgow Underground are more comprehensively reconstructed, with both new stations and new trains - though even there the outer stations of the Tyne Metro are unreconstructed; and some are indeed memorials of the Victorian age.

The nearest comparison with the German examples, in terms of the scale of the new system, is almost certainly the Tyne Metro. In the other cases, though undoubtedly there were significant improvements in accessibility and service levels, the psychological effect of a new system was not so evident. Therefore, most of the German case-study systems are qualitatively different.

The last point is one that does not come directly out of the case studies reported here, but is implicit. The British case-study cities have relied heavily on buses and in some cases - notably in South Yorkshire - have subsidised them very heavily to offer a real competition in terms of costs with the convenience of the private car. Therefore, the heart of this study is a comparison between rail rapid transit cities which are mainly German, and bus-based cities which are almost exclusively British. This needs to be borne in mind in reading the chapters that follow.

5 Pedestrianisation in British and German cities

This chapter parallels Chapter 4. It tries to set out the background to policies of pedestrianisation in the two countries, with special reference to the thirteen case-study cities and particularly to their city centres, where most of the pedestrianisation has occurred (though since the mid-1970s in Germany, it has also been extended to urban sub-centres and even to villages). First, it briefly outlines the history of pedestrianisation in the two countries - a history that, in Germany, goes back as far as the 1920s. Then it summarises the main facts about city-centre pedestrian schemes in the case-study cities, drawing on the statistical material in Appendix B. The emphasis throughout this chapter is on the evolution of pedestrian policies and of the resulting pedestrianised areas. Discussion of the impacts of pedestrianisation is reserved until Chapter 6.

Before any of this is done, however, some clarification as to concepts and to terminology is necessary. Monheim (1975, p.1) provides a useful guide:

1. The pedestrianised street: a street used only by pedestrians, with deliveries possible only at special daily hours; mostly rear deliveries; public transport access possible;

2. The pedestrianised zone: a network of pedestrian streets; here, too, public transport may have access;

3. The urban unit: this is similar to the environmental area of the British Buchanan report (Minister of Transport 1963). Residential streets are open only to cars belonging to local residents; no through traffic is allowed. This concept is directly derived from the Dutch concept of the 'Woonerf' (literally, 'Living Yard') (H. Monheim 1977, p.59). Thus a pedestrianised area may be part of an urban unit (Monheim 1975, p.1). Monheim's term 'urban unit' is however not generally used in Germany; the preferred term is 'Verkehrsberuhigung' (Environmental Traffic Management).

In this chapter, pedestrianisation is defined as the removal of traffic from existing city streets, which may be followed by suitable treatment in terms of paving, street furniture and other details. This treatment may be applied to a single street or part of a street, or to a whole network of streets. It may occur in central shopping streets (our primary concern here), or in streets connecting shopping areas with housing or recreation or urban conservation areas. Additionally, in Britain and to a lesser extent in Germany (Table 5.1), cities may redevelop part of their central areas as new pedestrian shopping precincts, either open or (as is more usual after 1970) enclosed. Such precincts may incorporate part of the former vehicle street system, but more often ignore it. Our main concern here is with pedestrianised streets in the strict sense, that is closures of vehicle streets; but it is necessary to bear in mind that the resulting estimates of lengths of pedestrian street, presented in the second half of this chapter for the thirteen case study cities, do not include precincts - or, either in Britain or Germany, pedestrianised squares.[1] Roberts (1981) gives figures showing that of 1,014 pedestrian units in British cities of which the type is known, 447 (44 per cent) are converted streets; 117 (11 per cent) are converted streets in which buses are allowed to penetrate; 214 (21 per cent) are uncovered purpose-built precincts; and 172 (17 per cent) are post-1945 covered shopping precincts. (A residue of 64 (6 per cent) consist of older shopping arcades.) Table 5.1 shows estimates of major purpose-built off-street covered precincts in German and British cities; here the figures are for gross area, including retail and storage space.

History of pedestrianisation in Germany

The idea of separating pedestrians from wheeled traffic is an old one; it can be traced back at least to Leonardo da Vinci (Mumford 1961, p.246). The practice goes back to about 1800, when the first covered shopping arcade was opened in Paris; thereafter, during the course of the nineteenth century, European cities vied with each other in the construction of magnificent arcades, which were a direct precursor of the covered shopping malls of the late twentieth century (Geist 1983). But none of these attempted to take traffic out of existing streets.

The real beginning of pedestrianisation occurred in Germany in the 1920s. Around 1929 (the exact date is not known), one of the main shopping streets in Essen (Limbecker Strasse) was closed to car traffic; twelve years later the main shopping street, Kettwiger Strasse, was closed. The reason was that the streets were simply too narrow to accommodate both pedestrians and traffic; the closures were also made possible by the completion of an inner ring road around the medieval central business district (Monheim 1980, p.41). About four years later Köln's main shopping street (Hohe Strasse) was closed. In 1931 Bremen

---

1) Monheim argues that in quantifying pedestrianisation, length (in metres) is better than area; doubling the width does not double the size. We follow him in this, but not in his recommendation that pedestrian squares should be measured by length and width.

rebuilt some narrow medieval lanes in its city centre, closing them to
traffic.   No other country at this time imitated Germany in
pedestrianising city centre streets, though in the United States Clarence
Stein's plan for the garden city of Radburn, New Jersey (1928), was the
first to embody complete segregation of pedestrians and cars within a
residential area (Stein 1951, p.42).

Table 5.1

The Thirteen Case Study Cities: Major City-Centre
Purpose-Built Covered Shopping Precincts

City	Gross floorspace (sq. metres)
Bremen	-
Dortmund	25,000
Essen	26,000
Köln	28,000
Hannover	60,000
München	54,000
Nürnberg	-
Glasgow	16,700
Leeds	38,100
Liverpool	37,200
Manchester	88,700
Newcastle	72,500
Sheffield	-

Excludes German department stores

Source:interviews, 1983-1984.

Postwar reconstruction

The bombing of German cities during World War Two made it possible to redevelop new street schemes, which were carried out more vigorously in some cities than in others. Kassel, in 1948, was the first German city to develop a complete plan for the reconstruction of its bombed central area which embodied a substantial pedestrianised area - though this was within the framework of a completely car-oriented plan for the city's development. Ironically, when in 1960 the city at last tried to implement the closure of the main shopping street - an integral part of the plan - there was violent opposition from retailers, which was only overcome in 1964 (Monheim 1980, p.44).

In the same year Bonn also closed its two most important shopping streets during the late afternoon (ibid., p.59). Aachen closed one of its narrow shopping streets in 1951 and Hannover followed five years later (ibid., p.71). By 1955 twenty-one German cities had closed at least one street to traffic, but only four of these were true pedestrian streets in the sense of having been totally landscaped. Even by 1963, of the forty-six cities with traffic-free streets, only nineteen had treated them comprehensively (ibid., p.45).

During the 1950s and 1960s, therefore, pedestrianisation in Germany tended to be ad hoc in character; few cities made complete plans for networks of pedestrian streets, and only a minority did more than simply bar streets to traffic. Nor, at this time, was the introduction of pedestrianised streets seen as a traffic restraint policy; on the contrary, pedestrianisation was an integrated part of an ideal shopping centre in the middle of the city for the car user. The model of these new shopping streets was the regional shopping mall common in the United States. In some cases public transport systems were integrated into the shopping scheme but this was not the rule. The idea was (and to some extent still is) to separate spatially the different modes of transportation. Parking spaces were provided close to the shopping street, or even as part of the building complex (e.g. Kassel, Essen and Köln).

Monheim classifies three types of development in pedestrianisation in Germany during the post-World War Two period (ibid., pp.38-67):

1. pedestrianisation planned deliberately after the last war as part of a new city concept (e.g. Kassel, Essen, Kiel)

2. the traditional city concept in which pedestrianisation was not originally planned, but was developed during the 1970s as a result of concern for issues of 'urban life', urban renewal, conservation, and environmental protection. This resulted in progressive pedestrianisation, often covering large areas in the city centre (e.g Nürnberg, Freiburg, Bonn, Osnabrück, Oldenburg).

Plate 5.1 Pedestrianisation in the Centre of Hannover

A typical example of pedestrianisation applied to a narrow street in the medieval core of the city, now largely given over to restaurants, bars and night clubs.

Plate 5.2 Pedestrianisation in München

The historic Marienplatz, showing the intense pedestrian traffic characteristic of the most successful German pedestrianisation schemes.

Plate 5.3 Pedestrianisation and U-Bahn in Nürnberg

The successful integration of a U-Bahn station entrance into a pedestrian
street in the centre of the city.

Plate 5.4: Pedestrianisation in Nürnberg

A corner of the historic <u>Altstadt</u>, below the castle.

3. the third type of city developed pedestrianised areas as a result of a trend away from car-oriented planning in favour of the 'rediscovery of the city' (e.g. Dortmund, Frankfurt, Duisburg etc.)

The German planners and retailers had various motives for these policies, which are summarised in Monheim's survey. About two-thirds of transport planners saw the most important aim of pedestrianisation as being the improvement of traffic conditions. The retailing sector saw it as an attraction to customers from the surrounding area (40 per cent). Urban planners had a much wider spectrum of aims, of which 30 per cent mentioned an attractive image and current urban design, recreation value in the city centre, more life in the evening (15 per cent); traffic improvement was mentioned by only 11 per cent of planners (Monheim 1975, p.15).

This demonstrates the fact that pedestrianisation is a way of resolving conflicts between different economic interests (Heinz, Hübner et al 1977). Though there is a kind of superficial conflict between car drivers and pedestrians, the real dilemma is the negative effect that cars have on retail trade; pedestrians who cannot shop in a relaxed atmosphere will spend little time in shops, will not look around and will very rarely do any impulse shopping. This has a particularly serious effect on the large department stores, which tend to be in the main city-centre streets (Monheim 1975, p.56). According to Heinz et al, the main aim identified by Monheim - the improvement of traffic (ibid., p.11) - is only a technical means to realise the real objective, the promotion of the local economy and especially of retailing (Heinz et al 1977, p.133). Thus, though traders were at first opposed to the schemes, now they often call for more pedestrianisation (ibid., p.135). Our own interviews with the representatives of trade and commerce (IHK) showed that in some cities pedestrianisation was strongly promoted (Bremen) but in others (Essen, München, Nürnberg) no further improvements were desired.

The progress of pedestrianisation

By 1960, 35 cities had at least one pedestrianised street; six years later, the number had risen to 63 (Monheim 1980, p.69). The last reasonably reliable figure on the number of cities which have pedestrianised streets was 350-400 in 1977 (ibid., p.69). But pedestrianisation has taken place in so many cities in the Federal Republic that an accurate count is impossible. Monheim's estimate, the best available, is that in 1984 there were more than 800 pedestrianised areas in the city centres and sub-centres.

Precise data on the current size of pedestrian areas in the Federal Republic is also difficult to obtain. There is no central source of information, so that data must be obtained from individual cities (and even these may not have accurate current figures).   The figures are conventionally presented in terms of length of pedestrian streets; large

squares are not included in the total. (Similarly, it is difficult to
make an exact comparison with British shopping precincts, where data are
usually given in square feet of shopping space.) Monheim's estimates
indicate that in the early 1960s the longest pedestrian streets were only
about 400-900 m. (ibid., p.70); but that later, the average length
increased from 646 m. (1960) to 1,554 m. (1967) to 2,185 m. (1973)
(ibid., p.70) and then again during the 1970s.

Today several of the largest German cities have pedestrian areas of
over 5,000 m., taking into account their central areas and also
neighbouring inner-city areas; for instance Stuttgart, Nürnberg, Hannover
and Frankfurt. In general therefore the largest pedestrian areas are in
larger cities, though city size and pedestrianisation size are not
directly correlated. Typical large cities tend to have pedestrian areas
of around 2,500 m., in contrast to the British cities in which the
average size is only 870 m. (not including pedestrian streets shared by
buses, taxis etc); even if one includes these streets, the average size
of British schemes is still only 1,620 m., 900 m. less than in Germany.

As a result, in many large German cities pedestrianisation of the
central area is to all intents and purposes complete; indeed, in some it
is extended to take in substantial lengths of shopping street in the
surrounding inner city (for instance the Lister Meile in Hannover). In
the period since 1970 the concept has been extended and varied, with many
individual experiments. There is considerable emphasis on the treatment
of the pedestrianised areas in terms of street furniture and also in
terms of street events (exhibitions, entertainment and the like). In
many cities there are experiments in extensive traffic restraint schemes
- for instance, limiting the speed of traffic over large areas, and
effectively giving priority to pedestrians even in vehicle streets (the
principle of Woonerven, or Verkehrsberuhigung).

Pedestrianisation in Britain

Early ideas

In the nineteenth century, British architects and planners pioneered
radical thinking on pedestrian precincts. Joseph Paxton, designer of the
Crystal Palace, proposed a Great Victorian Way which would connect all
the main termini with Piccadilly Circus. Ebenezer Howard proposed a
similar covered shopping arcade for his Garden City. Much later, in the
1930s and 1940s, the same ideas reappeared in the work of two architect
town planners, Sharp and Gibson. In one of Sharp's earlier publications
Town and Countryside (1932) he suggested arcades for shopping to protect
pedestrians from weather and traffic (Sharp 1932, p.187). Although Sharp
was mainly concerned to alleviate traffic congestion in the city centre
by a system of radial and ring roads (ibid., p.181), he actually proposed
pedestrianisation in his 1940 book, Town Planning:

Indeed there is much to be said for some at least of a town's shopping premises being situated on a street or square which is limited to pedestrian traffic (Sharp 1940, p.74).

Sharp's later plans for Exeter (1946) and Oxford (1948) included pedestrianised streets, although the one for Durham did not (Sharp 1946, pp.100-101; 1948, pp.214, 215).

At about this time, Gibson and Ford developed a city centre plan for Coventry which included some areas exclusively for pedestrian use. Ford stressed the need for areas where pedestrians could move freely and safely and was concerned about the problem of motor traffic and pedestrians in his shopping streets (Gregory 1973, p.88). During the war, Gibson developed a new city centre plan (1941) including an even larger pedestrian area, on the principles of the 1939 plan (ibid., p.89). As we will see, continuously - even until today - the main opposition against the 1941 plan came from Coventry's traders. They pressured the Borough to build a new road, bisecting the planned precinct, so as to allow street parking near to shops (ibid., p.92). The plan was therefore changed quite drastically: instead of the planned central amenity park near Pool Meadow, car park facilities and public buildings were substituted (ibid., p.93). By the time of the approval of the Development Plan in 1951, many of the original pedestrian features had already been lost. Still, Sharp's shopping centre in Exeter (Princesshay) and Coventry's shopping centre were the first purpose-built pedestrian areas in Britain. Princesshay opened about 1952, Coventry about 1952/53 (information from planning departments in Exeter and Coventry).

In 1942, H. Alker Tripp, Assistant Commissioner of Police for Traffic at Scotland Yard, published a small book, Town Planning and Road Traffic, which also included some ideas on the problem of city centre traffic (Tripp 1942). In his opinion, shoppers should not be allowed to be exposed to traffic, and he developed a plan for shopping centres in which the centre road and one cross road would be used only by pedestrians. This pedestrian 'cross' would be surrounded by a one-way street.

The best plan, when practicable, will almost certainly be to leave the existing main thoroughfare with their existing frontages severely alone and to provide new isolated conduits of such outstanding traffic merit as to draw all the through-traffic away from the old main streets .... if it allows any contact between pedestrians and vehicular traffic it is a faultily designed thoroughfare (ibid., p.66).

Tripp thus evokes a picture of life in the future traffic-free city which still represents a current ideal:

> The streets in the various precincts will then become town streets of the old-fashioned type. They will cease to be maelstroms of noise and confusion, and become companionable places, with an air of leisure and repose, such streets will provide a real promenade for the town dweller and a rest for jaded nerves. We shall be getting back to Merrie England (ibid. , p.77).

However, elsewhere in his book it is not quite clear if Tripp wanted to remove all car traffic from shopping streets or keep only the through traffic out of them (ibid., p.82).

Sharp, Gibson and Tripp's ideas may have influenced the layout of city centres in the two generations of British New Towns. However, it is not really clear if there was any influence and, if so, how powerful this was. Furthermore it is questionable which one of the three was the most influential. There is no evidence that Tripp's idea of precincts was known to German planners, though they have implemented its spirit more faithfully than in its homeland.

The New Town movement

Little attention has been given to the achievements of the British New Towns in terms of pedestrianisation. Interestingly, the first New Town, Stevenage, set an example which was not emulated anywhere else until the second generation of New Towns. Stevenage's first town centre plan embodied a pedestrian area with complete separation from vehicle traffic and noise in 1950. It was challenged in 1953, and the resulting plan was a complete reversal (Balchin 1980, p.271). However, in a public meeting in 1954, the public voted in favour of a pedestrianised shopping centre. A visit to Rotterdam by the responsible planners, plus much persuasion of the central government, finally made a pedestrianised shopping centre possible (ibid., pp.275-276). In addition, Stevenage also adopted the Radburn principle for its residential neighbourhoods.

Other New Towns of the first generation were not as successful; none of the other first fifteen New Towns emulated Stevenage in its attempt at pedestrianisation. Interesting features were introduced with Harlow and Crawley which included the old shopping street within their new pedestrian concept (Cherry 1972, p.170). Basildon tried a partial adoption of the Radburn plan (Osborn and Whittick 1963, p.177) whereas Corby failed to achieve any degree of pedestrianisation at all (ibid., p.309).

In the second generation of New Towns, Cumbernauld and Milton Keynes were the two most remarkable cases of pedestrianisation (Tetlow and Goss 1965, p.99; Milton Keynes Development Corporation 1970, p.281). Cumbernauld's concept of city centre pedestrianisation was a shopping street rather than a market square as in Stevenage. But for the first time in Britain and perhaps the first time in the world, the street was covered. Milton Keynes, one of the last new towns of the 1960s, has a covered shopping centre which represents the largest pedestrian precinct ever built in a New Town (Roberts 1981, p.102).

Pedestrianisation in the large cities

The first fifteen years after World War Two represented a period of inaction. Already in 1945 the city planner of Manchester, J.R. Nicholas, was complaining about the absence of central government and voice in redeveloping city centres (Nicholas 1945, p.186). The government responded to such criticisms in 1946 by publishing a major guide to The Design and Layout of Roads in Built-Up Areas, which suggested that city centres be planned on precinctual principles (though not necessarily on the basis of complete pedestrianisation), surrounded by an inner distributor road with car parking (Ministry of War Transport 1946). This was extremely influential for all towns in developing their post-war reconstruction plans. Unfortunately, with one or two exceptions of war-damaged cities (such as Coventry, Exeter and Plymouth), their implementation was long delayed by government expenditure limits.

The 1950s were marked by inactivity on the part of the central government on questions concerning urban transport and pedestrianisation (McKay and Cox 1979, p.166). But, as in Germany, by the late 1950s British cities were becoming seriously congested (ibid., p.166). Some cities, following the 1946 guidelines, were developing ambitious city centre plans including ring roads, urban motorways and pedestrianisation. One of the earliest was Newcastle, which developed a separate network system for pedestrians including open space, arcades and existing streets closed to traffic in 1960 (Tetlow and Goss 1965, pp.199-200). The plan also included moving pavements and a newly created pedestrian level with servicing and transport links at existing ground level (Galley 1973, p.223). This idea was taken up by Colin Buchanan in his 1958 book Mixed Blessing, in which he suggested:

> There is really only one way in which this can be done, and that is by arranging the pedestrian and vehicle circulation at different physical levels (Buchanan 1958, p.190).

Buchanan included also a 'practicable' suggestion for London:

> Yet there is one possibility for Oxford Street that could bring relief for an outlay which though heavy, would probably be less than for any other scheme yet suggested. The possibility lies simply in the elevation of the footways and the main shop window display to first floor level (ibid. , p.192).

In 1963 the often quoted and much discussed Buchanan Report was published (Minister of Transport 1963). The report was set up by the Ministry of Transport to study the long term development of roads and traffic in urban areas and their influence on urban environment (McKay and Cox 1979, p.167). The success of the report lies perhaps in the fact that it did not take a position for or against the car, but represented it - in a celebrated phrase - as:

a monster of great potential destructiveness. And yet we love him dearly (Minister of Transport 1963, n.p.).

This perhaps explains its enormous influence on Britsh planning practice in the mid-1960s - the period when, significantly, the great period of city rebuilding reached its height.

The effect can be seen in several of the plans for major British cities. Thus the Manchester central redevelopment plan showed large areas of open space and many pedestrian streets (Tetlow and Goss 1965, p.203). Liverpool had even more ambitious plans for pedestrianisation (ibid., p.208). It is also clear however that while some cities quickly developed plans for pedestrianisation, others did not do so until much later. What is not clear is why this time lag occurred. One is that a difference may have developed about the best way to achieve pedestrianisation. The City of London was one of the most enthusiastic advocates of Buchanan's proposal to banish pedestrians to an upper level throughhout the city centre, which however invoked opposition from shop owners, planners, and conservationists. David Lloyd, representing the Society for the Protection of Ancient Buildings, wrote in 1965 about the City's plans:

The walkway system, if anything like fully implemented, would have a devastating effect on the townscape of the city ... The city is traditionally an area for pedestrians and their convenience and safety should be a prior consideration. In most of the narrower streets, lanes and alleys, pedestrian movement should be considered to have priority, and, where these must be left open to traffic in order to meet servicing needs, vehicles should be compelled to move slowly (Lloyd 1965, pp.135, 137).

Pedestrianisation schemes in practice

In the literature on pedestrianisation in Britain, Norwich is generally cited as being the first city which carried out pedestrianisation in 1967. One suggestion is that ironically the scheme was the result of an accident, when a faulty sewer forced the city council to close London Street (MacDonald 1979, p.11). However, Norwich had already featured as one of the case studies in the Buchanan report, which had recommended the closure of London Street, the main shopping street for traffic. Buchanan was strongly supported by Alfred Wood, City Planner at the time, who only

Plate 5.5 Pedestrianisation in Glasgow

Integration of the new Trans-Clyde station, on the reopened Argyle line, with pedestrianisation of Argyle Street.

Plate 5.6 Pedestrianisation in the Centre of Sheffield

One of the more successful British city-centre schemes, showing provision for front-loading.

wanted a good excuse to close the road. Until 1967, local governments did not have the ability to close highways to traffic because no adequate law existed to allow such action (Roberts 1981, p.18).

Strangely enough, the example of Norwich did not result in a major wave of pedestrianisation. A very few conversions took place around 1967 and shortly after, and all were on a very small scale (see Roberts 1981, passim). But by 1971 several large cities had introduced pedestrian schemes. The largest ones by far were in Liverpool (1968) and Leeds (1970). According to Roberts, the number of pedestrianisation schemes was highest between 1972-1973, 1974-1975 and 1978-1979 (ibid.,p.18).

Britain and German pedestrianisation compared

Despite this, overall there are important differences in the scale and character of pedestrianisation as between British and German cities. In Germany, as earlier seen, most of the large cities have developed very large pedestrianisation schemes, thus implementing the ideas developed a half-century and more before by pioneer cities like Essen and Köln. But in Britain - with the exception of Leeds and Liverpool - the larger cities have not pedestrianised to the same extent. A further important difference is that in Britain the pedestrianised city centres are served by buses, with their inevitable environmental effects in terms of noise and pollution. No British city, with the exceptions of Glasgow, Newcastle and Liverpool, has been able to associate pedestrianisation with underground rail systems on the model so widely used in Germany.

Another critical difference is that the British approach to pedestrianisation has been more piecemeal than the German: individual streets, often quite small and unimportant, are pedestrianised but they are not connected up into an entire pedestrian area. Further, though some cities have gone a considerable way in the environmental treatment of their pedestrian streets, others have simply closed them to traffic - and are thus at about the same stage as German cities had reached in the mid-1950s. The fact that some streets have to accommodate buses inevitably limits the degree of environmental treatment that can be secured - though Germany offers many examples of bus-only streets comprehensively treated by elimination of the street-pavement division and the use of quietened bus engines: for instance in Trier and Mainz. Finally, however, Britain has embraced the idea of the new, entirely enclosed covered shopping mall more enthusiastically than has Germany - and this fact may explain the more limited approach to pedestrianisation of existing streets.

Pedestrianisation in the Case Study cities

Bremen

Bremen has what is by German standards an extremely modest pedestrianisation scheme, totalling only 700 metres. It was introduced relatively late (1974) and consists essentially of Bremen's high-quality shopping street, Sögestrasse, plus the main market; and a second street, Obernstrasse, is a pedestrian-plus-tram street. Additionally, the original medieval core - a network of narrow lanes with shops and restaurants - has been converted into a car-free area. Within the area of the medieval city there are some 9,000 parking spaces, only 500 of them short-term; it is proposed to increase this latter figure greatly in the near future. Plans include the upgrading of the Obernstrasse, which is now a popular shopping street, to give it a higher-quality image. Bremen is one of the few major German cities where it is still possible to extend pedestrianisation in the centre, and there is general concern in the city that this will be necessary to arrest the decline in retail trade which is now observed there.

Dortmund

Dortmund has a pedestrian area of some 1,405 metres plus three squares, mainly in the form of a long pedestrianised street (the historic east-west Hellweg). The scheme was initiated in 1963 and extended during the 1970s. At the time of the survey, public transport in the form of tram routes crossed this linear shopping street at right angles; since then, underground light rail has been introduced. Like most German cities, Dortmund's medieval core is surrounded by a wide ring street on which the main railway station (focus of the new S-Bahn system) is located. There are some 9,000 public parking spaces in the centre.

Essen

Essen's pedestrian area is very similar in size to that of its neighbour Dortmund: 2,000 metres. It was the first pedestrian area in Germany, dating probably from 1926 or 1929 (there is some doubt about the precise date). It still focuses heavily on the linear Kettwiger Strasse leading northward from the main railway station and the Limbecker Strasse leading off from this westwards, but now with a large extension eastwards to a new shopping area (Porscheplatz) constructed above the light rail station. There are about 8,000 public parking spaces in the centre, some 1,250 at short-term meters. The city would like to extend the pedestrian area to make it less linear in character; but, despite its status as pioneer, it is currently in conflict with the retailers who claim that further pedestrianisation might harm trade. They propose a large extension of underground parking in the centre, about which the city is unenthusiastic.

96

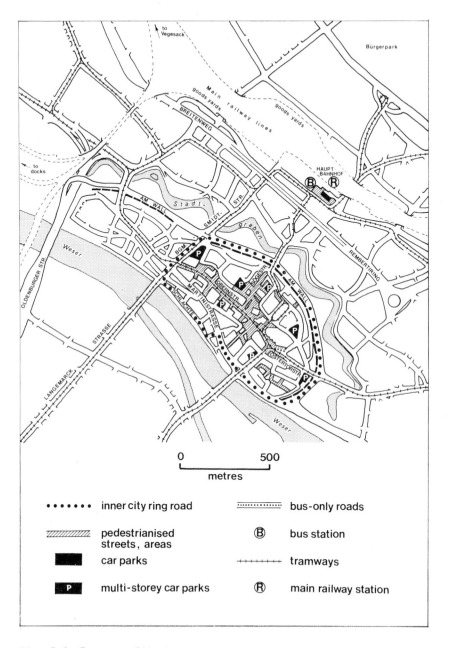

Fig. 5.1 Bremen: City Centre Pedestrianisation

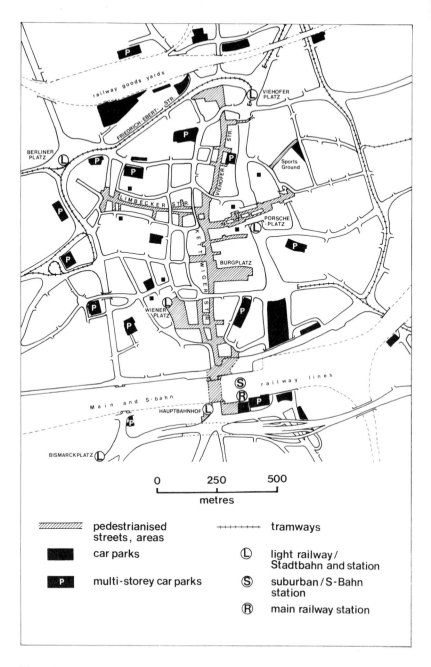

Fig. 5.2 Essen: City Centre Pedestrianisation

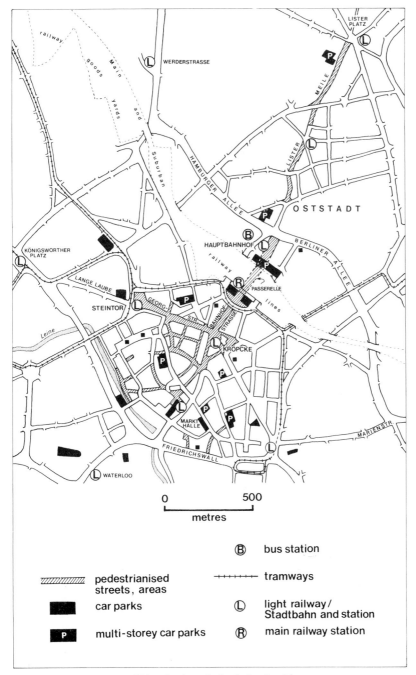

Fig 5.3 Hannover: City Centre Pedestrianisation

Hannover

Hannover's pedestrian area was initiated as early as 1956 but was extended in the 1970s in association with the underground light rail scheme then under construction. It is very extensive: some 3,500 metres or, including the adjacent inner-city shopping district of Lister Meile, over 5,000 metres. (The central area and the Lister Meile are both of such outstanding quality that they act as rival shopping centres.) The pedestrian area embraces much of the commercial core of the city. There is also a very extensive underground circulation and shopping area (Passerelle), designed to give a continuous connection between the city centre and the Lister Meile under the railway station and the large square in front of it; designed to incorporate a new shopping centre behind the station, it has not proved a very successful element of the scheme. The centre has public parking provision for nearly 14,000 cars, 5,800 of them in short-stay form on the streets around the pedestrian area.

Köln

Köln's pedestrian area was one of the first in Germany after Essen, beginning with the closure of the Hohe Strasse to traffic in 1930. The estimated size of the pedestrian area is now more than 3,000 metres occupying the two main shopping streets and some adjacent areas. Within the extended city centre area there are no less than 26,800 public parking spaces. However, in Germany the pedestrian area of Köln is regarded as rather problematic; Hohe Strasse, once one of Germany's premier shopping streets, has suffered decline and is now given over to cheap popular shops. The city is engaged on a plan for major upgrading and extension of the pedestrian area.

München

München has the most celebrated pedestrian area in Germany and possibly in the world. The first part was opened in 1972 to coincide with the 20th Olympic Games; following its success, the area was extended in 1975 and 1981. It is now possible to walk through a continuous pedestrian street from the railway station to the historic Marienplatz, a distance of just over 1 km.; the total length of pedestrian streets is about double this. There are 13,250 public parking places, of which 10,000 are in multi-storey garages and the remainder on the streets. The underground S-Bahn runs directly under the main pedestrian axis to a major interchange with U-Bahn lines under the Marienplatz. Some small parts of the pedestrian network (not on the main axis) are shared with trams. The system is substantially complete and no further major extensions are planned.

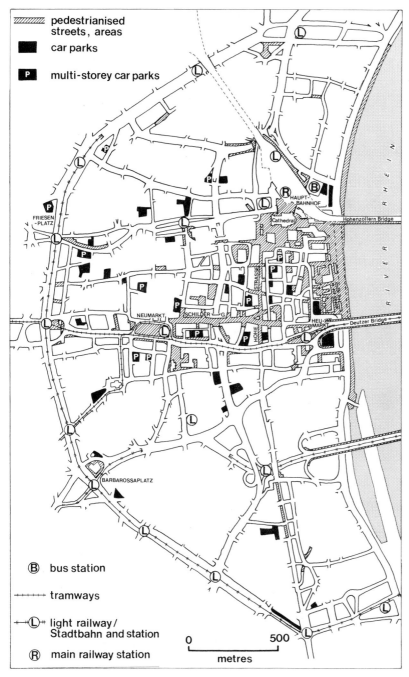

Fig. 5.4 Köln: City Centre Pedestrianisation

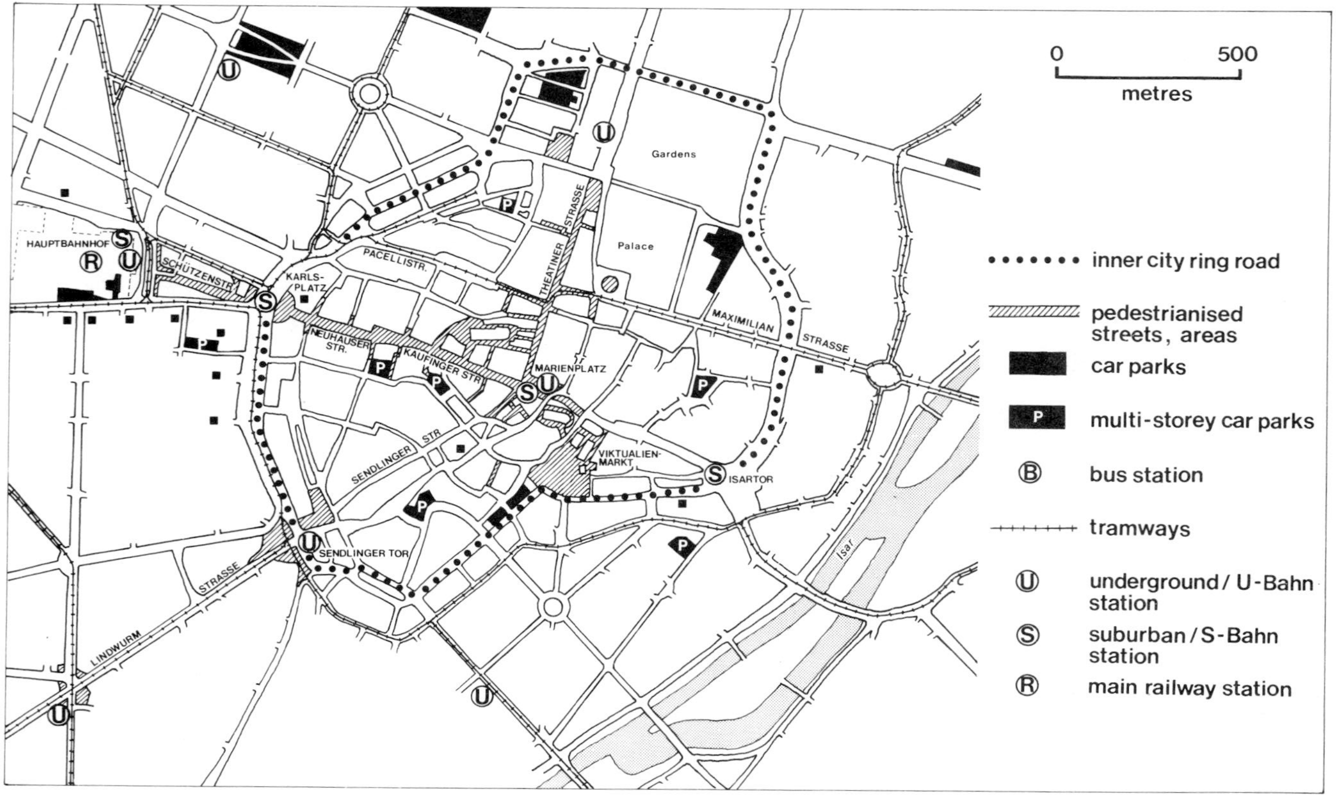

Fig. 5.5 München: City Centre Pedestrianisation

Legend:

- inner city ring road
- pedestrianised streets, areas
- car parks
- multi-storey car parks
- Ⓑ bus station
- tramways
- Ⓤ underground / U-Bahn station
- Ⓢ suburban / S-Bahn station
- Ⓡ main railway station

Map labels: MAXIMILIAN STRASSE, Gardens, Palace, THEATINER STRASSE, MARIENPLATZ, VIKTUALIEN-MARKT, ISARTOR, Isar, PACELLISTR., NEUHAUSER STR., KAUFINGER STR., SENDLINGER STR., SENDLINGER TOR, KARLS-PLATZ, SCHÜTZENSTR., HAUPTBAHNHOF, LINDWURM STRASSE, STRASSE

500 / metres / 0

102

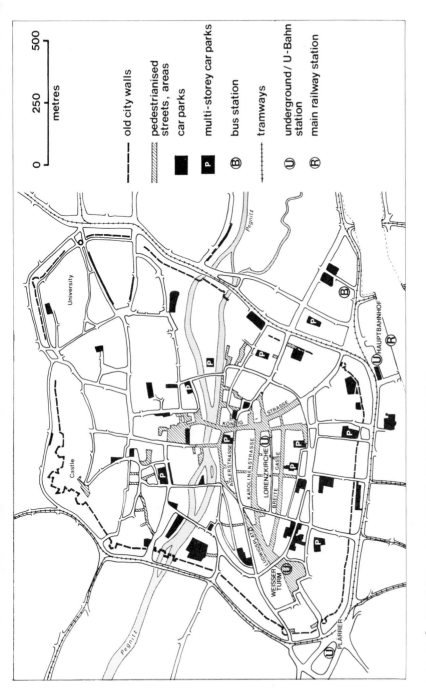

Fig. 5.6 Nürnberg: City Centre Pedestrianisation

The legend of the figure reads:

— old city walls

pedestrianised streets, areas

car parks

P multi-storey car parks

Ⓑ bus station

tramways

Ⓤ underground / U-Bahn station

Ⓡ main railway station

metres
0 250 500

Labels on the map include: University, Castle, Pegnitz, KÖNIG STRASSE, ADLERSTRASSE, KAROLINENSTRASSE, LORENZKIRCHE, BREITE GASSE, LUDWIGSPLATZ, WEISSER TURM, HAUPTBAHNHOF, PLÄRRER

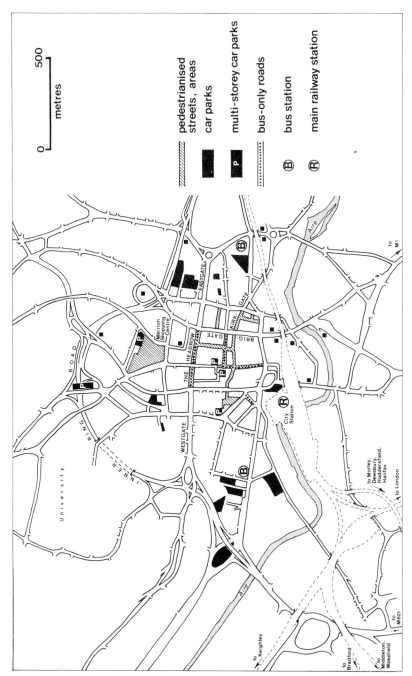

Fig. 5.7 Leeds: City Centre Pedestrianisation

Scale:
0 — 500 metres

Legend:
- pedestrianised streets, areas
- car parks
- P multi-storey car parks
- bus-only roads
- Ⓑ bus station
- Ⓡ main railway station

Nürnberg

Though small-scale pedestrianisation of individual streets occurred in
the 1960s, the city took its decision to pedestrianise the central area
in 1972. The result is one of the most extensive schemes of city-centre
pedestrianisation in the Federal Republic, totalling some 5,000 metres of
streets and squares. Since the scheme embraces large parts of the
medieval centre of the city, no further extensions are planned - though
several schemes for environmental traffic management are under
discussion. A special feature of the Nürnberg plan is the outstanding
quality of the detailed treatment. The pedestrian area has three
underground stations, of which the most important (Lorenzkirche) is at
the core of the medieval city. Most of the 5,000 public parking spaces
are at the periphery of the pedestrian area, though some are
unfortunately located in the very centre.

Glasgow

Glasgow's pedestrian area, initiated in 1972, is relatively modest: 895
metres consisting essentially of the pedestrianisation of Sauchiehall
Street, the main popular shopping street of the city, and Buchanan
Street-Argyle Street; the two are so far unconnected. One branch of the
Argyle Line passes under Argyle Street, with a station about half-way
along it. There are some 9,900 public parking places in the city centre.

Leeds

In 1970 Leeds was one of the first British cities to pedestrianise its
city-centre streets, as part of a comprehensive traffic plan of 1969
which also entailed the construction of a motorway around the city centre
together with implementation of traffic restraint and bus priority within
the centre: the so-called Leeds Approach. The plan was implemented in
two stages, in 1970 and 1972. By the mid-1970s there was a 2.5 km.
network (partially continuous) of pedestrian and restricted-access
streets in the city centre. There are 12,800 public parking spaces in
the area. There are plans to extend the system to make it a continuous
network embracing virtually the whole shopping centre of the city.

Liverpool

The scheme, begun in 1968, is extensive by British standards, embracing
some 2,000 metres (including bus-only streets). It covers an extensive
area including the new St John's Precinct (not part of this calculation)
and adjacent traditional shopping streets such as Church Street and Bold
Street. Central Station, an interchange between two Merseyrail lines, is
located under Church Street.

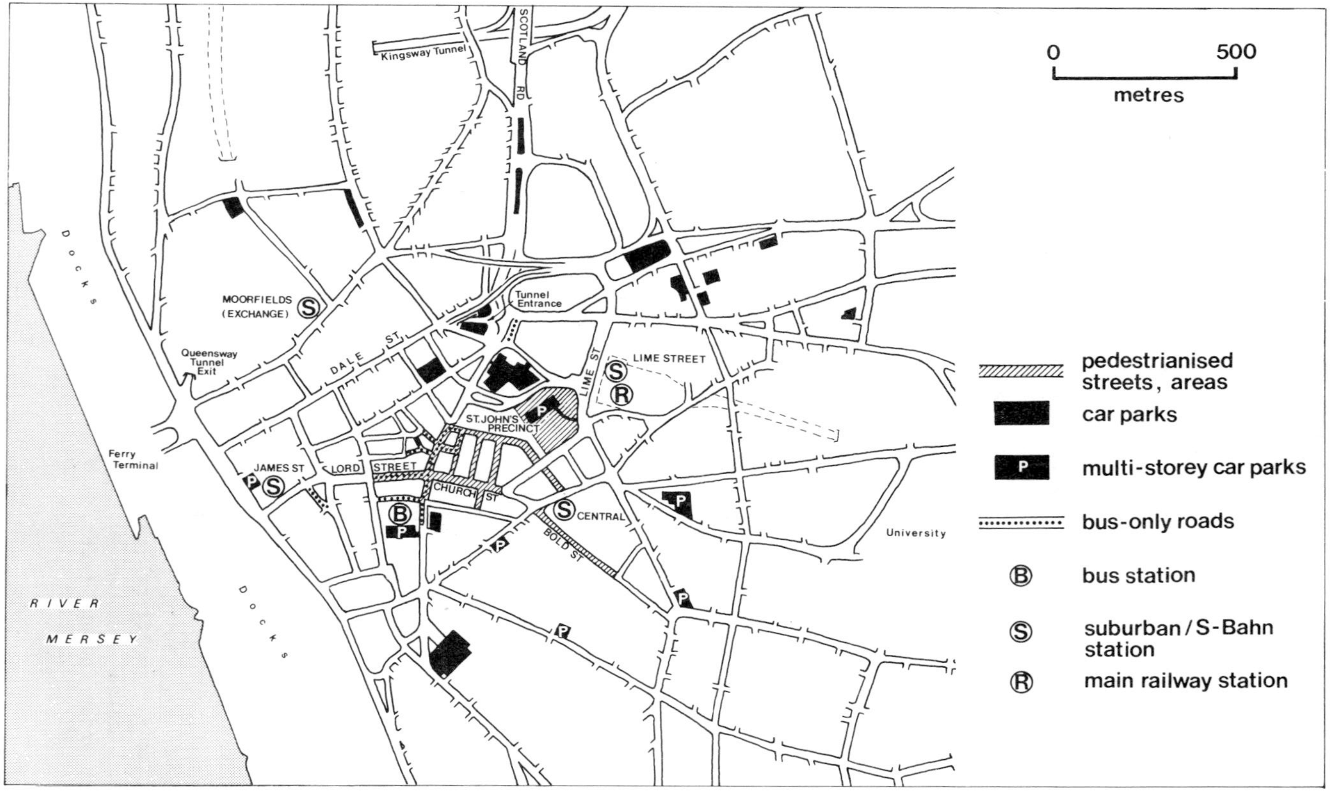

Fig. 5.8 Liverpool: City Centre Pedestrianisation

Legend:

- pedestrianised streets, areas
- car parks
- P multi-storey car parks
- bus-only roads
- Ⓑ bus station
- Ⓢ suburban/S-Bahn station
- Ⓡ main railway station

Scale: 0 — 500 metres

Map labels: University, LIME STREET, LIME ST, Ⓡ, Ⓢ, Ⓢ CENTRAL, BOLD ST, P, P, SCOTLAND RD, Tunnel Entrance, Kingsway Tunnel, ST JOHN'S PRECINCT, CHURCH ST, STREET, LORD, DALE ST, JAMES ST, Ⓢ, Ⓑ, P, MOORFIELDS (EXCHANGE) Ⓢ, Queensway Tunnel Exit, Ferry Terminal, DOCKS, RIVER MERSEY, DOCKS

Manchester

The pedestrian area, developed between 1976 and 1983, consists of a network of the city's principal shopping streets (

The pedestrian area, developed between 1976 and 1983, consists of a network of the city's principal shopping streets (Market Street, St Ann's Square and King Street) together with some bus-only streets. This network is connected directly to the Arndale Centre, the largest covered shopping precinct in Britain (88,700 square metres gross area), which is built at a high level beside and across Market Street. The total length of pedestrian and bus-only streets, 2,150 metres, makes this one of the most extensive in Britain. There are some 16,000 parking spaces in the central area, over 9,000 of them short-stay.

Newcastle

The scheme, introduced between 1971 and 1975, embraces some 1,300 metres of bus-only streets forming a network around the giant Eldon Square covered shopping precinct (72,500 square metres gross area). A Metro station at Monument, in the heart of the network, provides direct access into the Eldon Square mall. There are nearly 13,000 parking spaces in the central area.

Sheffield

Sheffield has a quite extensive pedestrian area including the city's main shopping street, The Moor, as far as Fargate, Chapel Walk and Exchange Streets as well as several narrow streets between Norfolk Street and Union Street. Several other principal shopping streets (High Street, Haymarket, Castle Street) are restricted to buses and access traffic. These pedestrian streets are however interrupted by busy distributor roads, necessitating that pedestrians cross by underground passages. In terms of detailed treatment and design this is one of the best British pedestrian schemes, comparing well with German examples. No extensions are planned, but it is intended to widen the footways in the bus-only streets.

Summing up

Detailed survey confirms the overall impression from the statistical comparisons of Chapter 4: that German cities have pedestrianised their principal central shopping streets earlier, and more comprehensively, than have British cities. The difference, though appreciable, is not great; and a number of our British case study cities have extensive pedestrian areas. Further, British cities tend to have larger purpose-built precincts than their German examples, including at least two very large ones.

The main difference in the quality of the pedestrianisation lies rather in the fact that because of their extensive rail and light rail investment programmes, the major German cities have been able to integrate the two concepts so that city-centre workers and visitors can travel directly by new rail systems to emerge in the heart of the pedestrian area. This makes public transport relatively more attractive in comparison with the car and in turn aids both transit and the restraint of the private car. It is to this aspect of the comparison that we turn in Chapter 6.

6 Impacts: pedestrianisation

We now turn to the core of this study: the impacts of rail rapid transit and of pedestrianisation. Necessarily these are difficult to separate. In those cities - particularly the German ones - where city centres were pedestrianised at approximately the same time as rail rapid transit was introduced or improved, the impacts of the two may be inextricably mixed. Nevertheless, for analytic purposes we should make the effort to separate them.

Much of this chapter is derived from existing recent sources - in particular, the excellent studies of pedestrianisation in the Federal Republic by R. Monheim (Monheim 1975, 1977, 1980). For British cities, the evidence is more fragmentary. Ross Davies' very detailed study of the centre of Newcastle upon Tyne is however interesting to compare with similar studies of pedestrianisation in Germany (Davies 1984). First, then, the overall evidence will be reviewed, both from the copious German sources and from the more limited British ones. The chapter will end with three detailed studies: of the effects of pedestrianisation in München, and in Nürnberg and of a new covered pedestrian precinct in Newcastle upon Tyne.

Following these studies, we can logically divide the effects of pedestrianisation into two groups: positive and direct - on the flows of pedestrians, and on the volume of shopping and other business activity in the centre, and negative and indirect, through effects on rental levels in the city centre and on shopping activity in other shopping areas within the city - notably of shopping streets close to the pedestrianised area, and also other shopping sub-centres in the inner or outer suburbs.

Impacts of pedestrianisation in the Federal Republic

Positive impacts: pedestrian flows, liveliness, and increase in walking distances

The most obvious index of the success of pedestrianisation, and the one most likely to be associated with an increase in shopping and other commercial activities in the centre, is provided by the actual numbers of

Table 6.1

Changes in Pedestrian Flows after Closure and Pedestrianisation

City and street	Year of closure	Year of reconstruction	Period of observation	Annual average change in flow
Aachen, Adalbertstr.	1957/63	1976	1962-74	2.1
Bamberg, Grüner Markt	1971	1976	1965-72	6.9
Bonn, Remigiusstr.	1948/66	1968	1962-70	-0.4
Braunschweig, Schuhstr.	1957/64	1964	1959-65	5.5
Bremen, Sögestr.	1961	1973	1955-62	7.6
Darmstadt, Ernst-Ludwig-Str.	1969	1969	1969-72	6.0
Hamburg, Spitaler Str.	1968	1968	1963-70	3.7
Herford, Gehrenberg	1968	1968	1968-69	31.0
Mannheim, Planken	1975	1975	1970-75	2.6
Mülheim, Schlossstr.	1973	1974	1962-74	-0.1
München, Kaufinger Str.	1970	1972	1960-74	1.3
Nürnberg, Breite Gasse	1966	1970	1964-75	6.3
Osnabrück, Grosse Str.	1972	1972	1972-75	8.7
Wiesbaden, Kirchgasse	1970	1971	1971-73	1.5

Source: Monheim 1980, pp.88-89.

pedestrians. In Germany there have been many studies of this effect in individual cities, which are however somewhat difficult to compare because they were made at different dates (and on different days in different months), sometimes with special complicating factors such as bad weather or holiday periods. Monheim (1980) has however sought to compare the results by a standard technique, which shows the average annual increase in pedestrian flow between two survey dates. (This is a simple arithmetic average, not a compounded figure.) Table 6.1 is derived from his work; it attempts to show the average increase for the period which covers the street closure and, where possible, the subsequent comprehensive pedestrian treatment. It shows that, in nearly every case, there was a substantial increase in pedestrian numbers following pedestrianisation.

Monheim's complete analysis was based as 26 comparable observations including 13 not shown in Table 6.1, but excluding the anomalous result from Herford. In terms of yearly average change, seven showed virtually no change (between -0.9 and +0.9 per cent), nine showed small increases (between 1 and 5 per cent) and ten showed large increases (5-10 per cent). The biggest increases were generally observed immediately after closure. Of the seven cases of no change, five were in two cities - Braunschweig and Mülheim - and are to be explained by changes that took place in the pedestrianised area (Monheim 1980, p.90).

Further analysis shows that the biggest increases in flow were not in the 'pure' shopping hours of the late morning (1100-1200) but in the mid-day period between 1300 and 1500, especially between 1400 and 1500. Thus the main factor in the increased activity is the use by workers in their lunch period (ibid., p.90). These changes are explained by Monheim primarily by two factors: first, the possibility of using the street in a more interesting and less direct way, not merely to get to one's destination by the shortest possible route; and secondly, the increased accessibility to the centre, especially by public transport (ibid., p.91), which made the pedestrianised cores relatively more attractive in comparison with sub-centres and out-of-town shopping centres. Here again, in Germany it is very difficult to separate the effect of pedestrianisation from that of the concurrent inauguration of rail transit. Thirdly, Monheim concludes, the enhanced environmental quality of the pedestrian streets attracted people from other streets, which might lose trade absolutely as a result.

Monheim's analysis further indicates that the biggest pedestrianised areas show the largest increases in pedestrian traffic, both during daytime shopping hours and during the evening. Big daytime increases were reported for only 45 per cent of the areas with less than 500 m. of pedestrian street, against 57 per cent for those with between 500 and 1,000 m. and no less than 70 per cent for those with over 1,000 m. The increases in evening hours and on Sundays (when shops are shut by law in Germany), though less spectacular, were also significant (Table 6.2).

In the Federal Republic no less than 69 per cent of all visits to the city centre are carried out for shopping purposes (Monheim 1980, pp.176-177). Other reasons are window shopping (the most important one); to have a meal, coffee etc. (about 16 per cent); to visit a theatre, cinema or similar entertainment or to have a date. If all data are analysed then only 30 per cent come only for shopping reasons and about 30 per cent for shopping and recreation activities (Monheim 1980, p.181). An interesting detail is that some pedestrian areas are also very busy on Sundays, when all shops (but not restaurants) are shut in Germany.

It seems there is no significant difference between pedestrian areas in cities which have a good urban environment (historical city centres) and other cities.   On a Sunday we visited Münster, which is famous for its old historic city centre, now extensively pedestrianised; it was crowded with people. But, on the same day, the pedestrianised area in Dortmund - a centre without particular historic character - was also packed.

Table 6.2

Changes in Passenger Flow after Pedestrianisation, by Size of Pedestrian Area

Period	Size of pedestrian area	Cities according to per cent change			
		Decrease	No change	Small increase	Large increase
Business hours	Under 500 m.	7	13	35	45
(92 cases)	500-1,000 m.	0	13	30	57
	Over 1,000 m.	0	0	30	70
	Total	2	10	32	57
Evenings	Under 500 m.	8	58	31	4
(86 cases)	500-1,000 m.	3	50	28	19
	Over 1,000 m.	0	43	18	39
	Total	5	50	26	50
Sundays	Under 500 m.	4	48	41	7
	500-1,000 m.	0	37	40	23
	Over 1,000 m.	0	26	39	35
	Total	2	37	40	21

Source: Monheim 1980, p.77.

The success of pedestrianised areas depends in part on the distance pedestrians are willing to walk. This is longer than planners think. A survey of Infas (not published) showed that on average pedestrians in Essen walked 1,200 m. and in Düsseldorf 1,550 m. Car users walked shorter distances than people who came on foot to the city centre - Essen: 724 m. (car users), 1,625 m. (pedestrians); Düsseldorf 1,050 m. (car users), 2,475 m. (pedestrians). Other surveys also showed higher average distances in other cities. Similar results can be shown for journeys to work in the city centre. In München, users of public transport modes walked about 700 m., car users 1,500 m., all figures for return trips (Monheim 1977, p.22). Monheim points out that the willingness to walk depends on the purpose of the visit.

The liveliness of the city centre and the pedestrianised areas also depends on the closeness of inner city areas, and their density. In Frankfurt, 22 per cent of all city centre visitors lived less than 1.5 km. distant, of whom 73 per cent came on foot or bicycle; only 34 per cent came from outside the city. Of those coming from outside, but within 10 km. of the centre, 71 per cent used public transportation; of those coming from greater than 10 km. distant, the proportion was only 63 per cent. In Düsseldorf and Bonn, 20 per cent of the population who visited the city centre live no further away than 1 km., and most of these came on foot or bicycle (Monheim 1977, p.25).

Positive effects: pedestrianisation and mode of transport

This evidence indicates clearly that the use of the pedestrian area is intimately related to the mode of transport used to reach it. In the Federal Republic, the dominating concept of pedestrian areas until today has still been to offer an optimal accessibility of the city centre to private car owners. In general, the retailing firms have always demanded an increase in the accessibility of pedestrian areas by building fast city ring roads and tangents, as well as an increase in the rear accessibility of shops, and most importantly, an increase in parking space.

However, in recent years the large cities have often planned pedestrianisation and public transport as one concept. The optimal solution has always been to have public transport stops inside the pedestrianised area but - if possible - to put the actual public transport line underground. Monheim reported in 1975 that out of 500 pedestrian zones in German cities, only twenty-eight had surface tram or bus traffic in them; however, twenty-two of these had no intention of removing it (Monheim 1975, p.29); they report satisfactory results, with very few accidents. Transport and urban planners in Bremen mentioned that pedestrianised streets with a tram line gave a much livelier impression in the evening than streets without public transport.

The question then is how this dual policy - on the one hand seeking to improve car access to the edge of the central pedestrian zone, on the other hand improving public transport - has affected the mode of transport that is used. On this question, there have been two major surveys in the Federal Republic. One, by Monheim, surveyed fourteen cities of different sizes; another, by BAG (a co-operation of retailing shops), undertook surveys in 1965, 1968, 1971, 1976 and 1980. Monheim's survey analysed pedestrians, whereas the BAG surveys focused on department-store shoppers. It perhaps goes without saying that the use of transportation mode was different between the two groups. Department

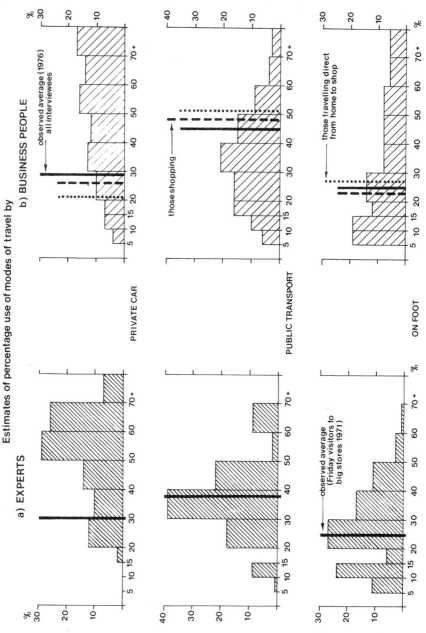

Fig. 6.1: Overestimates by Experts and Business People of Car Use

store shoppers use the car more often than pedestrians (most department stores provide their own parking facilities). However, both surveys show clearly that the use of the car has been over-estimated by planners and retailers. Urban and transport planners and retailers both estimated car use twice as high as in reality, and the proportion of pedestrians half as high (Monheim 1977, p.27). Monheim sees the main reason for the planners' over-estimate in the fact that most of them are car users. Fig. 6.1a shows the estimates of car use by 74 experts, and the actual results of the BAG survey in 1971; Fig. 6.1b shows the over-estimate of car use by business people in Düsseldorf in comparison with the actual use of transport modes in 1976. In actuality, just over 40 per cent of shoppers used cars. But over 60 per cent of the experts thought that more than 50 per cent would do so, and 33 per cent of them thought that more than 60 per cent would do so.

In Monheim's report of 1980, a more detailed picture is given of the use of different transportation modes, based on the BAG surveys of 1965, 1968, 1971 and 1976 for all cities surveyed. Table 6.3 includes the results for all cities above 500,000.

Table 6.3

Federal Republic of Germany: Use of Transport Modes in City Centre Department Stores, Major Cities[a]: Friday

	Car	Public transport	Foot
		percentage	
1965	26.8	54.5	16.4
1968	29.8	54.4	14.4
1971[b]	28.7	54.7	12.7
1971[c]	29.1	54.3	14.2
1976[d]	32.6	52.3	12.8
1980	27.4	60.0	9.0

a) Above 500,000 population.
b) City within 1971 boundaries.
c) City within 1976 boundaries.
d) Based on a sample of cities about 50 per cent bigger than in 1965.

Source: Monheim 1980, p.196, based on BAG surveys; BAG 1981, unpublished; figures exclude Berlin.

Table 6.4, which extracts data for the seven case study cities, shows
an increase in the weekday use of public transportation modes, especially
in cities which have heavily invested in new public transportation
systems. München shows the highest proportionate use of public transport
in Germany, even exceeding Hamburg and Berlin. Table 6.5 shows that there
has even been a notable increase in the use of public transport on
Saturdays, although the use is then generally much lower than during the
Monday-Friday working week; on Saturdays, the use of cars is 43 per cent
higher than on weekdays.

Monheim's work shows further that there is a notable difference in the
use of the car by sex and by age: younger people travel by car more than
older people; similarly, men use the car more than women (Monheim 1980,
pp.199-200). Further, Monheim's own survey on the use of transportation
mode showed an even lower percentage of car users. The BAG surveys
included only visitors from home to the city centre to visit department
stores, whereas Monheim points out that many trips to the city centre do
not start at home, but have origins which might be between home and
centre - jobs, school, public services. On average only 63 per cent of
pedestrians in the city centre come directly from home (ibid., p.200,
based on eight cities) (Table 6.6). Direct comparison between Monheim's
results and those of BAG show significant differences in the proportion
of pedestrians (Table 6.7).

The reason why car use for shopping is relatively low may have to do
with the availability of cars. Although more than 65 per cent of
households in Germany owned a car in 1983, less than one-third of its
members have the use of it during the day (BAG 1980). This is
particularly true for women who still do most of the shopping.

Modal split surveys show the generally high use of public transport by
city-centre workers in cities above 500,000. Blivice shows for employees
in München's city centre that about 70 per cent used public transport, 18
per cent walked and only 12 per cent used the car (Monheim 1977, p.25).
Such use of public transport cannot however be found for the other cities
studied.

Positive effects: shopping turnover

Nearly all firms in pedestrianised streets report an increase in
turnover, often not immediately after the introduction of
pedestrianisation but after pedestrianisation has been established for a
couple of years. Hermanns gives figures of an average increase of 30-40
per cent in Köln's pedestrianised streets, and for the main shopping
street Hohe Strasse at Christmas, 50-100 per cent (Hermanns 1972, p.5).
In Essen turnover and customers increased by between 15 and 35 per cent
after implementing pedestrianisation (Essen Stadtplanungsamt, 1971,
p.38). An FfH (Forschungsstelle für den Handel, Berlin) survey in

Table 6.4

**Federal Republic of Germany: Use of Transport Modes to City
Centre Department Stores in the Seven Case Study Cities: Thursday**

(a) Car

	Percentage		
	1971	1976	1980
Bremen	25.7	27.7	28.2
Dortmund	36.6	42.1	37.6
Essen	31.1	42.0	32.2
Hannover	28.0	31.9	26.1
Köln	38.7	36.4	28.8
München	24.4	19.7	15.7
Nürnberg	-	-	37.8

(b) Public transport

	1971	1976	1980
Bremen	57.6	58.4	56.8
Dortmund	43.8	41.4	45.6
Essen	55.0	45.2	55.6
Hannover	55.7	56.9	61.4
Köln	48.0	47.4	58.1
München	64.0	73.5	76.0
Nürnberg	-	-	43.8

(c) On foot

	1971	1976	1980
Bremen	11.7	9.7	9.5
Dortmund	18.8	15.4	13.7
Essen	12.5	11.1	10.6
Hannover	12.0	9.3	8.9
Köln	12.5	12.7	10.2
München	8.8	5.2	5.7
Nürnberg	-	-	33.4

Source: Monheim 1980, p.198, based on BAG surveys; BAG 1981.

Table 6.5

Federal Republic of Germany: Use of Public Transportation to City Centre Department Stores in Selected Cities: Saturday

	1976	1980
Hamburg	50	53
München	60	67
Frankfurt	38	49
Köln	28	37
Essen	29	33
Berlin	-	49

Source: BAG 1981.

Table 6.6

Federal Republic of Germany: Mode of all Journeys to City Centre, in Selected Cities

	A	B
Car	28	29
Public transport	29	31
On foot	39	36
Other	4	4

A: Survey in 8 cities

B: Survey in 14 cities: Aachen, Opladen, Soest, Leverkusen, Bonn, Düsseldorf, Koblenz, Essen, Dortmund, Bielefeld, Bochum, Hamm, Mülheim, Bonn-Bad Godesberg.

Source: Monheim 1980, p.201.

Table 6.7

Table 6.7

Federal Republic of Germany: City Centre Pedestrians Travelling from Home; Mode used to reach City Centre, in Selected Cities, Thursdays

	Monheim all pedestrians	BAG (1976) department store visitors
Car	34	39
Public transport	31	34
On foot	31	22
Other	4	5

Source: Monheim 1980, p.20.

Nürnberg showed that after pedestrianisation was implemented two-thirds of establishments showed an increase, 55 per cent an increase of more than 5 per cent. One third of businesses claimed turnover stayed the same and about 5 per cent reported a decline in turnover. 60 per cent of the 103 establishments believed that the turnover increase was the result of pedestrianisation (Nürnberg Stadt 1979, p.23). Similar figures can be shown for most German cities, the increase in turnover reflecting a dramatic increase in the number of pedestrians. (Here, it should be noted that in many cases parallel streets become so unpleasant to walk in - because of an increase in car traffic or because of loading and unloading, or both - that people are 'channelled' into pedestrianised streets.)

Negative effects of pedestrianisation: land use effects

The financially strongest business premises will tend to be successful in bidding for sites within the pedestrianised area; they will exclude other activities with less ability to pay the rents that are demanded, which will either go out of business or be relegated to the periphery of the centre or to sub-centres. Thus H. Monheim points out that non-commercial uses, small restaurants, cafes, and similar activities are generally lacking in pedestrianised areas (H. Monheim 1977, p.127).

This view is supported by at least two surveys. Heinz and Hübner et al point out that the retailers who are opposed to pedestrianisation are mainly small traditional traders. They are the first who will suffer:

because of rent increases they will have to give up their premises. Chain stores take over traditional shops and are willing to pay 30-40 per cent more rent (Heinz, Hübner, et al 1977, p.135). However, it is difficult here to separate the effects of pedestrianisation from the effects of general changes in the retailing structure - which, to our knowledge, have not been examined.

Another survey, by the FfH, researched eleven cities in the Federal Republic of Germany. Most of the cities studied had around 100,000-300,000 inhabitants. Two larger cities were included (Köln and Nürnberg). The main question asked concerned how far pedestrianisation changed the retailing structure in the cities studied. On average, shops belonging to branches such as textiles, clothing, shoes, hardware, household effects and home requirements had increased, whereas food shops and other branches declined (FfH, 1978, p.115). Generally, shops found in pedestrianised streets are more specialised. There is also a tendency for the development of what in German are called 'Schnelldreher': shops selling highly fashionable articles that change very quickly.

There may also be a strong displacement effect on dwellings inside the pedestrianised areas. Until now, there has been much more housing stock still available even in Germany's largest city centres than in comparable British city centres. One effect of pedestrianisation is that housing is changed into business premises, offices, or luxury flats. The original population is then forced to leave the area. An even more serious effect can be seen in inner city areas which are affected by the diversion of traffic. The resultant decline in environmental quality will exacerbate the out-migration of the better-off population, and again, a negative selection process will take place. German planners have been well aware of this problem and have worked to prevent it, with some success. Certainly, it appears that so far the German cities do not suffer an inner-city problem on the scale of many of their British counterparts.

The FfH found that since the opening of pedestrian streets, average shopping rents increased around 50 per cent (Table 6.8).

The results below should be treated with caution, because:

1. only every fifth shop owner questioned knew the rent before pedestrianisation was carried out;

2. the time since pedestrianisation was established varies greatly;

3. as can be seen from the average rent tables in Table 7.9a and b (Chapter 7), in some cities (e.g. Köln, München), rents outside the pedestrian area increased more than inside it. It is questionable indeed whether rent increases are mainly due to

pedestrianisation; it is far more likely that they result from displacement of certain kinds of retailing by others, though certainly pedestrianisation may have had an additional effect;

4. it is not clear if the rent increases reflect inflation-corrected rents.

Table 6.8

Federal Republic of Germany:
Shopping Rent Increases in Pedestrianised Cities

City	Monthly rent per sq. m. in establishment		Rent increase	Date of pedestrianisation
	1977	Before pedestrian- isation		
	DM	DM	per cent	
Wolfenbüttel	13.50	11.25	21	1967
Stade	11.85	8.50	30	1970
Rheine	19.80	16.50	47	1970
Unna	17.05	11.45	74	1967
Hildesheim	19.00	13.95	55	1968
Offenbach	32.30	26.20	52	-
Oldenburg	19.65	12.50	32	1967
Augsburg	24.75	15.20	63	1962
Gelsenkirchen	31.20	9.75	75	1956
Nürnberg	38.50	16.35	55	1967,1970,1972[a]
Köln	60.10	31.60	95	1930,1970,1974[a]

a) Dates shown are for first closure of street, not for formal pedestrianisation treatment. Where more than one date is given, streets were closed in stages.

Source: FfH 1978, p.34; Monheim 1975, pp. 240, 223, 209, 230, 152, 196, 96,

Negative effects: on transportation

As pointed out above, in nearly all cases pedestrianisation means an increase in the traffic flow in areas close by. As car-customers are seen as being very important (having more spending power), enough parking space therefore has to be provided as close as possible to the pedestrianised areas. Most Chambers of Commerce demand in addition new urban motorways, ring roads etc., which are often built. However, some German cities have adopted deliberate traffic restraint policies.

Negative effects: indirect

In general the success of pedestrianisation is measured by planning officials and representatives of commerce in terms of the increase in the number of pedestrians in the city centre and, even more important for the retailing trade, in the increase in turnover there. However, the success of an improved city centre is invariably made at the cost of other shopping centres. Basically if one assumes that the total amount of money spent in a city-plus-hinterland can only marginally increase, then a significant increase in the consumption in the city centre implies a decrease somewhere else, often in shopping centres relatively close to the city centre (Monheim, H., 1977, p.126; also our survey).

Impacts of pedestrianisation in Britain

In comparison with Germany, there has been little research on the effects pedestrianisation has had or might have on British city centres. Although the British literature on pedestrianisation is considerable, most of it is in the form of short articles on a particular pedestrian scheme. There are, however, several exceptions, especially the work carried out by TEST (Transport and Environmental Studies). An interesting dissertation written by J.F. Cashmore is comparable with the most important German literature on pedestrianisation. Cashmore concludes that within the planning profession pedestrianisation is positively regarded (Cashmore 1981, pp.5-6), but that traffic engineers tend to believe that it can only be successful if combined with construction of high-capacity inner distributor roads and provision of rear access for loading and unloading. Generally it is feared that congestion on alternative traffic routes in the centre would occur, including worse accessibility for car users, or decline in car speeds on the roads around the central area, which also would contribute to a slower and less reliable bus service. Cashmore concludes that 'none of these factors usually deteriorates to the extent forecast ....' (ibid., p.39).

Positive impacts: pedestrian flow

There is much more information available in Britain on the changes in
pedestrian flows than on increases or decreases in shopping turnover. In
contrast to German cities, the information is only available for a small
number of cities.   There are also no counts over a period of time in
order to measure changes in the number of pedestrians.   The records are
better for smaller cities than for bigger ones.

    Roberts' study notes an average increase of 29 per cent in the number
of pedestrians in Durham (Roberts 1981, p.68; TEST 1981, p.30).   Parker
and Hoile mention an increase of 36 per cent in London's Carnaby Street
after the traffic was removed (Parker, Hoile 1975, p.24).   Exactly the
same percentage increases were found after Broad Street in Reading was
closed to private cars, and also during the experimental closure of
Briggate in Leeds in 1972.   In Norwich's London Street an increase of 45
per cent was counted.   But there are also pedestrianised streets in
which either no change at all was observed (Cornmarket, Oxford: bus-only
street), or even a decline in the number of pedestrians was established:
Church Street, Liverpool declined 15 per cent over a 12-month period
during the introductory period (Cashmore 1981, p.47).

    In contrast to Germany we have little evidence in Britain of how the
pedestrianisation flow varies between   different streets in city centres.
Davies' work on Newcastle upon Tyne, which provides an outstanding
exception, is discussed below; it indicates that the opening of the Eldon
Square Shopping Centre significantly changed the pedestrian flow
(Bennison, Davies 1980, p.65) and that the opening of a new Metro station
had an even more dramatic effect on the change in pedestrian flows
(Davies 1979, 1984). Several studies indicate that pedestrians tend to
stay longer in a pedestrian street than in an unpedestrianised street; a
good example is the monitoring study in Commercial Road, Portsmouth (Ove
Arup 1973, para. 7.5.6).   Similar results have been found in many German
cities (Monheim 1978).   One can assume that changes in the pedestrian
flow occur when bus stops are altered, although little research has been
carried out on this question (Ove Arup 1973 para. 7.5.6).

    In Leeds, one of the largest city-centre pedestrianised areas in
Britain, the authorities conducted surveys after the scheme was
introduced (significantly, without a single objection) in December 1970.
There was a 9 per cent increase in pedestrian flow inside the pedestrian
area compared with a 6 per cent decrease on streets outside it. 94.4 per
cent of those surveyed (over half of them shoppers) were in favour of
pedestrianisation.   Retailers reported virtually no change in trade
(Wyborn 1973, pp.256-7).   Subsequently, research in Leeds has sought to
find a link between increases in pedestrian flow and increases in
shopping activity.   The data suggest a positive connection between the
changes in the number of people entering shops and sales (Cashmore 1981,
p.48).

Positive impacts: shopping turnover

One undoubted obstacle to pedestrianisation in Britain, even after thirty-two years of experience in over a hundred British cities and some 1,450 separate pedestrian schemes, has been the continued opposition of many traders (Roberts 1981, p.95; Cashmore 1981, p.8). Cashmore concludes that 'the effect on retailing trade is little understood ....' (ibid., p.130) and that there is little hard evidence because of the reluctance of Chambers of Commerce and shopkeepers to give precise sales information (ibid., p.49). An OECD study in 1978, which involved responses from 105 cities, quotes results from only thirteen British cities of which half had not noticed any change in sales. In comparison, nineteen German cities were included in the survey of which twelve (63 per cent) recorded an increase in turnover (Roberts 1981, p.84).

The Civic Trust conducted a study on the effect pedestrianisation had on trade, which collated the results from previous British and other studies, some as early as 1966. The information on turnover covered only five cities (Durham, Hereford, London (Carnaby Street), Watford, Norwich). One interesting result came from Durham, which showed a decline of 20 per cent in turnover after the introduction of pedestrianisation. An additional survey including 84 answers in the same city showed that, between 1975 and 1979, 52 per cent reported an increase in trade, 44 per cent reported no change, and 3 per cent thought trade had declined (Roberts 1981, p.30). There is further evidence in some British cities that there was in general an increase in turnover, but most of these cities are small or middle-sized (Bridlington, Hull, Lincoln, Bangor, Chichester, Norwich, Portsmouth). Information on large cities is given only on Manchester (Market Street and Deansgate), Leeds and London (Carnaby Street) of which London is clearly a special case (Roberts 1981, pp.81-86, Cashmore 1981, pp.49-51). However, no real comparison can be made because the information is not standardised over time.

Given this fact, it is not surprising that there is also a lack of information on the factors that might influence the increase or decrease of turnover in a pedestrianised street. Cashmore points out that 'there is remarkably little information on where the increase in turnover comes from, whether it is confined to the area pedestrianised, whether at the expense of other shops in the town centre, or of shops in other towns altogether' (Cashmore 1981, p.50).

Negative effects: decline in turnover

Neither in Britain nor in Germany has much attention been given to a puzzling phenomenon that is reported in a minority of cases: those pedestrianised streets in which there has been a fall in turnover. Some pedestrianised streets have experienced either a slight or even a dramatic fall in turnover shortly after pedestrianisation was introduced: for instance Church Street in Eccles, Greater Manchester (Cashmore 1981, p.50); the case of Durham, reported above; Baker Street, Brighton; George Street, Hove (internal information). It appears that several of these cases were second or third class shopping streets, where many shops live on very low profit margins and are sensitive to a decline in customers which might occur in the first few months of pedestrianisation. Furthermore, trades may fear rent increases and/or increases in rates in pedestrianised streets, which can be lethal for shops with a small profit margin. However, we have no firm evidence on these questions.

In London's Carnaby Street, a survey two years after the closure in March 1972 revealed that more retail managers reported a decline in sales than an increase. However, this was a period when Carnaby Street was in relative decline after its phenomenal boom period of the late 1960s (Myatt 1975, pp.30-32). This well illustrates the difficulty of separating out the influence of pedestrianisation from other factors.

Case Studies: München

In the early 1960s the first discussions took place on pedestrianisation of the old historic part of München's city centre (between Karlsplatz and Marienplatz). The city of München saw two preconditions as necessary for such a scheme:

1. the construction of an Underground and S-Bahn system which would focus on the city centre (Marienplatz), and

2. the construction of a ring road around the old historic city centre (Altstadtring).

In 1972, the pedestrian area from Karlsplatz to Marienplatz and the U- and S-Bahn system were opened at the beginning of the 20th Olympic Games. The increase in pedestrian use was dramatic: whereas in 1966, 72,000 people were counted between Karlsplatz and Marienplatz, in 1972 the number had increased to 120,000 on one day. It is estimated that between 1972 and 1980 the number of pedestrians increased by about 80 per cent, excluding holiday months (München Landeshauptstadt 1980, p.3). The City of München had seen the promotion of pedestrianisation **not** as a measure for supporting the retailing trade, but as a result of a planned restructuring of the city centre. The retailing turnover between Karlsplatz and Marienplatz however increased by about 40 per cent but retailing turnover at the edge of the city centre (outside the pedestrian zone) declined by 15 per cent.

After the first success, the largest open market in München - the Viktualienmarkt, near the Marienplatz - was pedestrianised in 1975. The scheme included new street furniture in the form of a hundred new lamp posts, forty new trees and three new fountains. The open air pub (Biergarten) offers seats for three hundred people. In the same year the Theatinerstrasse was pedestrianised, thus connecting the Marienplatz northwards. Then, in 1980/81, two other streets close to the Marienplatz were pedestrianised, although one, the Sendlinger Strasse, was not completely closed to traffic; the pavement was widened between 2.50 m. to 5.50 m, the roadway for cars was narrowed from 10.00 m. to 7.00 m, allowing short period parking for cars on both sides. The other, the Schützenstrasse, is the street which leads from München's main station to the Karlsplatz and further on to Marienplatz. The traveller arriving by train can therefore now reach the city centre through a completely car-free street network. Schützenstrasse has always been a problem area (cheap hotels, porn shops etc.); it will be interesting to observe the effect of pedestrianisation.

The costs of the entire scheme were relatively modest:

Karlsplatz - Marienplatz : about 12 million DM including street furniture (fountains, seats etc.), 240 DM/sq. m.

Viktualienmarkt : about 3.31 million, 140 DM/sq. m.

Theatinerstrasse : about 2.38 million DM, 150 DM/sq. m.

Sendlinger Strasse : about 1.0 million DM, of which 280,000 DM was paid by adjoining owners.

Schützenstrasse : about 1.42 million DM, of which 680,000 DM was paid by owners.

The City of München thus paid the total costs between Karlsplatz and Marienplatz and on the Viktualienmarkt. For the other streets the City of München received a contribution (20-30 per cent of total cost) from the retailing organisation and the owners of the houses along the pedestrianised streets.

The total length of the pedestrianisation in the city centre is about 2,000 m. excluding Viktualienmarkt which has 22,000 square metres. Nearly all streets have back street delivery apart from the Schützenstrasse. The Viktualienmarkt has both back and front deliveries. Trams still run through part of the Theatiner Strasse. There are 8,000 parking spaces available.

The pedestrianised area in München is often cited as the best example of pedestrianisation in Europe (München Landeshauptstadt, 1980, p.11). According to the Bavarian Organisation of Retailing (BOR) (Landesverband des Bayerischen Einzelhandels), hardly any negative effects have been noted in the pedestrianised zones of the city centre. There has been some change in the pattern of shopping towards mass articles but there has so far not been a change in the social-economic structure of the customers. Shops with high profit margins, which often change quickly, are hardly seen in the pedestrian zone, in contrast to cities such as Köln. There has also been no strong trend towards a change in the structure of shops.

Although department stores and branches have increased in number, this trend can be seen all over Germany, and is not specific to pedestrianised zones. Shops immediately outside the pedestrian area have not suffered in the long run, because the flow of pedestrians in the pedestrian zone is so high (up to 20,000 per hour in peak times) that many people seek neighbouring streets in order to move faster. There is a great deal of specialisation in the side streets, and no striking structural changes have been observed there either. Though rents increased rather strongly after pedestrianisation, forcing some old-established firms to leave, such changes have been observed in other major German cities.

Clearly more research is needed on the question of why München's pedestrianisation has been so successful in comparison with other German and British cities. There might be several reasons:

1. A nearly intact historic city centre with an attractive layout of streets; there are also several important historic monuments in the city centre, which attract tourists.

2. An extremely good public transportation system which focuses directly on the city centre.

3. A good mixture of shops, restaurants and cafes, not so much in pedestrianised zones but rather behind or close to the pedestrianised zone.

4. Many important institutions in the city centre or close by, such as banks and other public institutions. Most of the civil service jobs are in the city centre. As German shop hours are very inflexible, shopping - or part of the shopping - has to be done during lunch hours, which increases the liveliness of the pedestrianised zones.

5. Different cultural habits, a pleasant climate, strong southerly winds, many sunny days.

6. A coalition of powerful interest groups in München who favour large-scale pedestrianisation.

Nürnberg

Nürnberg's pedestrian centre is one of the most thoroughly researched in the Federal Republic. The city has carried out pedestrian counts since 1963 (Monheim 1984, private correspondence). As early as 1961 a small passage connecting two major department stores was closed to traffic (Monheim 1980, p.51). Then, in 1964, a narrow but important part of a shopping street (Breite Gasse) was closed to traffic and later converted into a pedestrian street (Nürnberg Stadt, 1979, p.2). At that time, and indeed throughout the 1960s, the concept of pedestrianisation barely existed; the city then favoured a car-oriented city centre with only small and isolated pedestrian 'islands' (Monheim 1980, p.51). But the success of the first pedestrianised street, in terms of increased pedestrian flow, led in 1972 to a decision by the city to develop a more comprehensive pedestrianisation concept for the city centre.

The plan evoked fierce opposition from retailing and motoring organisations, including private car parking firms, extending in one case to a six-year legal action against the city (Monheim 1984, private correspondence). Despite this the pedestrian area was extended from its previous 840 m. to 1,830 m. in 1972 (Nürnberg Stadt, 1979, p.4). A further extension took place after 1975, and progressively the entire city centre was converted into a car-free, elaborately landscaped zone 5 km. long - a process which in 1984 was virtually complete.

The completion of the underground system was always seen as a major contribution to the success of the pedestrianisation scheme. But several other factors have proved significant. These include the combination of several refurbished houses into a new department store, new multi-storey parking facilities and systematic enhancement of the historic character of the city. During the major market period in the weeks before Christmas, which brings heavy tourist traffic, the city since 1978 has developed a park-and-ride system; all tourist buses must use the facilities, and visitors receive free underground tickets for their onward journey to the city centre (Nürnberg Stadt, 1979, p.12).

Pedestrian counts during this pre-Christmas period show that the number of pedestrians nearly doubled in the city centre between 1967 and 1977 (Monheim 1980, p.96; Monheim 1984, personal correspondence). Apart from a decline in 1978, which was due to special circumstances, all three major shopping streets experienced a rapid increase in pedestrian traffic after their closure to the motorised traffic. The oldest, Breite Gasse, was converted into a full pedestrian street in 1966; its popularity rose from then until 1974, and again from 1977 to 1980, though since then it has lost some pedestrian traffic. Karolinenstrasse was the busiest shopping street in Nürnberg immediately after the war. It then lost popularity until 1976 (with only a slight upward movement after 1972). Its pedestrianisation in 1978 caused a return to its old popularity. The Königstrasse - the second major shopping street, leading from the main railway station to the Lorenzkirche in the heart of the city also increased sharply in popularity after closure. The Nürnberg experience thus shows that pedestrian streets develop in what might be called waves of popularity.

These increases have been obtained at the cost of some other city-centre streets, which have lost pedestrians. The most dramatic case is not in the city centre itself, where pedestrian flows seem to have been at worst static (Monheim 1980, p.101), but in the Südstadt, an inner-city sub-centre close to the city centre, where the main shopping street lost 28 per cent of its pedestrians between 1967 and 1976 (ibid., p.101) and has almost certainly lost more people since the latter date.

Newcastle upon Tyne

There have been no similarly detailed studies of British pedestrianisation schemes; the nearest approach, by the Leeds city authorities, has already been summarised. However, a very detailed study has been made of a British scheme which is of interest because in some ways it is comparable with the largest German schemes (Davies 1984). When Newcastle's Eldon Square Centre was opened in 1976, it was the largest purpose-built shopping centre in Britain and possibly in Europe (73,000 sq. m.), including a large department store and over one hundred specialised stores. Situated in the heart of the central shopping area, it has easy links to the traditional shopping streets outside. In its first year of opening its turnover was some 30 per cent of the central area total, which itself had grown by some 12-13 per cent as a result of the opening of the centre.

However, the interesting point about Eldon Square, in comparison with an ordinary pedestrianisation, was the dramatic shift in trade which resulted. Davies estimates that of the total turnover of the Eldon Centre - £63 million - no less than £23 million was taken from existing streets in the central area. A similar amount was diverted from other major centres of the Tyneside region, with other shifts from smaller centres. Most of the impact was felt along the main traditional shopping street of the city just outside the Eldon Centre, Northumberland Street. In the first year, much concern was felt in the city about these effects, particularly as the main streets began to wear a neglected and careworn look. However, within the following three years, a quite remarkable recovery of trade occurred: as against 51 vacant shops in the central area just prior to the opening and 69 a year after opening, by the end of 1979 there were only 27 (Davies 1984, p.283).

Davies' explanation for this is interesting: before the opening of Eldon Square the whole city centre was under-shopped and a number of major national multiples were not represented. These multiples occupied most of the units within the new centre, leaving vacant shop units in the old shopping streets. Then, encouraged by the City Planning Department, smaller independent retailers moved into the empty shops. The likelihood then is that over time the injection of a new shopping precinct brings about a growth in the turnover of the entire central shopping district, with a particular increase in smaller independent shops in the older streets.

The new centre has also had an effect on other shopping centres in the surrounding region. Within the Tyneside agglomeration, the major district shopping centres experienced a 9 per cent decline in their durable goods turnover, but this constitutes a small part of their total trade which mainly consists of convenience goods. In the three years 1976-9, the three nearest centres were closely monitored, but in none of them could any shop closures be attributed to competition from Eldon Square. The centre most seriously affected is Gateshead, just across the river Tyne. But several factors were at work here, including problems of design of the Gateshead centre. There was a bigger percentage impact on centres outside the agglomeration, such as Durham City, Morpeth and Hexham; but in this ring, general population growth and increased spending levels have more than compensated. So overall, Davies concludes, the indirect effects of Eldon Square have not been at all serious.

The Case Studies: Conclusion

The case studies, in one important respect, help to confirm an impression from the early overall comparison. There has been less pedestrianisation in British cities, and much less sustained interest in its results, partly - or even mainly - because the introduction of pedestrian shopping into Britain has come by a different route: the construction, in the hearts of British cities, of totally new shopping precincts. In this respect Eldon Square is just an extreme example of a phenomenon that can also be seen in Manchester (Arndale Centre), Liverpool (St John's Precinct), Nottingham (Victoria Centre), Birmingham (New Street Centre) and many others. The main differences, as against the German method of pedestrianising whole networks of existing streets, are two. First, the British method involves a large and sudden injection into the city centre of additional shopping floorspace; secondly, unless done with particular sensitivity, it can greatly disrupt the physical structure and streetscape of the city centre; and thirdly, its location must modify existing patterns of pedestrian movement in a way that is not true of the German system. Whether a city can absorb such sudden changes seems to depend in some measure on the general prosperity of the city itself and also of its surrounding region. In this regard, it is perhaps significant that Newcastle, as the regional capital of what has traditionally been one of the most depressed regions of Britain, has apparently been able to absorb these changes without excessive strain.

Our primary focus in this study has been on pedestrianisation in the strict sense. But, as we now move to consider the effects of rail rapid transit in some cities as against trends in those cities without it, it will be necessary to bear in mind that pedestrianisation in this sense is by no means the only kind of major change that has been occurring in German or British city centres. Big increases in retail floorspace, or changes in the character of existing floorspace - whether through pedestrianisation or through new shopping precincts or through major new department stores - are bound to have a major impact on city-centre activity and thus on the potential impact of rapid transit.

7 Impacts: rail rapid transit

We now turn to the final task, and the hardest: to try to assess the impacts of rail investment, both _directly_, in terms of passenger levels and the financial performance of urban passenger transport undertakings, and _indirectly_, in terms of the effects on urban activity patterns.

It is difficult because - as already explained in Chapter 1 - other changes, simultaneously occurring, cannot be held constant. We cannot assume that, had rail investment not occurred, earlier conditions would necessarily have prevailed. In all western cities, public transport tends to lose passengers to the private car. It tends to become less self-supporting, more in need of central or local government subsidy. In increasing numbers of cities, people are moving out and economic activity is shrinking; this further reduces the number of potential passengers and thus the viability of the public transport system.

Apart from this basic conceptual difficulty, there are more localised technical problems. Not every city provides data in the same way. Some may not provide certain data at all. It is particularly difficult to compare certain kinds of data, for instance on rental levels, between two different countries. Nevertheless the attempt needs to be made.

A final difficulty, which also provides a starting point for the analysis of this chapter, is to establish the date or dates from which impacts are to be measured. This would be easier if the investment took place, and began to produce effects, at one point in time. But a feature of urban rail investments (and indeed, to a smaller degree, pedestrianisation) is that they tend to occur in stages, sometimes quite small: part of a line will be opened, then an extension, then a second line, and so on. It is therefore necessary to look at the impacts onward from each of these points. Table 7.1 sets out, succinctly, the most important dates for each of the thirteen case study cities.

In München, Nürnberg, Glasgow and Liverpool the critical city-centre rail investments were thus concentrated into one or two years. In Essen, Hannover, Köln and Newcastle, they occurred over a more extended period. In Bremen, Dortmund, Manchester, Sheffield and Leeds no such investments had been made at the time of the survey.

Table 7.1

The Thirteen Case Study Cities: Opening of Light Rail
or Rapid Rail Stations in the City Centre

Bremen   :   None

Dortmund   :   None

Essen   :   1977 Hauptbahnhof (central railway station)
                 1981 Porscheplatz (new shopping precinct)

Hannover   :   1976 Hauptbahnhof (central railway station)
                 1979 Kröpcke (main city centre station)

Köln   :   1968 Hauptbahnhof (central railway station)
                 1974 Completion of 20.4 km. city centre network

München   :   1972 Marienplatz
                 1972 Hauptbahnhof (central railway station)

Nürnberg   :   1978 Weisser Turm
                 1978 Lorenzkirche
                 1978 Hauptbahnhof (central railway station)

Glasgow   :   1979 Buchanan Street (Argyle Line)
                 1980 Buchanan Street (Underground)

Leeds   :   None

Liverpool   :   1977 Lime Street (Loop)

Manchester :   None

Newcastle   :   1980 Haymarket
                 1984 System completion
                 1977 Moorfields (Link)

Sheffield   :   None

Source: Interviews and correspondence.

It is important to bear in mind that in all the cities - both those that invested in rail and those that did not - extensive schemes of city centre pedestrianisation were also occurring. Appendix B gives the details. It shows that pedestrianisation began earlier, and extended over a longer period, than rail investment.

Direct effects

<u>Passenger levels</u>

Table 7.2 shows figures for total public transport passengers for the thirteen cities at selected dates. Critical dates from Table 7.1 are indicated by lines. There is a clear secular tendency toward contraction, but this is strikingly halted or even reversed in several of the German cities during the 1970s, when the rail investments were coming onstream. Although the relationship is not a precise one, it appears that those cities that invested in rail managed at least to modify the loss of public transport passengers. Thus, in München, traffic fell by 2.2 per cent between 1963 and 1971, but rose by 17.3 per cent in the corresponding eight-year period after the opening of the rapid transit system in 1972. In Köln, where the main event was the opening of a nearly complete city-centre network in 1974, traffic had fallen by 9.2 per cent in the ten years 1963-73 but thereafter remained approximately static. In Hannover, where the major openings of the new system were in 1975 and 1979, traffic was relatively static between 1967 and 1975, but thence rose by 24.2 per cent to 1982. In Essen, where the main developments occurred in 1977 and 1981, traffic had fallen by no less than 21.5 per cent in the ten years 1967-77 but thence rose by 10.1 per cent to 1982. Finally, in Nürnberg - where the city centre system opened in 1978 - traffic had been almost static over the ten-year period 1967-77 (and had fallen by 8.7 per cent in the immediately preceding four-year period, 1973-77), but thence rose by 18.3 per cent from 1977 to 1982.

There are however some puzzling features about the two cities in the control group which did not invest in transit in this period. In Dortmund traffic remained virtually static over the fifteen-year period from 1967 to 1982. Essen, the city most nearly comparable with it, did show some recovery after the transit openings of 1977 and 1981. In Bremen, there was a sharp recovery of passenger traffic between 1977 and 1979 followed by a fall; here, however, the 1979 figure is known to be suspect.

In interpreting these figures, it is important to remember that all kinds of other factors may have had an influence. Thus in the German economy as a whole, but especially in the Ruhr area, the period after 1975 was marked by recession and increasing unemployment, with obvious effects on passenger movements. Additionally, the construction of transit in some cities may have caused an artificial effect by disrupting

Table 7.2

The Thirteen Case Study Cities: Public Transport Passenger Trips, 1963-82

Number of passenger trips per year in 1000s

Year	Bremen	Dortmund	Essen	Hannover	Köln	München	Nürnberg
1963	132,840	109,523	135,021	142,492	185,442	295,196	124,789
1967	98,886	83,918	103,880	104,674	164,872	276,485	113,880
1971	84,360	83,662	99,268	107,530	170,823	288,710	122,228
1973	86,775	84,993	95,786	112,477	168,903	307,000[c]	120,081[a]
1975	90,355	89,672	95,054	109,576	176,145[b]	296,960	117,169
1977	88,083	79,384	81,523	120,997	167,282	313,722[c]	109,622
1979	111,529[d]	78,735	81,770	130,763	168,485	338,712	121,344
1981	109,015	82,989	92,208	130,099	171,750	351,156	128,445
1982	102,772	77,950	89,780	136,122	164,675		129,721

a) From 1973 onwards, different calculations - see Appendix B.
b) Köln: increase of passengers because of boundary changes in 1975.
c) München: passenger figures from the year before.
d) Bremen: Change in the counting system, number of some season ticket holders were calculated too low.

135

Table 7.2 cont'd

The Thirteen Case Study Cities: Public Transport Passenger Trips 1963-82

Number of passenger trips per year in 1000s

	Glasgow[e]	Leeds[e]	Merseyside[e]	Greater Manchester	Tyne & Wear	Sheffield[e]
1963	480,400	203,601	-	936,000	-	226,700
1967	374,700	192,410	-	796,000	-	193,900
1971	292,500	164,000	-	575,000	-	171,100
1973	244,000	166,874	-	552,000	-	166,500
1975	203,300	151,580	301,000	546,000	281,100	168,000
1977	199,800	131,440	274,000	462,000	297,600	163,000
1979	185,700	121,794	243,000	425,000	303,100	174,000
1981	161,300	96,301	216,000	377,000	305,100	174,000
1982	148,900	96,460	244,000	358,000	310,500	177,000
1983	-	-	-	347,000	-	-

e) Figures apply to cities not to the PTE area.

Source: VÖV 1964, MVV 1983, Appendix B
PTE Strathclyde, internal information.
PTE West Yorkshire, internal information. Figures for Leeds from 1974 onwards represent about 53 per cent of total passenger trips in West Yorkshire.
PTE Merseyside, internal information.
PTE Greater Manchester, internal information at 31 March of each year.
Tyne and Wear County Council, Tyne and Wear PTE 1983.
PTE South Yorkshire, internal information.

surface traffic in the years immediately before the opening of the new system. Clearly, also, these figures cannot pretend to any kind of rigorous statistical significance. Nevertheless, for what they are worth, they do seem to show that transit investments in the German cities had some influence on general traffic levels.

There is further support for this in the detailed evidence on choice of transport mode in the seven German case-study cities, which we already reviewed in Chapter 6 (Table 6.4). We saw there that those cities that invested in rail had a quite dramatic shift towards the use of public transport in the immediately following period: Essen, Hannover and Köln from 1976 to 1980, München from 1971 to 1976. In Bremen and Dortmund, where no investment occurred, there was no such major shift.

The British evidence however suggests very different conclusions. All the systems in Table 7.2, with the exception of Sheffield and Tyne & Wear, were suffering from serious traffic contraction during the 1960s and 1970s. In two out of the three cities with new transit developments - all of them opening between 1977 and 1982 - there was no evident impact on this pattern of secular decline. Thus, between 1977 and 1982, traffic in Glasgow declined by 26.8 per cent, and on Merseyside by 18.9 per cent. The exception was Tyne and Wear where traffic rose by 10.1 per cent. But even here, it should be noted that much of this increase actually occurred between 1975 and 1979, that is before the opening of even the first section of the Metro in 1980. All we can say is that in two of the three cities that did not invest in transit, the contraction was even more precipitous: 36.4 per cent in Leeds and 34.4 per cent in Greater Manchester. Sheffield, which also made no transit investment but followed a policy of heavily subsidised low fares on its buses, achieved an increase in traffic of 5.4 per cent.

These British results are so different from the German ones that they are worth pursuing in more detail. Data on journeys to work, from the British 1981 Census, allow us to do this (Table 7.3). These figures are for entire cities; equivalent figures for city centres were not yet available at time of writing. (There are, as yet, no equivalent Census figures for Germany.) This makes it clear that, with the exception of those cities that had major boundary changes, employment in British cities was sharply declining during the 1970s; there were thus less work journeys to be shared by the modes. Within these reduced totals, cars gained massively everywhere at the expense of buses, reducing the percentage share of the latter by between 10 and 22 per cent and leading to percentage declines in bus work journeys by up to 40 per cent. However the really significant point about this table, for the purposes of this study, is the very small share of all journeys that is made by rail (and, where appropriate, by Underground) and the negligible change in that share during the 1970s. In both Glasgow and Liverpool, where rail improvements occurred during this period, rail work journeys actually fell in number and even, in the case of Newcastle, in share of total. The fall in Newcastle was particularly drastic, but here the 1981

Table 7.3

Journeys to Work in British Cities: Mode of Travel of those Working in the Area, 1981

City	Date	Total workforce 000s	Train 000s	%	Bus 000s	%	Car 000s	%	Bicycle, Motor bike 000s	%	Foot 000s	%	Other 000s	%
Glasgow[a]	1971	426,330	46,890	11.0	209,750	49.2	95,780	22.5	2,100	0.5	56,020	13.1	15,790	3.7
	1981	360,240	43,320	11.7	130,610	36.3	133,740	37.1	4,720	1.3	45,670	12.7	3,180	0.8
% Change 71–81		-15.5		-7.6		-37.7		+39.6		+124.8		-18.5		-79.9
Newcastle	1971	152,650	8,580	5.6	71,040	46.5	44,700	29.3	1,760	1.2	20,730	13.6	5,840	3.8
	1981	168,750	6,410	3.8	60,910	36.1	73,840	43.8	3,540	2.1	19,250	11.4	4,800	2.8
% Change 71–81		+10.5		-25.3		-14.3		+65.2		+101.1		-7.1		-17.8
Liverpool	1971	324,840	24,220	7.5	140,870	43.4	89,990	27.7	7,310	2.3	45,890	14.1	16,560	5.1
	1981	258,770	22,290	8.6	83,230	32.2	104,130	40.2	8,690	3.4	29,850	11.5	10,580	4.1
% Change 71–81		-20.3		-8.0		-40.9		+15.7		+18.9		-35.0		-36.1
Manchester	1971	335,360	24,740	8.1	138,980	45.5	103,500	33.9	7,270	2.4	42,930	14.1	17,940	5.9
	1981	295,090	21,460	7.3	82,940	28.1	139,800	47.3	12,110	4.1	29,870	10.1	8,910	3.0
% Change 71–81		-12.0		-13.3		-40.3		+35.1		+66.6		-30.4		-50.3
Sheffield[a]	1971	266,180	1,810	0.7	126,500	47.5	84,330	31.7	2,850	1.1	38,200	14.4	12,490	4.7
	1981	253,860	1,980	0.8	97,940	38.6	112,900	44.5	4,900	1.9	28,280	11.1	7,860	3.1
% Change 71–81		-4.6		+9.4		-22.6		+33.9		+71.9		-26.0		-37.1
Leeds[a]	1971	255,630	5,490	2.1	120,750	47.3	77,140	30.2	3,600	1.4	35,320	13.8	13,330	5.2
	1981	317,640	5,930	1.9	81,290	25.6	160,340	50.5	10,680	3.4	45,490	14.3	13,910	4.4
% Change 71–81		+24.3		+8.0		-32.7		+107.9		+196.6		+28.8		+4.4

a) Major boundary changes 1971–81.

Source: Census 1971, England and Wales Workplace Tables 1981, Workplace and Transport to work.
Census 1971, Scotland Workplace Tables 1981, Scotland, Workplace and Transport Tables.

Census was held some seven months before the opening of the main city centre link (though after the opening of the first section of the Tyne Metro from Tynemouth to Haymarket). All in all, Table 7.3 confirms the impression in Table 7.2 that the new systems did not make much impact on the pattern of journeys in these major British cities.

Essen

Traffic on Essen's new light rail system grew during early years of operation. On the first line, U18 between Essen central station and Mülheim, the numbers nearly trebled in four years (1977: 2,127,052; 1981: 5,864,610). This is despite the fact that the line runs in the middle of the Ruhrschnellweg, an urban motorway, with difficult crossings and somewhat unattractive stations. With the opening of the U17 (central station to University) the number of passengers increased to 9,837,400 in 1982, though they declined to 9,080,525 in 1983 (Essen VAG, internal source) - mainly as a result of the level of unemployment in the city, one of the highest in the Federal Republic.

Hannover

A major study by the Hannover Transport Authority for the German Federal Ministry of Transport (USTRA 1983b) aimed to analyse all the significant impacts of the opening of Hannover's first light rail line in 1976. It is a pioneer pilot study commissioned as an aid to the methodology of cost-benefit analysis, which the Federal Government hoped to apply to all major future public transport investments. It looked both at direct operating effects and at indirect impacts (which are discussed in a later section of this chapter).

The southern part of the new line offered more frequent services than before. The speed increased from 19.6 km./hr. on the old tram service in 1968 to 24.0 km./hr in 1982 (USTRA 1983b, p.80). There was thus a time saving of 21.6 per cent from Oberricklingen to Fasanenkrug, the two original terminal stations of the line. Passengers on the line as a whole increased by 46.6 per cent per day, and on the southern section of the line by more than 60 per cent (USTRA 1983b, p.81).

Most importantly, there was a big increase in generated traffic - people who had previously not used the public transport system: some 18-25 per cent a day (ibid., p.81). These 'new' passengers travelled mainly in the periods 0800-0900, 1500-1600 and 1800-1900, that is outside the rush hours. (The working day normally starts at 0800 and shops shut at 1830.) The study concluded that there are three main reasons:

1. increased importance of the city centre;

2. delayed return travel of city centre employees because of shopping after finishing work;

3. increase in the use of light rail by the employees of department stores and shops in the city centre (ibid., pp.81-83).

On the second line (Line B North), the increase of traffic was nearly 35 per cent (ibid., p.34). Overall, during the period 1969-79 - which included the opening of the first section of the new transit system in the city centre - total passenger traffic on the transport authority system rose by some 45 per cent from 108 to 156.2 million - a figure comparable with that in the early 1960s, before the secular decline in traffic began (Grossraumverkehr Hannover n.d., p.19). Between 1976 and 1980 it was estimated that on all transport authority lines within the city, there has been newly generated traffic of more than 20 per cent.

Köln

In Köln the former Rheinuferbahn (Rhineside Railway), an old inter-urban rail line that ran from the southern suburbs of Köln through to Bonn and Bad Godesberg, was modernised and connected into the city-centre light rail network in 1978. There was an immediate increase in passengers. On the stretch between Marienburg and Rodenkirchen - the first section of the old system, outside the city limits, traffic on the Rheinuferbahn fell from 8,700 to 5,700 passengers per day between 1965 and 1977. At the latter date the tram line connecting the terminus inwards to the city centre was carrying 7,100 passengers a day. By 1979 the new through system had 18,100 passengers a day (Kölner Verkehrsbetriebe AG Köln-Bonner Eisenbahn AG 1980, p.81).

München

The opening of the new transit system in München in 1972 was followed by a large and sustained increase - representing a doubling of traffic - within three years, followed by a more modest annual increase from 1975 to 1982 (Table 7.4). Surveys suggest that there was a steady increase in the percentage of retail customers who travelled by public transportation: from 64.1 per cent in 1971 to 73.5 per cent in 1976 and to 76.0 per cent in 1980 (Monheim 1980, pp.196, 198; BAG 1981). Interestingly, the old tram system experienced a passenger decline of 28.6 per cent in 1981; the underground lines also registered a decline, but the number of passengers increased even further on the S-Bahn lines (MVV 1982a, pp.8, 19) and more than counteracted the declines on the other two modes.

Table 7.4

München: (Verkehrsverbund) Public Transport Passengers, 1972-1982

Year	Number of passengers (in millions)
1972	203
1973	358
1974	395
1975	405
1976	412
1977	417
1978	432
1979	449
1980	451
1981	463
1982	464

Source: MVV. 1982a, p.8; 1983, p.7.

Nürnberg

In Nürnberg the new system has been successful in reversing a long decline in public transport patronage. Nürnberg's unique 100-year series on passenger numbers shows that this decline began in 1956 and continued steadily until 1970; thence, there was a generally upward trend, and in 1981 more trips were made on public transportation than in 1956, with a further increase to 1982. Table 7.5 gives details on the basis of the historic system of counting; modified in 1973, this method may give figures that are about 10 per cent too high. Particularly notable is the fact that with the opening of the city centre underground stations in 1978, the number of trips nearly trebled. The significant increase of trips in 1981 has been the result of the opening of the underground line to Fürth.

Table 7.5

Nürnberg: Public Transport Passengers, 1955-1983

Year	Total trips	Trips by tram	Trips by rapid rail
1955	161,742	103,802	
1956	167,826	134,349	
1957	136,694	111,244	
1958	129,022	105,246	
1959	128,921	104,830	
1960	130,287	104,803 (break in series 61-66)	
1967	113,881	82,644	
1968	105,458	75,192	
1969	112,511	79,860	
1970	116,217	81,339	
1971	122,433	83,944	
1972	119,395	82,095	
1973	124,062	81,423	6,674
1974	138,087	88,860	10,184
1975	144,170	89,315	13,251
1976	144,615	87,410	14,085
1977	137,213	81,257	11,140
1978	148,317	74,763	26,404
1979	154,152	74,050	30,686
1980	164,405	75,118	34,307
1981	169,548	65,261	41,827

Source: Nürnberg Stadt, Städtische Werke, GMBH, internal statistics, Appendix B.

Newcastle upon Tyne

The Transport and Road Research Laboratory have published several impact studies on the Tyne and Wear Metro. As this is the only substantial new public transport system in Britain, most research has been concentrated on it.

The North Tyne loop and South Shields lines carried about 30,000 passengers a day before they closed in 1979. The new Metro carried 165,000 passengers a day or 50 million a year in 1983, 16 per cent of total public transport passengers (Tyne and Wear PTE 1984, p.14).

The forecast for this stage of the Metro opening and for this year was 30 million.   The corresponding forecast of passengers after the Metro was in full operation (i.e. from Spring 1984) was to carry 190,000 passengers a day or about 62 million per year (TRRL 1982, p.9).   It appears therefore that total patronage of the system was certainly well up to forecast and if anything ahead of it.   This seems to confirm the earlier evidence that the Tyne Metro system is the only British example of a rail transit improvement that did have a significant impact on urban travel patterns.

Bus passengers declined around 30-40 per cent in all areas close to the first part of the Metro to be opened.   In areas away from the Metro, the decline was only 4 per cent. (It should be realised that even the total Metro system, as completed in 1984, serves only one-third of all the metropolitan county's population within 15 minutes' walk; this catchment area is extended by bus feeders, but these merely divert, not replace, the previous bus traffic: (ibid., 1982, p.4.) No significant change in car traffic was found on the Tyne Bridge; but TRRL points out that this is a positive conclusion because it had been forecast that the bridge would become even more congested (ibid., 1982, p.9). A large drop in road traffic (of 1,700 vehicles a day) occured on Sunderland Road which runs parallel to the Metro line from Heworth to Gateshead (ibid., p.9).

Glasgow

The Glasgow Rail Impact Study (GRIS) was commissioned at the same time as the Tyne and Wear Impact Study, in 1978 (Martin and Voorhees Associates 1982, p.3).   The study was commissioned by Scottish Development Department, the TRRL, Martin and Voorhees Associates and Strathclyde Passenger Transport Executive (SPTE).   The study lasted four years and was based on surveys before and after the opening of the new services (ibid., p.3).

Between 1978 and 1980, before the re-opening of the underground, travel declined by 8 per cent on average.   Average daily bus journeys declined 13 per cent, while BR had an increase of 8 per cent (ibid., 1982, p.18). GRIS points out that 'passenger numbers had been declining on both BR and the Underground up to the time of the investments' (ibid., p.25).

After the Argyle line opened in 1979, 27 per cent more journeys were made on the BR services concerned than the previous year. A high proportion of the new journeys were short-distance.   Immediately after the opening 40 per cent more journeys were made than in the year before, but an increase in fares reduced the growth rate (ibid., p.25). As was also seen in the Hannover impact study, traffic increased mainly at off-peak and was nearer to central Glasgow or in the local travel area around Glasgow. However 75 per cent of these new passengers had only switched from another mode of public transport (bus) to the train, but 19 per cent switched from car to train (ibid., p.41).

After the Argyle line opened there was an increase of 43 per cent in the number of weekday shopping trips. Shopping trips to the city centre rose by 51 per cent on weekdays but shopping journeys to other places fell by 12 per cent (ibid. p.53). This change may have some importance for Glasgow's city centre because central Glasgow had declined as a major shopping centre for west central Scotland with the growth of other suburban centres; between 1971 and 1981, retail floorspace in Glasgow declined by 20 per cent (ibid., p.52). Similar results were found for journeys by underground (ibid., p.53).

An increase in leisure journeys also occurred after the opening of the Argyle line. Leisure journeys account for about 20 per cent of off-peak rail journeys during week days and nearly a third during Saturdays. The number of total BR leisure journeys increased 54 per cent on week days and 15 per cent on Saturdays (ibid., p.60). It should be remembered here that car ownership in the Clydeside region, at only 142 per thousand population in 1981, is still very low by the standards of most western European urban areas.

The effect of the underground system was more difficult to analyse, for a number of reasons. First, the system was completely shut for reconstruction between 1977 and 1980, leading to a complete loss of the former passengers and their redistribution on to other modes. Then, after the reopening, only a limited service was provided. There was also a fare increase of 25 per cent, and a tunnel failure near Govan at the end of August 1981. GRIS calculated that there was an increase of passengers of 18 per cent, but this number was adjusted to compensate for the partial service operating. However 10 per cent of the underground traffic was diverted from the bus, basically because the underground is cheaper. GRIS concluded that 'there is no evidence for a substantial increase in traffic associated with the modernisation of the underground' (ibid., p.30). Later passenger figures show a further modest increase, to 11.8 million in 1982-3 and to 12.5 million in 1983-4, as against just over 10 million on the unreconstructed system in 1976 (information from SPTE).

The main reason for this disappointing result is that many of the potential customers had disappeared. During the 1960s and 1970s Glasgow experienced such great population losses (22 per cent between 1971 and 1981 alone; up to 40 per cent in some inner city wards - (Strathclyde Regional Council 1983, p.15) that the success of the modernised system was seriously compromised. The most highly frequented part of the underground is between the city centre (Buchanan Street) and the University (Hillhead, at the north-west corner of the centre). On this section, the old BR station of St Enoch is being redeveloped, and a new shopping centre is to be built. In contrast, the southern part of the underground circle runs through housing areas, formerly developed at a very high density, which have been demolished, and through the dock area (Govan) which is supposed to be redeveloped for private housing (interviews with the PTE). Much of the area around the south circle

stations is still derelict, or has a few high-rise council housing
blocks, with wide expressways. Hardly any passengers enter or leave at
these stations.

Indirect effects

Retail turnover

If rail investment is to have any immediate effect on the city centre, it
should be on retail turnover. It is not possible to measure this
accurately, neither for the German case study cities nor - because of the
lack of a Census of Distribution in 1981 - for British cities. Although
data for turnover are available for German city centres for the year
1978, important stretches of transit opened after this date in Essen,
Hannover, Köln and Nürnberg.

Table 7.6 shows the available data. They do not demonstrate any clear
impact of rail investment. Between 1967 and 1978 - the period when rail
investments were occurring in some of the German cities but not in others
- turnover in the city centres of Bremen and Dortmund, which did not
invest, increased by 81.9 and 29.9 per cent respectively. In comparison
the growth was 66.1 per cent in Essen, 92.5 per cent in Hannover and
137.5 per cent in München. This last figure is particularly interesting
because it confirms the impression emerging from the München traffic
figures in Table 7.4. The comparison between Dortmund and Essen is also
interesting, though in 1978 the Essen light rail system was only
partially open.

For Köln and Nürnberg we have only comparable figures for turnover over
a time period for the entire city. Köln shows a marked increase of 130.4
per cent corresponding with the completion of the city-centre light rail
system in 1974. Nürnberg, where the U-Bahn was just about to open in
1978, shows only a 17.9 per cent rate of growth. This very poor record
may result in part from the disruption of the central shopping area by
the underground works.

Retail rental levels

An increase in turnover should logically be followed after a short
interval - reflecting the average length of leases - by an upward
movement of rents. We were fortunate in obtaining excellent unpublished
rental data for both German and British cities, which are set out in
Table 7.7 and Table 7.8. The original German figures have been corrected
for inflation and have then been translated into £ per square foot to
facilitate direct comparison with the British figures. We also
interviewed estate agents in all cities where rail investment had
occurred, asking them whether they thought it had had an effect.

Table 7.7 shows no noticeable impact of rail investment. Neither do

Table 7.6

Retailing in Selected German Cities

	Bremen	CBD[a]	Dortmund	CBD[e]	Essen	CBD
Shopping turnover (000 DM)						
1959[d]	1,047,028	-	1,158,351	-	1,624,200	440,600
1967	1,908,475	698,944	1,815,360	891,874	2,034,290	794,872
1978	4,130,670	1,270,340	4,281,688	1,807,845	2,289,305	1,319,964
Employment[b]						
1960	26,344	-	27,456	-	37,300	9,609
1968	29,221	10,022	27,478	13,204	30,424	11,801
1979	27,382	9,114	27,509	11,710	28,951	8,333
of which part-time:						
1960	-	-	-	-	-	-
1968	5,572	1,604	4,103	1,880	4,962	1,773
1979	8,924	2,904	8,033	3,075	8,934	2,471
Establishments						
1960	5,778	-	4,855	-	6,525	326
1968	5,378	623	4,207	817	5,015	384
1979	3,900	559	3,698	798	4,322	401
Floorspace[f] in sq.m.						
1960	-	-	770,500	-	-	-
1968	891,459	241,132	773,900	-	776,832	270,893
1979	1,261,386	303,472	1,252,000	378,300[e]	1,211,934	301,100

Table 7.6 Cont'd

	Hannover	CBD	Köln[g]	CBD	München	CBD	Nürnberg	CBD
Shopping Turnover (000 DM)								
1959[d]	1,233,522	–	1,799,537	–	2,306,072[c]	828,209[c]	971,071	–
1967	2,028,282	981,304	3,315,023	–	4,281,267	1,448,267	2,918,467	–
1978	4,248,637	1,889,098	7,638,699	429,665	10,228,586	3,440,323	3,440,323	1,145,709
Employment[b]								
1960	28,047	–	41,969	–	52,085[c]	17,236	21,664	–
1968	28,600	13,068	42,160	–	52,981	18,906	28,194	–
1979	25,889	11,646	44,379	11,441	59,031	21,308	22,134	8,956
of which part-time:								
1960	–	–	–	–	–	–	–	–
1968	6,607	–	7,914	–	10,709	–	5,094	–
1979	7,863	3,197	12,890	3,324	15,204	4,313	5,974	2,523
Establishments								
1960	5,448	–	8,545	–	13,238[c]	1,646[c]	3,983	–
1968	4,593	748	6,963	–	9,668	1,235	3,479	–
1979	3,311	643	7,136	911	8,925	1,342	2,857	616
Floorspace[f] in sq. m.								
1960	–	–	–	–	–	–	–	–
1968	839,299	308,787	1,283,000	–	1,782,000	–	917,305	–
1979	1,107,000	398,000	1,990,200	397,100	2,248,100	416,600	1,089,300	302,600

a) CBD = Central Business District – see Appendix B: basic data.
b) Shopowners are excluded from the employment statistics because they were listed for the first time in 1979.
c) Change in the statistical count; figures for 1960 cannot be strictly compared.
d) All figures are for city size at 1960, 1968 or 1979; boundary changes occurred in most cities.
e) Innenstadt West, no comparison with CBD of Essen possible.
f) Geschäftsflächen, gross floor space.
g) Figures in Köln are not comparable between 1968 and 1979 because of boundary changes in 1975.

Sources: Essen Stadt, Amt für Statistik und Wahlen, 1982.
       Dortmund Stadt, Amt für Statistik und Wahlen, 1982, 1983.
       München Landeshauptstadt 1984a
       Bremen Statistisches Landesamt (unpublished material).
       Nürnberg Stadt, Amt für Stadtforschung und Statistik, 1983.
       Nordrhein-Westfalen Land, 1962.
       Nordrhein-Westfalen Land, 1970.
       Köln Stadt (unpublished material).

the British figures for Glasgow or Newcastle (Table 7.8). In Germany there was a general tendency for city rents to increase through the 1970s, thence stabilising. In Essen there was a slight increase after 1977, the year of opening of the first light rail section in the centre; however, rents here did not rise in line with other cities during this period, almost certainly because of economic recession in the Ruhr area. Hannover actually shows a fall in rents after the opening of the first light rail line, reflecting a sharp increase in available retail floorspace after the opening in 1974 of the underground Passarelle and the subsequent completion of several major department stores in the city centre. Our estate agent in Hannover thought that rents were higher round the light rail stations, both in the city centre and in the suburbs; this was the only city that produced this response. Rents increased after 1979, the date of opening of the main city-centre station (Kröpcke), but similar increases were observed in other cities (e.g. München) where no particular developments were occurring at that time. Further, Table 7.9 shows that in some German cities, rents for small shops in the city-centre fringe - outside the main pedestrian area - rose faster than in the pedestrianised core.

The one instance of real impact seems to occur in Nürnberg. There, after the opening of the three city-centre stations on the U-Bahn (1978), there was a sharp increase in inflation-corrected rents. But, as just noticed, similar increases were occurring in other cities. Neither in Nürnberg nor elsewhere does there appear to be any connection between rental changes and openings of city-centre stations.

Retail floorspace

If rail investment does influence activity levels in the city centre, one of the most telling indices - at least after a short time lag - ought to be the total amount and the character of the retail floorspace there. Table 7.6 has already given information on this point for the entire period.

The evidence in Table 7.6 provides no definitive evidence of any generative effects of rail investment in German cities. This could well be because the effects would appear only after 1979, the last date for which figures appear in the table. For Köln and München, the two cities where substantial light rail and rapid rail investment occurred in the mid-1970s, no separate figures for CBD floorspace are available for 1968; both cities showed big increases between 1968 and 1979, 23.9 per cent in Köln and 26.2 per cent in München. In Hannover, where the first rail development in the centre was in 1975, there was an increase of 31.8 per cent in the city but only 28.9 per cent in the CBD. But in Essen, Dortmund and Nürnberg, three cities without any notable rail investment in the period, the respective increases city-wide were 61.7, 56.0 and 17.8 per cent. For Bremen, separate city-centre figures give an increase of 26.3 per cent. It would be hard to see in all this any evidence of the impact of rail.

Table 7.7

Annual Shop Rents for Small Shops in Selected German Cities, Prime (1a) Locations, Corrected for Inflation, in £/sq.ft.

	1977	1979	1980	1981	1982	1983
Bremen	27.88 (26.89)	46.00 (41.48)	46.00 (39.32)	48.79 (39.38)	48.79 (38.00)	48.79 (36.71)
Dortmund	39.03 (37.64)	50.19 (50.19)	50.19 (42.90)	50.19 (40.51)	50.19 (39.10)	50.19 (37.76)
Essen	39.03 (37.64)	41.82 (37.50)	-	41.82 (33.75)	48.79 (38.00)	47.40 (35.66)
Hannover	22.30 (21.50)	25.09 (22.62)	30.67 (26.21)	30.67 (24.75)	30.67 (28.89)	30.67 (23.08)
Köln	32.06 (30.92)	41.82 (37.70)	55.76 (47.66)	55.76 (45.00)	55.76 (43.34)	55.76 (41.96)
München	33.46 (32.27)	39.03 (35.19)	50.19 (42.90)	55.76 (45.00)	55.76 (43.43)	55.76 (41.96)
Nürnberg	22.30 (21.50)	30.11 (27.15)	33.46 (28.62)	39.03 (31.50)	41.82 (32.57)	41.82 (31.47)

1 sq.m. = 10.76 sq. ft.
Figures in brackets are inflation-corrected rents x 100
Assumed exchange rate: £1 = 4DM

Source: RDM. All figures can only be seen as a guideline.
Statistisches Bundesamt 1977, 1983 (Index of Living Costs).
Dortmund Stadt 1984 (Index of Living Costs).

Table 7.8

Annual Shop Rents in Selected British Cities, Prime Locations (Zone 1), Corrected for Inflation, in £/sq.ft.

	1978	1979	1989	1981	1982	1983
Glasgow	53 (42.23)	59 (41.46)	73 (43.48)	73 (38.87)	79 (38.78)	83 (38.99)
Leeds	35 (27.89)	41 (28.81)	46 (27.40)	50 (26.62)	52 (25.53)	55 (25.83)
Manchester	50 (39.84)	50 (35.14)	50 (29.78)	47 (25.03)	45 (22.09)	45 (21.14)
Newcastle	45 (35.86)	50 (35.14)	60 (35.74)	65 (34.61)	70 (34.36)	77 (36.17)
London Knightsbridge	165 (131.47)	165 (115.95)	165 (98.27)	165 (87.86)	165 (81.00)	185 (86.90)
Oxford Street	227 (180.88)	313 (219.96)	240 (142.94)	180 (95.85)	180 (88.37)	196 (92.06)

Figures in brackets: inflation-corrected rents x 100

Source: Debenham Tewson & Chinnocks 1983

Table 7.9

Monthly Rents (in DM) for Small Shops in (a) Centre Core, and (b) Centre Fringe Locations in German Cities

(a) Centre core[b]

	1972	1973	1974	1975	1976	1977	1979	1980	1981	1982	1983
Bremen	90	100	80	60*	110[a]	100	165*	165*	175*	175*	175*
Dortmund	90	100	100	-	90*	140	180	180	180	180	180
Essen	120	40*	100	-	140*	140*	150	-	150*	175*	170*
Hannover	130	130	130	80*	80*	90*	100*	110*	110*		
Köln	110*	125*	120*	125*	110*	115*	150*	200*	200*	200*	200*
München	90	100	100	120	110	120	140	180	200	200	200
Nürnberg	65*	65*	70	70	70	80	108*	120	140	150	150

(b) Centre fringe[c]

	1972	1974	1976	1977	1979	1980	1981	1982	1983
Bremen	60	54*	60	60	60	65*	65*	65*	
Dortmund	45	60	60	80	80	80	80		
Essen	75	80	25	70*	45*	80	35*	35*	35*
Hannover	50	70	45*	45*	43*	50*	50*	50*	50*
Köln	26*	60*	45*	70*	110*	125*	110*	125*	
München	40	50	60	60	65	80	90	100	100
Nürnberg	35	40	40	40	55*	63	90	80	60

* Average value

a) There is the likelihood of a misprint in 1976, see Table 1976 RDM rents were much more likely 110 than 25 – 30 DM.

b) Business center: approximately equal to pedestrian area.

c) Location can be defined as being outside the pedestrian area.

Source: RDM. All figures given can only be seen as a guide line.

Office rents

Evidence is also available for British cities of prime office rents.
This is set out in Table 7.10. Again, it is difficult to establish any
substantial impact of rail investment. True, rents did rise in Liverpool
in 1980/1, three years after opening of the Loop and Link; in Newcastle
in 1980 the year of opening of the first section of the Metro; and in
Glasgow in 1981/2, two or three years after opening of the Argyle
Line/Underground. But against this must be set the fact that Manchester
showed a sharp rise in 1982/3 without any investment at all; and that
Leeds and Sheffield, which also had no rail developments, showed steady
rises in rental levels throughout the period.

Some case studies

Earlier, looking at direct impacts, we saw that in Britain there have
been before-and-after studies in both Glasgow and Newcastle upon Tyne.
These also sought to cover the indirect impacts of the new transit
systems. There have been comparable studies for Hannover and for Hamburg
and München. Together they provide some valuable detailed evidence.

Hamburg and München

A pre-study of these two cities was commissioned by the Federal
Government and published in 1978 (BMBau 1978). It found a paradoxical
result: Hamburg, which was one of the first German cities to develop U-
and S-Bahn systems, grew rapidly until World War Two but thence stagnated
(ibid., p.27); München, in contrast, lacking a rapid rail system before
1972, grew strongly between 1950 and 1970. It appeared that Hamburg's
transit system was actually a factor encouraging the outward movement of
people leading to depopulation in the zone within 5 km. of the centre
(ibid., p.28). Hamburg's population tended to concentrate along the
public transportation axes, a tendency that in München occurred only
after the opening of the U- and S-Bahn in 1972. But closer to the
centre, transit appeared to have the effect of aiding the displacement of
residential populations by workplaces (ibid., p.75). Beyond this, the
BMBau study does not deal very specifically with city-centre effects.

Hannover

As already noted, this study (USTRA 1983b) aimed to develop a method to
analyse the full effects of the first light rail line in the city, which
was the first in the Federal Republic, as an aid to the Federal
Government in the cost-benefit analysis of major public transport
projects. It looked both at direct or primary effects (discussed earlier
in this chapter) and - most importantly - at secondary effects. It
looked particularly at the city centre, two inner city areas and areas
around two peripheral interchanges) (ibid., p.XI).

Table 7.10

British Case Study Cities: Prime Office Rents and Rates

	1973/74	1974/5	1975/6	1976/7	1977/8	1978/9	1979/80	1980/1	1981/2	1982/3
(1) Rents (£ per square foot)										
Glasgow	1.75	2.50	3.00	4.00	4.00	4.25	4.25	4.25	5.00	5.00
Leeds	1.75	2.00	3.75	4.00	4.00	4.25	4.50	5.00	5.25	5.25
Liverpool	1.00	1.25	2.25	2.75	3.50	3.50	3.75	4.75	4.75	4.75
Manchester	1.75	2.00	3.00	3.00	2.50	2.75	3.25	3.75	4.25	5.25
Newcastle	1.50	1.50	1.75	2.25	2.50	2.50	2.75	3.25	3.25	3.25
Sheffield	1.00	1.25	1.75	2.50	2.25	2.25	3.00	4.25	4.75	4.75
(City of London)	16.00	22.00	18.00	12.00	13.50	15.00	18.00	22.00	24.00	26.00
(2) Rates (£ per square foot)										
Glasgow	1.20	1.30	1.50	1.70	1.90	1.30	1.40	2.00	2.70	3.20
Leeds	0.70	0.90	1.00	1.00	1.00	1.10	1.30	1.60	2.10	2.40
Liverpool	0.50	0.60	0.60	0.70	0.80	0.80	1.00	1.30	1.60	1.80
Manchester	0.70	0.80	1.00	1.10	1.30	1.40	1.50	1.90	2.40	2.70
Newcastle	0.70	0.90	1.20	1.20	1.20	1.40	1.60	2.10	2.70	3.00
Sheffield	0.60	0.80	0.90	1.00	1.10	1.20	1.40	1.90	2.60	3.10
(City of London)	3.30	4.70	7.40	8.20	8.80	8.80	9.20	11.20	14.20	16.60

Source: Debenham Tewson and Chinnocks 1982.

153

It is generally assumed that Hannover had insufficient retail floorspace until the mid-60s. In particular, before 1967 the city had only one large department store (ibid., p.98). Between 1965 and 1982 the situation changed dramatically with the opening of four new department stores, though two have already closed again. The Passerelle, a half open tunnel which connects the city centre with the Oststadt, opened in 1974 with a large number of small retailing shops (Stadtplanungsamt Hannover, interview 27.2.84). The study could however establish no connection between the decisions of the department stores to settle in the city centre and the completion of line A (USTRA 1983b, p.100). The Lister Meile, an important high-quality inner-city shopping area along the new line, increased its retail floorspace but this could have also been the result of pedestrianisation, urban renewal and traffic improvements in the area (ibid., pp.100-103). Several large office firms did however move to the terminus of line A between 1974 and 1976 (ibid., pp.104-105) and later to other stations.

Private investments around the main station and in the city centre generally accelerated after 1970, with a particular concentration in 1974-5, the time of construction of the line. There were also several public investments, such as extension of the main station, post office etc. Between 1969 and 1979 these totalled DM 126,430 million, giving a total for public and private investment of DM 410-460 million (ibid., p.113). Although this sum looks impressive, the study cannot prove that all of it was connected with the opening of the light rail line A. Many investments indeed have clearly nothing to do with it, especially most of the private investments around the inner-city area of the Lister Meile.

Nürnberg's Südstadt

Südstadt is an inner city area of Nürnberg, located south of the city centre and quite close to it; however, it is separated by the main railway lines, which act as a kind of barrier. The Südstadt has always been an important shopping centre, and has about 80,000-100,000 inhabitants. A large department store was set up as early as 1928/29 (Schoken), and there were a reasonable number of shops for the middle and upper middle class which then constituted the resident population of this part of the city. Today the Südstadt is a typical inner-city area with an above-average percentage of old people and of foreigners.

Part of the centre's importance for shopping reflected the fact that it was always an important public transport interchange; in 1967, there were about 573 trams a day in both directions, one of the busiest interchanges in Nürnberg (Nürnberg Stadt, Arbeitsgruppe 1972, p.16). This was at first enhanced by the new underground, the first line of which was actually built inwards from Langwasser (a satellite town) towards the city centre, reaching Südstadt in 1975 and bringing customers from Langwasser into the sub-centre. Shop rents around the underground station rose considerably, and shops close to the underground station had higher turnover figures than shops further away. There was a tendency for shops to centralise around the station (interview with local estate agent specialising in retail property).

Three years later, the underground at last reached the city centre. Now, passengers from Langwasser could reach the city centre directly in 12-13 minutes instead of 30-40 minutes (ibid., map 18). As a result shop rents in the Südstadt dropped even lower than before the underground was built. Even in major shopping streets, such as the Allersberger Strasse, and U-Bahn Aufsessplatz, actual rents are below the level 5-6 years ago. Some Südstadt shops even moved to the city centre. Whereas 1,800 DM/sq. m. (£450/sq. m.) was paid in 1983 for top locations in the city centre, even the top location in Südstadt (U-Bahn Aufsessplatz) can command only 480 DM/sq. m. (£120/sq. m.) (private interview).

For years the city has seen the Südstadt as a problem area. It has made improvements such as pedestrianisation, one-way streets, upgrading of residential areas, and landscaping. However, after the opening of the city-centre underground stations, shopkeepers' complaints increased to a degree that could not be ignored by the city authorities. They commissioned a report on the possibilities of further retailing development in the Südstadt.

The consultants (GfK) interviewed 789 shopkeepers in the Südstadt in 1983. 54 per cent expressed worries about stagnant or declining turnover (GfK 1983, p.3). They saw the main reason as the improvements in the city centre: its pedestrian area was far larger and more attractive; the underground brought customers directly into the city centre instead of changing in Südstadt. Others blamed the construction of a large shopping centre in the Südstadt, which had harmed trade of existing shops, and a host of miscellaneous factors like amusement arcades, foreign shops, low-grade pubs, and the presence of traffic (ibid., p.21).

The report made it clear that shopkeepers in the Südstadt see their main competition as being the city centre (ibid., pp.13-15). The Südstadt had 499 million DM (£125 million) purchasing power (1983) of which 410 million DM (£103 million) stayed in the Südstadt, 68 million DM (£17 million) went to the city centre, and 90 million DM (£23 million) were spent by customers living outside the Südstadt (ibid., p.78). The consultants' recommendations include creating a better retail mix (more clothing shops, stationers and art materials shops), strengthening of the main shopping area, better clustering of shops, more parking space, improvement of the housing stock and more pedestrianisation (ibid., pp.88-93).

If these measures are taken, the report suggests, Südstadt will stabilise its essential role as a subcentre. It remains to be seen whether this will happen. Meanwhile, Südstadt is a classic instance of the impact of transit on an inner-city subcentre.

Newcastle upon Tyne

Shopping. In Newcastle it appeared that shoppers transferred to the new Metro both from bus and private car. The figures for shoppers travelling to the city centre of Newcastle on Saturdays can be seen from Table 7.11:

Table: 7.11 Newcastle upon Tyne: Shoppers' Use of Transport Mode

	before opening of Metro per cent	after opening of Metro per cent
Walk	5	5
Bus	56	51
Car	33	30
Train	4	4
Metro	-	6

Source: TRRL 1982, p.13.

Traders, asked in 1982 what effect the Metro might have on their business, answered:

    trade would increase : 33 per cent

    trade would decrease : 14 per cent

    stay the same   : 30 per cent

Traders who believed in an increase cited changes in the pedestrian flow as the cause (TRRL 1982, p.13). The opening of Monument and Centre metro stations in November 1981 'has pulled the centre of gravity of the city centre (in terms of numbers of shoppers) southwards. The greatest increase in activity has been close to Haymarket and Monument stations' (ibid., p.13.).

Other impacts

The TRRL impact study looked at several other areas in which secondary effects could occur, such as employment, land use planning, planning applications, housing and office development, employment and residential vehicles. In most of these areas, no effects or negligible effects were found. In most cases interviews or surveys were carried out before and after the Metro opened. The interviews on housing and office development showed that the Metro was a selling point for private developers but no more. The same is true in most of the German cities we studied. Especially in an area like München, close proximity to an S- or U-Bahn station was mentioned as an additional asset of the property. Office developers in the city centre see public transport provision and car parking provision as being equally important (interviews).

As already noticed in Chapter 6, some negative effects on a sub-centre, similar to those observed in Germany, can be found in Gateshead. The Gateshead District Council has prepared a development brief for a major shopping complex next to the Metro station. So far none of the developers approached have been interested in the site. 'Some store managers in Gateshead have been complaining about a loss of trade due to the opening of the Metro' (TRRL 1982, p.23). The similarity with the negative effects in the Südstadt in Nürnberg and in Bornheim in Frankfurt is apparent. This effect also occurred in some sub-centres in other cities we studied; shopping centres too close to the city centre will suffer if they are not made attractive.

Glasgow

Shopping. Surveys made on trends in retail turnover near underground and Argyle line stations showed no detectable impact from rail investments between 1978 and 1981. According to GRIS, 'there are already some indications of impact: increase in certain types of planning applications in the relevant areas: signs of a positive effect on property values and change in the pattern of central area pedestrian activity. Other evidence is insubstantial'. (Martin & Voorhees Associates 1982, p.63). Pedestrian activity appears to have shifted eastward on Argyle Street and to have increased in Trongate Street, both around the Argyle Street station (ibid., p.65). An increase occurred in planning applications for retail, offices, storage and manufacturing development in the inner area served by the Argyle line and the Underground between 1979 and 1980 (ibid., p.64).

A comparison

It is instructive to try to summarise the overall conclusions of the Glasgow and Newcastle impact studies with those of two others: one for München, and one for the San Francisco Bay Area. This is done in Table 7.12.

Table 7.12

Comparison of Impact Study Conclusions:
Tyne and Wear, Glasgow, San Francisco Bay Area, München

(Numbers in brackets refer to page numbers in the reports cited)

	Tyne & Wear	Glasgow	Bart	München
Industry	no effects (18)	very slight increase in planning applications	no impact	little effect; some effect on small scale industries which were displaced by the growth of service sector activites; rapid rail effect cannot be isolated
Land use impacts	will take time, no effects yet. (19)	general increase in planning applications for retail, office etc. (64). No systematic change of vacant land in the area served by new rail service (67)	land use impacts have not been realised	it is assumed that there was some strong effect - a clear picture is not possible; rapid rail effects cannot be isolated
Office development	little impact (17)	increase in planning applications for office development	no redistribution of office space (V)	increase in office development but rapid rail effects cannot be isolated
Housing property values	little impact, slight increase in property values around stations (17)	little impact, slight increase in house prices around stations (64)	little impact, slight increase in house prices	strong increase in property values around stations (Kreibich 305 and BMBau 89). However the difference between land prices close to stations and general land prices declined completely by 1981 (ASF 50)

Table 7.12 Cont'd

Shopping	one third of the traders think Metro will increase trade (13)	no detectable impact, increase in shopping trips (53)	sale data show no advantages for stores near Bart locations few merchants near Bart Stations feel that location enhances their sale. Survey data suggest a potential shift in shopping pattern towards stations (VII + VIII)	probable increase of shopping in the city centre but no hard data available
Employment	no positive finding	work trips stayed the same	no impacts	increase of employment in the city centre
Population	no comments	slight population increase but not certain if not a statistical mistake. (67)	no impact	decline in population in the core area and inner city areas, strong increase of population in areas with good rapid rail accessibility (EWBau 87, Kreibich, 302)
Environment	decline in road traffic in the Gateshead area; Tyne Bridge (9)	stretches of motorway serving the same area as Argyle line were not built (67)	no comments	environmental improvements decline of car pollution in the city centre about 25%, decline of CO - 25%, CH - 35%, NOX - 44%, 50-25% between 1970-1973. Decline in road traffic in the city centre and decline of car accidents
Effect on urban core area	increase of pedestrian flow towards the Haymarket and Monument Stn (13)	improved access to the city centre (68); increase in pedestrian activity in the city centre (65)	passenger increase at an average rate of 9%, total impacts either not clear or insignificant (117-119)	increase of service sector activities, mainly banks, insurances, specialised retailing shops; decline in food retailing and strong decline of population. Decline of use of motor car

Table 7.12 Cont'd

Trips	no comparable figure available for buses or road traffic before and after Metro opened	27% more trips after Argyle Line opened (25) little peak traffic growth (5%), increase in off-peak travel 28%, on Saturday 37% (27). There is no evidence for a substantial increase in traffic associated with modernisation of the underground (30)	only information on accessibility and time savings are given (36-40)	number of passengers doubled in 10 years (1972: 203 million and 1981: 461 million) (MVV 82a, 8)
Accessi-bility	no comments	no comments	Bart improves the level of transit service but there is still no clear superior alternative to automobile travel especially during off peak hours	increase of off-peak accessibility in many local authorities outside the city of München travel time from these local authorities by public transportation to the city centre is about 30% lower than by car

Source: Tyne and Wear: TRRL 1982.
    Glasgow: Martin & Voorhees Associates 1982.
    San Francisco: Dyett M., Dornbusch D. et al 1979.
    München: BMBau 1978b; Kreibich 1978; MVV 1982a.

The British studies indicate therefore that there is little city-centre impact in Newcastle but an increase of planning applications for retail and office development in Glasgow. On the other hand a substantial minority of Tyneside traders think that Metro will increase trade while in Glasgow there is no discernible effect. There is rather more positive effect in the München case than in any of the other three, but even here the impact on either office or shopping development cannot be clearly distinguished.

Our questionnaire study

Because neither the statistical data nor previous case studies give a very direct picture of the impact of transit, we determined to try to make our own direct survey of business people in our thirteen case-study cities. Necessarily this had to be somewhat limited. We asked local Chambers of Commerce, branches of major retailing organisations and managers of major department stores for their experience of recent changes in business activity in their city centres. In general the response rate was very satisfactory at about 50 per cent; the response from Chambers of Commerce and from retailing organisations was however much higher than that from department stores. The response from one German department store was particularly difficult because research and related questions are centralised in a single national office. So we cannot claim that the results are completely representative for the retailing trade.

The questions were designed to permit a free choice of answer. Respondents were free to tick more than one of the multiple choice answers, and many did so. So, in the presentation of results (Table 7.13), the answers do not sum to a consistent total.

We first asked directly about the effect of rail transit: **Do you think that construction of a rapid rail system has had/would have an effect on your city?** In Germany every respondent except two believed that rail (or light rail) transit had positive effects on retail trade in the city centre. In Britain three-quarters of respondents agreed, but one-quarter actually thought that the effect would be negative. The respondents who gave a positive reply, whether in Britain or Germany, believed that transit increased the number of shoppers in the city centre while reducing car parking problems and traffic congestion. Here there was an interesting national difference: British answers stressed the problems of parking and congestion, while German answers indicated that transit had reduced them.

We then asked a question about pedestrianisation: **Has pedestrianisation improved turnover for most traders in the City centre?** Here, British and German responses were virtually identical. Twenty-one respondents

Table 7.13

Responses to the Questionnaire Survey of Business People in British and German cities

	German cities			British cities		
	With transit	Without transit	Total	With transit	Without transit	Total
Effect of transit on retailing in city						
Positive	10	4	14	4	7	11
Negative		1	1	1	3	4
Neutral		1	1			
Impact of pedestrianisation on turnover						
Positive	8	4	12	4	5	9
Negative					2	2
Neutral	3	2	5	1	0	1
Don't know	1		1		3	3
Impact of transit on turnover: city centre						
Positive	3	1	4	4	6	10
Negative					1	1
Neutral	5	4	9	1	1	2
Don't know	1		1		2	2
Impact of transit on turnover: sub-centres						
Positive	3	2	5		2	2
Negative	1		1	5	5	10
Neutral	4	3	7			
Don't know	2		2		2	2
Importance of planning policies						
Pedestrian-isation	2	2	4	3	4	7
Suburban rail				4	2	6
Light rail/ underground				1	1	2
Pedestrian-isation and light rail/ underground	1		1	1		1
Parking	7	2	9	4	8	12
None of these	3	2	5			

Table 7.13 Cont'd

Future of Retailing

Increase	4	1	5	2	6	8
Decrease	2	2	4	3	1	4
Neutral	4	3	7			
Don't know					2	2

Biggest Turnover Increase

Big centres	3	1	3	2	7	9
Big sub- centres	3	3	6		1	1
Suburban	2	3	5	2	2	4
Small towns	5	2	7			
Villages		1	1		1	1
Don't know				1	1	2

Source: Own Questionnaires.

(twelve German, nine British) thought that pedestrianisation had increased turnover, but two correspondents (both British) reported that it had declined, four (three of whom were in Britain) reported no change and three British respondents could not say.

Next we asked an identical question on transit: **Do you think construction of a rapid rail system has increased/would increase turnover in the city centre?** The British responses were very similar to those on the pedestranisation question: ten said yes, one no, two said no change and one did not know. In contrast a large majority of German answers indicated that no change had occurred as a result of the introduction of transit. Only four reported an increase: Dortmund, München (twice) and Nürnberg. Asked whether such a system would increase trade in sub-centres almost all British respondents thought not, while in Germany five answered yes and seven were neutral.

We also asked: **Which of the following planning policies would be important for retailing in the city centre?** We listed improved suburban rail, a light rail system, pedestrianisation plus light rail, parking and ring roads; we also asked for respondents' own ideas. Both the German and the British respondents put better parking overwhelmingly in first place (nine of out of nineteen German replies, twelve out of twenty-eight British ones). The British, who tended to give multiple answers to this question, also quoted pedestrianisation (seven times) and suburban rail (six times). Five German correspondents, oddly, seemed to think that there was no planning policy that could achieve any effect.

A question on the future of shopping also brought very different answers. Asked: **How do you see the future of retailing in your city?**, the great majority of German responses suggested that there would be no change, while the British replies tended to see the future much more positively: eight out of fourteen expected an increase. Similarly, asked where the major increases in turnover would occur in the future, the majority of German respondents quoted sub-centres, suburban centres and small towns while a majority of British respondents cite big-city centres. This is rather remarkable in view of recent trends in British retailing.

Conclusion

The historical-statistical evidence reviewed in this chapter strongly suggests that no definite effects on city-centre activities or economic levels can be ascribed to the opening of new rail rapid transit systems there. It is clear that many other forces are simultaneously working to shape the fortunes of city centres, of which public transport accessibility is only one. Some cities that invested heavily in rail recorded only moderate increases in activity; others recorded large increases; but equally, other cities that invested nothing, or negligibly, recorded good results. We conclude that the explanation for city-centre prosperity must lie elsewhere.

Nevertheless, the questionnaire survey reveals that on the whole retailers in the cities - whether or not they have direct recent experience of transit in their own city - share a strong belief that both it, and associated pedestrianisation policies, have an impact on retail trade. The major difference is that when asked directly about impact on city-centre turnover, the Germans - both in transit cities and in non-transit cities - are neutral while the British - again in both kinds of cities - are strongly positive. These answers are difficult to reconcile with others that suggest strongly that better parking, both in British and German cities, is the most important factor for the health of retailing. It appears that German retailers, who have had more experience of transit, are sceptical about it while the British remain enthusiastic - but both are in no doubt about the importance of car-based shopping. As Monheim has shown (Fig. 6.1) however, they may over-estimate its significance.

8 Summing up

It is time to sum up. This in a way is easy, because the evidence is fairly clear. That is not to say that it always agrees; we have seen some important differences between the German experience and the British, for which there are good explanations.

We first saw that in both countries there was a parallel shift in transportation policies in the mid-1960s. Down to then, the main emphasis had been on providing extra highway capacity for rising numbers of cars. When this was applied to the cities, it soon came to be seen as self-defeating and environmentally destructive. The new policy was based on traffic restraint and on improvement in the quality of public transport in order to win back lost passengers. Capital expenditure was substantially diverted from road investment to public transport. In the larger urban areas, unified passenger transport authorities were set up, sometimes covering one city and its hinterland, sometimes - as in the Ruhr or Greater Manchester - a whole set of neighbouring cities.

Because buses inevitably shared in general traffic congestion, there was a tendency to favour rail-based solutions. This was much easier in German cities than in British ones, because the British had scrapped their trams while with few exceptions the Germans had not. These trams often ran on reserved track as light railways in the suburbs and outside the cities. They suffered from street congestion in their inner-city and central-city sections, so the logical answer was to put them underground there. This is why the usual German urban rail investment has been in light rail. The British found this difficult because they had nothing to start with. In the one case where they did it, the Tyne Metro, they used old British Rail track.

The British had also let their urban railways deteriorate to a greater extent than the Germans. They had actually closed some (on Tyneside and in Glasgow) and had under-invested in others, allowing electric services to revert to diesel, for instance. However this meant that there was scope for refurbishment at modest cost, as was achieved in Glasgow and Liverpool. The resulting systems have some points in common with the German S-Bahn systems, though they are not so ambitious or so expensive.

True new underground systems are rare, even in Germany, because of their high capital cost. But both München, a city of nearly two million people, and Nürnberg, a city of only half-a-million, have built them. The latter case is rather as if Bristol or Leeds had built a new tube.

And both West Berlin and Hamburg have made major extensions to their established systems. In comparison all Britain can show is the refurbishment of the Victorian Glasgow underground, an inner-city circle line, plus two new tube lines in London.

So Germany has built generously while Britain has built relatively little. Twenty-one German cities have essentially new transit systems; Britain, stretching some definitions, has three. Further, the German cities are medium-sized places, most no larger than the average major British provincial city. The question is whether the Germans are right. It is not self-evident, because the new systems might not justify their construction costs.

At the same time almost all German cities have pedestrianised their central shopping streets more generously than have British ones. Whereas the typical British city has pedestrianised one or two streets, the typical German city has pedestrianised a whole network of streets, sometimes amounting to a large part of the entire central area, turning it into a vast pedestrian zone. We have to be careful about making comparisons here because the British have put more resources into construction of new pedestrian shopping precincts, some open, some (especially in more recent years) covered. But the overall effect is that German city centres are much more car-less than British ones. Even the casual visitor cannot fail to notice this.

These two policies are associated. The Germans can afford to create car-less centres because they can bring people in to work and shop by their new public transport systems. Evidently, even from casual observation, many are doing so.

It happens that German cities appear to be in better economic health than many British ones. With a few exceptions, they do not suffer as yet from the inner-city blight that afflicts so many large British cities. The statistics confirm that though they are beginning to lose people on the model earlier set by Britain, they seem to be more successful in retaining their position as employment and service centres. The obvious question is whether their transport policies have helped. This question was the starting-point of our study.

We approached it by taking representative cities, chosen to be broadly comparable as far as possible in terms of size and character. Finally, we looked at thirteen: seven in Germany, six in Britain. We wanted both cities that had invested in transit, and cities that had not. The problem was to find transit cities in Britain and non-transit ones in Germany. (If we had started much later we would have found it even harder: one of our cities, Dortmund, opened transit soon after we surveyed it.) Though we could never pretend any rigorous statistical proof, we wanted to see if the transit cities had done better than their non-transit counterparts.

There were two ways of looking at the effects. First were direct or primary effects: the numbers of passengers the new systems carried in comparison with the systems they replaced, the sources from which new passengers were drawn, the factors that seemed to have attracted them. These however were only a means to an end. The critical point was, secondly, the indirect or secondary effects on patterns of activity in the city centres, as measured by floorspace, employment, shopping turnover, or rents.

We wanted if possible to distinguish the effects of pedestrianisation from those of transit, since all the cities had some of the first while not all had the second. In practice this was almost impossible, since the cities that introduced transit did so at about the same time as they introduced pedestrianisation; in Germany, the two were often deliberately coupled. The general evidence everywhere is that pedestrianisation of streets is followed by big increases in pedestrian flows on those streets, especially at lunchtime and in early afternoon. German evidence is that where transit is available to pedestrianised zones, high proportions of all travellers use it.

The German evidence, which is thoroughly researched, is that the increase in pedestrians is followed by an increase in trade. The majority of shops report more turnover. This may have a negative effect, in that rents rise and bigger, more profitable establishments tend to push out the older traditional trades, who contributed something to the character of the city. And there will be increased pressure to turn housing into shops or offices. (Part of these pressures may arise from general structural causes, independent of pedestrianisation.) Finally, there is a strong suggestion that enhanced trade in the pedestrian centre may come at the expense of sub-centres in the inner city or suburbs.

The British evidence is much more fragmentary, because the research has not been done, especially in larger cities. For what it is worth, it indicates that the results are similar. Pedestrian flows markedly increase. Most shops report increased trade, though a minority report a fall. There is some evidence that some pedestrianised streets suffered a serious drop in trade, though special factors may have applied. These may have been lower-order shopping streets, where most of the shops lived on low profit margins and were very sensitive to even small short-term losses in trade.

The evidence on the direct impact of rail transit is equally clear, albeit contradictory. In Germany, new transit systems attracted passengers, sometimes in large numbers. In some cases (Hannover, Nürnberg) these restored the passenger levels of twenty years previously, when car ownership was much lower. In one (München), it actually did better than that. But, on the limited evidence available, it appears that the effect of transit did depend to some degree on the general economic prosperity of the city. Within the depressed Ruhrgebiet, Dortmund did not open a new transit system in the period of our study;

Essen did. But both cities suffered drastic losses of passengers on their public transport systems. Finally, Bremen - one of the few German cities that did not invest in new transit systems, but progressively modernised its tram services - actually saw an upturn in passengers in the late 1970s.

The British experience supports this to some degree. Liverpool and Glasgow, both cities with serious problems of economic contraction and out-migration of people, rehabilitated and extended their existing rail transit systems during the late 1970s. But in neither was there a significant effect in terms of passengers. The Glasgow Argyle Line attracted passengers, but most had simply transferred from buses. The Glasgow Underground did not even attract many people, and the reason is clear: while the system was being planned and built, the passengers had disappeared. The exception is the Tyne Metro, which had big increases in passengers after opening. It is significant that this is the only truly new British system, and that it took the place of an essentially derelict rail service.

The critical question is whether increases in passengers were followed by increases in economic activity. Here, even in Germany, the overwhelming weight of the evidence is negative. Retail turnover in Bremen and Dortmund, which did not invest, showed a bigger increase than in Essen and Nürnberg, which did (and where the increase was negligible). The increase in Köln and München was broadly of the same order as that in Dortmumd. Similarly, rents - corrected for inflation and reduced to comparable figures per unit of floorspace - demonstrate no noticeable effect of rail investment. In Germany, cities that had no or negligible rail investment appear to have had increases in floorspace at least as great as those cities that had a lot. Thus Dortmund's growth was greater than Essen's; Nürnberg's growth was negligible. British cities showed some rises in office rents after opening transit - sometimes with a two- or three-year time lag - but so did cities that did not. Detailed case studies, made in a number of British and German cities - Glasgow, Newcastle, Hannover - similarly failed to establish a significant impact.

All kinds of qualifications must of course be entered. The data are not as good as anyone would like. They are often fragmentary and - since the cancellation of the British Census of Retail Distribution - by no means uniform. Their timing is often unfortunate in relation to the dates of opening of transit, or of pedestrianisation. The number of cases is far too small to permit rigorous statistical conclusions - but so is the total number of cases in the wider universe. All we can say is that the verdict is, in the hallowed Scottish words, not proven.

It may be that time will enter a different verdict. Neither retailers, nor even more so property developers, are necessarily sensitive to the opportunities that transit and pedestrianisation convey. In a decade or more, perhaps they will begin to respond and the impact of transit will at last be demonstrated. But not yet.

These negative conclusions receive final backing from our own direct polling of city-centre retailers. Those in Germany, who should know, were on the whole cautious and sceptical about the influence of transit. They were also sceptical of the future prospects of city centres, and were inclined to think that the best futures were outside them in suburbs or small towns. Those in Britain, most of whom have no direct way of saying, were far more enthusiastic. They went so far as to confirm their belief that the city centres had the best retailing prospects of any kind of shopping area, despite the fact that many of them have clearly lost trade in recent years. We found this response to be perhaps the most surprising, and the hardest to interpret, of all the data in our research.

It confirms a disturbing general impression that significant decision-makers in Britain, who should be drawing on good quality research, are simply basing their investment and location decisions on hunch, in defiance of the evidence - fragmentary and poor as that may be. There may be a kind of vicious circle, whereby ignorance produces no demand for hard evidence, the lack of which then simply confirms the ignorance.

The Germans, who have commissioned a great deal of research and are concerned to learn from it, seem to conclude that transit investment has not had much effect on the city. It may have helped delay the process of decline; but that process has been delayed in non-transit cities also. In Britain, whose cities are clearly facing much larger and more immediate problems, transit investment certainly has not helped stem the decline of Glasgow or Liverpool, though it may have done something for Newcastle.

At the end of the study, the only fair conclusion is that the processes of urban growth and decline have deep and subtle causes, so far imperfectly understood. Transit investment is in large measure irrelevant to these processes, though it may affect some of them at the margin. Rail cannot save the city, if the city is going down, because the forces that are taking it down are far wider and far deeper than mere questions of accessibility. That is not to deny the potential importance of transport investments to the regeneration of a city's economy. It is to say that they would need to be planned in the context of a far better understanding of that city's malaise.

That problem is addressed in a very wide range of literature, which could not adequately be summarised here. It is clear that many historic functions of the European city have contracted very rapidly and suddenly, and may well continue to do so. They include much of manufacturing, except for very local needs and highly specialised lines; warehousing; and transportation, including railways and ports. Everywhere, the city is becoming increasingly a provider of services rather than a producer or handler of goods. But in some of the larger cities, even some of the more routine service functions are tending to leave in search of lower rents and lower salary levels in smaller towns. At the same time, many specialised service activities - including the media, design, financial services, health services, tourism and entertainment - continue to show rapid growth. Many of these do so in the core of the city and in selected inner-urban areas - especially those areas seen as having a good ambiance and good environmental quality.

Positive action by the city's planners can do much to encourage this: by a careful blend of sympathetic renewal in some places and careful rehabilitation of old built stock in others, by enhancement of the quality of the local environment - including especially the creation of good pedestrian spaces - and the encouragement of the right mix of activities that are sympathetic and even symbiotic to each other. In all this, transport policies have an important role to play. There can be no doubt, from the experience of the German cities in our case studies, that citizens and visitors do respond to efficient, fast, comfortable, well-designed public transport by patronising it. In the process, they raise the potential of the city centre on which the new systems focus. The important point is to realise that this is merely potential. Transport improvements by themselves can never achieve anything; they merely facilitate urban change. They have not had an obvious or marked effect on the structure and organisation of the city, even in Germany - though that may well happen in time. It will only happen, however, if other urban policies make it do so.

Appendix A: Glossary of technical terms

Environmental Traffic Management: see **Verkehrsberuhigung**.

Light Rail Transit (LRT): A public transport system intermediate between a tram (streetcar, trolley) and a full underground rail system; see Table 1.2.

Linienlänge: see Route Length.

Pre-Metro: A term originally used in French-speaking cities (e.g. Brussels) to refer to a Stadtbahn-type system (q.v.) designed in such a way that it can eventually be upgraded into a true U-Bahn (q.v.); thus stations are designed with platforms longer than presently needed, sometimes with two levels to adapt from low-loading to high-loading cars.

Route Length (Route Mileage): Total length of all public transport routes in a city or system. Compare Track Length.

S-Bahn: An upgraded suburban commuter rail system, operated by the national main-line rail network (DB, BR); generally involves some new track length, segregation from Inter-City tracks, new or upgraded stations; may involve new tunnelling under city centre; see Table 1.2.

Stadtbahn: A particular form of Light Rail (q.v.) introduced into German cities; involves a combination of underground tracks in city centre, reserved surface tracks outside city centre, partial signal control, and short trains with cars of tramcar type.

Streckenlänge: see Track Length.

Track Length (Track Mileage): Total length of all tracks in a city or system. May be shorter than route length (q.v.) because several routes share the same track.

U-Bahn: This widely used German term can give rise to confusion. Strictly, it refers to a true Underground railway (Heavy Rail) with full signalling and full-length trains, generally of standard track gauge though perhaps of restricted rolling stock gauge (cf London Underground, New York Subway, Paris Metro). The München and Nürnberg systems are true U-Bahn systems in this sense. However other cities (e.g. Essen, Frankfurt am Main) use the designation U1, U2, etc., to refer to routes that are in fact Stadtbahn systems (q.v.) Some of these may be Pre-Metro systems (q.v.), designed for eventual upgrading to true U-Bahn systems.

Verkehrsberuhigung: systems of traffic management designed to mitigate the environmental effects of motor traffic, either by excluding it entirely from a street or area, or by modifying driver behaviour (e.g. speeds). Methods include pedestrian streets or areas, bus- or tram-only streets, 'sleeping policemen' (speed bumps), traffic mazes, and Woonerven (Dutch, literally Living Yards: spaces designed to be safe for pedestrians and for playing children while still accepting slow-moving or parked traffic).

Appendix B: Thirteen case study cities: basic data

1   BREMEN

1.1   Basic Data   1970   1981   1982

Population

	1970	1981	1982
Population CBD[a]	21,950	15,953	15,953
Population city	593,182	555,118	553,261
Population density (city)	18.7/ha	17.0/ha	17.0/ha
Population regional[b]	1,004,119	1,021,299	1,021,880

Area in hectares

	1970	1981	1982
Area CBD	312	312	312
Area city	32,672	32,672	32,672
Area region	370,329	370,329	370,329

a) Stadtteil Mitte; 111-113
b) Regional population, all local authorities which are in
   proximity of 30 km of Bremen. Regional population including the
   city of Bremen.

Source: Bremen Land, Statistisches Landesamt 1972.
        Bremen Land, Statistisches Landesamt 1981, 1982.
        Niedersächsisches Landesverwaltungsamt 1982, 1983.

1.2   Economic Data

Census of Population 1970	CBD	City
Total employment by residence	9,002	252,677
Employment in:		
Industry (excluding construction and mining)	1,968	82,132
Trade and transportation	2,025	46,813
Other tertiary activities	4,581	104,817

	CBD	City
Total employment at workplace	74,135	315,585
Employment in:		
Industry (excluding construction and mining)	6,011	105,217
Trade and transportation	34,978	100,344
Other tertiary activities	29,940	80,762

Source: Bremen Land, Statistisches Landesamt 1972.

Socially insured workers and employees

	1974	1978	1979	1980	1981	1982
Agriculture, forestry, power, water and mining	4,770	4,649	4,654	4,694	4,600	4,590
Manufacturing industries	90,794	76,119	76,658	77,299	75,775	73,263
Construction	19,062	15,786	15,513	16,225	15,966	13,770
Distributive trades	46,958	45,124	45,330	45,506	45,504	43,831
Transportation and communication	36,723	33,940	33,573	33,690	32,165	32,482
Finance and insurance	10,566	9,938	10,219	10,338	10,488	10,515
Service activities)		43,650	45,480	47,026	47,769	47,162
Non-profit organisations and private households)	53,831	3,956	4,013	4,068	4,226	4,405
Territorial authorities and social insurance)		12,805	12,816	12,570	12,549	12,116
Total	262,704	245,967	248,256	251,471	249,054	242,106

174

Date: 30 June

Source: Statistisches Bundesamt 1980, 1981, 1982.
         Statistisches Handbuch 1975-1980.
         Bremen Land, Statistisches Landesamt 1981.

Unemployment in percentage

    1983   :   13.0
March 1984   :   14.1

Source: BAFA 1983, 1984.

1.3   Transportation

Modal split   1976

		PT	:	IT
Trips (not including pedestrians and bicycles) total trips during 24 hours		33	:	67
Trips between city centre and the city (origin and destination)		54	:	46
Trips total, excluding city centre (origin and destination)		26	:	74

Source: Dorsch Consult 1977, pp.50, 68.

Trips (total) including bicycles (B)

PT	IT	B
25	55	20

80 per cent of traffic with destinations in Bremen used the car; 20 per cent of public transportation users have a car available.

Source: Dorsch Consult 1977, pp.116, 120.

Today, bicycle traffic has increased, and is higher than 20 per cent.

Source: Interviews in Bremen.

Public transportation

No S-Bahn system, no Verkehrsverbund
Opening of the first stretch of a
light rail line   :   1976

175

```
Network (km., track length) 1982:     Number of routes/services

Light rail   :    10                              -
Tram         :    57                              6
Bus          :   243                             38
```

50 per cent of all passengers are carried by trams.

Source: Bremer Strassenbahn AG 1984, internal statistics.
        Total trips per year: see Table 7.2.

Car ownership per 1,000 inhabitants

```
1950   :     13
1970   :    232
1982   :    358
```

Source: Bremen Stadt 1984.

1.4   Pedestrianisation in the City Centre

Total length of pedestrianisation   :   about 700 m   excluding the
                                         market

Date of first inception   :   1974

Pedestrianisation concept   :   linear[a]
Future of pedestrianisation   :   increase of size planned by
                                         IHK (Chambers of Commerce)
                                         and planning office

Loading provision   :   mostly rear

Parking provision (inside the
medieval city)   :   5,000 short time parking
                                         spaces

Private and public parking spaces (inside the medieval city) about
9,000 (stand 1976).
Total parking spaces (inside and outside the medieval city:
Altstadt, Bahnhofsvorstadt, Ostertor) about 19,400, public parking
spaces 11,000, private 7,800, illegal 600 (figures does not include
parking spaces on Bürgerweide).

a) Linear: pedestrianisation is defined as being the pedestrianisation of streets which are mostly unconnected so that they do
   not form a consistent area of pedestrianisation.

Areal: pedestrianisation covers several streets (main and minor) and squares as one connected area; roads for motorised traffic hardly ever cross pedestrianised streets.

Source: Bremen Handelskammer 1982, p.9.
Bremen Stadt 1982.

2 DORTMUND

2.1 Basic Data

	1970	1981
Population		
Population CBD[a]	11,576	9,751
Population city	646,954	608,908
Population density (city)	23.1/ha	21.6/ha
Population regional[b]	700,000	-
Area in hectares		
Area CBD[a]	177.8	177.8
Area city[c]	28,017	28,017
Area region[b]	-	-

a) Stadtbezirk 'city'.
b) Mittelbereich des Oberzentrums Dortmund, as defined: according to the Landesentwicklungsplan in Nordrhein Westfalen.
c) All figures for 1970 are calculated on the basis of 1975 boundaries.

Source: Dortmund Stadt, Amt für Statistik und Wahlen 1978, 1983.

2.2 Economic Data

Census of Population 1970	CBD	City
Total employment by residence	5,951	254,027
Employment in:		
Industry (excluding construction and mining)	1,424	94,101
Trade and transportation	1,404	56,089
Other tertiary activities	2,793	60,590
Total employment at workplace	56,716	276,775
Employment in:		
Industry (excluding construction and mining)	6,501	92,021
Trade and transportation	21,560	69,334
Other tertiary activities	24,902	66,782

Source: Dortmund Stadt, Amt für Statistik und Wahlen 1978.

Socially insured workers and employees

	1974[a]	1978	1979	1980	1981	1982
Agriculture, forestry, power, water and mining	25,693	25,491	25,705	25,423	25,293
Manufacturing industries	68,693	70,882	66,692	65,400	60,149
Construction	19,049	19,898	19,714	19,795	18,303
Distributive trades	36,508	37,933	37,383	36,949	35,493
Transport and communication	11,249	11,741	11,517	12,054	11,736
Finance and insurance	8,923	9,591	9,924	10,190	10,441
Service activities	38,315	41,612	42,045	42,470	41,998
Non-profit organisations and private households	3,402	3,629	3,831	3,856	4,028
Territorial authorities and social insurance	11,247	9,797	9,807	9,644	9,484
Total	239,847	223,083	230,645	226,723	225,785	216,925

Date: 30 June

a) No detailed data available for 1974.

Source: Statistisches Bundesamt 1980, 1981, 1982.

<u>Unemployment in percentage</u>

```
      1983  :  15.0
March 1984  :  16.5
```

Highest unemployment rate in the German case study cities.

Source: BAFA 1983, 1984.

3 Transportation

<u>Modal split</u>

	1963-1965	1973-1974	
Trips (weekdays)			
Dortmund	PT : IT	PT : IT	P
	40 : 60	32 : 68	-
	- : -	23 : 48	29

	1973-1974
Trips to and from the city centre and some other urban areas (Brackel, Eving, Hörde, Huckarde)	38 and more by PT
Trips to and from the urban districts in the south and Mengede	26 and less by PT

There is some difference between:

	PT	:	IT
commuters	40	:	60
students and pupils	75	:	25
shopping trips	43	:	57
visit and pleasure trips	29	:	71
official, business and other trips	11	:	89

Without consistent development and improvement of public transportation the share will fall to about 20 per cent for public transport
in the year 2000.

Modal split was on average in the Federal Republic of Germany on
weekdays (1975):

```
   PT   :   IT
  25.7  :  74.3
```

179

Modal split for local authorities with more than 500,000 inhabitants, which do not have either an S-Bahn and/or U-Bahn system, was:

PT	:	IT
36	:	64

With the opening of the first S-Bahn line in Dortmund it is believed that the modal split of 1973 can be kept.

Source: Dortmund Stadt 1975 p.25, 1977 pp.38, 80, 81.

Public transportation

(No detailed information of the public transportation system could be obtained.)

Opening of the first S-Bahn line to Bochum: September 1983. Opening of the first stretch of light rail: May 1983 (tunnel: 1.5 km.). The Dortmunder transport authority is part of the Verkehrsverbund Rhein-Ruhr.

From 3 June 1984 there are three new light rail lines (U41, U45, U47).

Network (km., route length) 1983:   Number of routes/services:

Light rail	:	12
Tram	:	98
Bus	:	about 400

- not known -

Total trips per year: see Table 7.2.

Source: Anon 1984a, 1984b.
        VRR 1983.
        D.M.f.W.M.u.V.d.L.N.-W. 1976/77 p.16.

Car ownership per 1,000 inhabitants

1963	:	124
1976	:	305
1981	:	361

Source: Dortmund Stadt 1977 Teil B, p.12.
        Dortmund Stadt Amt für Statistik und Wahlen, 1982

2.4   Pedestrianisation in the City Centre

Total length of pedestrianisation : 1,405 m. not including three squares

(Total sq.m.   : 33,060)

Date of first inception   : 1963
Date of last inception   : 1976

Pedestrian concept   : linear and areal[a]
Future of pedestrianisation   : extension planned but including car lanes

Total cost (1963-1976)   : 4,171,500 DM; in most cases half was paid by adjoining property owners

Loading provision   : rear and front

Parking provision in the
city centre (1974)
Public parking spaces   :   9,000
Private parking spaces   :   6,700
Total   :   15,700

It is planned to increase parking provision by 3,300.

a) See above under Bremen, pedestrianisation.

Source: Dortmund Stadt 1977, pp.85, 86.
According to information from the town planning office new parking spaces are planned for short-term parking (high parking costs).
Information on pedestrianisation given by town planning office.

3   ESSEN

3.1   Basic Data

	1970	1981[b]	1983
Population			
Population CBD[a]	4,602	3,712	3,526
Population city	698,434	653,319	642,391
Population density (city)	35.9/ha	32.2/ha	32.7/ha
Population regional[b]	-	-	-

Area in hectares

Area CBD[a)	92.5	92.5	92.5
Area city	19,476	21,024	21,024
Area region	-	-	-

a) Statistical area 01.
b) According to Landesentwicklungsplan 1970, regional population is about 2 million.

Source: Essen Stadt, Amt für Statistik und Wahlen 1972, 1981, 1983.

3.2 Economic Data

Census of Population 1970	CBD	City
Total employment by residence	2,467	274,313
Employment in:		
Industry (including construction and mining)	793	136,001
Trade and transportation	670	65,773
Other tertiary activities	989	70,349
Total employment at workplace	34,498	298,548
Employment in:		
Industry (including construction and mining)	1,713	146,983
Trade and transportation	17,441	74,199
Other tertiary activities	14,434	76,229

Source: Essen Stadt, Amt für Statistik und Wahlen 1972, 1980, 1981.

Socially insured workers and employees

	1974	1978	1979	1980	1981	1982
Agriculture, forestry, power, water and mining		21,518	20,951	19,851	19,047	18,668
Manufacturing industries		61,518	61,517	59,497	59,439	56,931
Construction		21,656	21,699	21,920	21,123	20,371
Distributive trades		42,201	43,201	41,746	41,637	39,824

Transport and communication	12,387	12,655	12,753	13,078	12,381
Finance and insurance	7,570	7,769	8,101	8,037	7,923
Service activities	46,285	50,996	53,963	54,304	54,375
Non-profit organisations and private households	5,935	6,211	6,336	6,440	6,500
Territorial authorities and social insurance	9,277	8,882	9,174	9,261	8,719
Total	249,271	227,997 233,709	233,341	232,366	225,692

Date: 30 June.

Source: StatistischesBundesamt 1980, 1981, 1982.

Unemployment in percentage

        1983   :   12.4
  March 1984   :   13.5

Source: BAFA 1983, 1984.

3.3 Transportation

Modal split   1965

Trips (destination and origin   PT   :   IT
in Essen and destination or   46   :   54
origin in the transportation
region of Essen) (about 215,000
population in 1975))

                                                       1975

Trips (destination and origin   PT   :   IT
in Essen and either destination   27   :   73
or origin in the transport region
of Essen

Modal split (weekdays) 1975

PT	:	IT	:	B	:	P
19	:	52	:	3	:	26

B = Bicycles
P = Pedestrians

Source: Ingeniergruppe Aachen 1975, pp.30, 31.

Public transportation

The Essener transportation authority is part of the Verkehrsverbund Rhein-Ruhr.
Opening of the first light rail line : 1977

Network (km., route length) 1982:   Number of routes/services

Light rail	:	10	2
Tram	:	71.2	17
Bus	:	313	60
Duobus	:	2.5	2

The track gauge of trams is different to that of the light rail (tram: about 1 m., light rail 1.433 m)

Source: Essener Verkehrs AG 1982.

Trips per year for Trams/Buses/and Light Rail in millions

	1962	1964	1966	1968	1970	1972	1974	1976	1978	1980	1982
Tram	97.1	87.9	76.1	62.4							
Light rail								2.9	5.2	9.8	
Bus	41.1	43.6	40.3	35.2							
Total	143.2	131.5	116.4	97.6	97.5	99.9	95.4	85.8	83.0	91.1	89.4

Source: Essener Verkehrs AG 1982, p.15.
        Essener Verkehrs AG 1984, internal statistics.

Finance in million DM

	Costs	Income[a]	of which subsidies are	in %
1970	76	68	8	10.5
1972	93	85	4	4.3
1974	118	82	28	23.7
1976	136	100	28	20.6
1978	166	112	38.5	23.2
1980	198	121	63	31.8
1982	195	116	65	33.3

The Verkehrsverbund has some small additional income (since 1980)
8.5 million DM (1980) and 6 million DM (1982).

a) Excluding income of Niessbrauch.

Source: Essener Verkehrs AG 1982, p.15 (own calculations).

Car ownership per 1,000 inhabitants

1960	:	70
1975	:	260
1981	:	369
1982	:	382

Source: Essener Verkehrs AG 1984, internal statistics.
        Essen Stadt 1979, p.20.

3.4   Pedestrianisation in the City Centre

Total length of pedestrianisation : 2,000 m not including all the
                                     squares.

Date of first inception   : 1929 (exact date not known)
Date of first inception after
the Second World War   : 1959
Date of second inception   : 1966
Date of third inception   : 1977

Pedestrian concept   : still more linear than
                                     areal[b]
Future of pedestrianisation   : increase of size planned by
                                     planning office

Loading provision   : mostly rear

```
                    Parking provision in the city
                    centre[a]
                    public parking space            : about 8,000
                    parking meters                  : 1,250
                    multi-storey parking space      : 6,500
                    private parking space           : about 3,000 not exactly known

                    a) City Centre - see basic data
                    b) See above under Bremen, pedestrianisation

Source: Essen Stadt 1971.
        Essen Stadt 1980, p.78, Reschke 1979,
        internal information.
```

4   HANNOVER

4.1 Basic Data	1970	1981	1982
Population			
Population CBD[a]	15,006	11,523	11,177
Population city	522,603	554,575	549,414
Population density (city)	39/ha	27/ha	27/ha
Population regional[a]	1,068,400	1,073,459	1,078,502
(Grossraum)			
Area in hectares			
Area CBD[a]	222	222	222
Area city	13,500	20,400	20,400
Area region[b]	210,000	228,900	228,900

```
                    a) Stadtteil Mitte; 011-018.
                    b) Including Hannover.

Source: Grossraum Hannover 1977.
        Hannover Landeshauptstadt, 1982.
```

4.2 Economic Data

Census of Population 1970	CBD	City
Total employment by residence	7,806	270,816
Employment in:		
Industry (including construction) and mining)	2,523	115,379
Trade and transportation	1,822	60,641
Other tertiary activities	3,448	92,947

	CBD	City
Total employment at workplace	82,807	401,055
Employment in:		
Industry (excluding construction and mining)	7,620	151,943
Trade and transportation	35,381	96,878
Other tertiary activities	25,929	121,448

1976		
Total employment at workplace	81,704	366,819
Employment in:		
Industry (excluding construction and mining)	7,114	114,772
Trade and transportation	32,852	86,385
Other tertiary activities	29,259	141,592

Source: Grossraum Hannover 1978.
Hannover Landeshauptstadt 1973.

Socially insured workers and employees

	1974[a]	1978	1979	1980	1981	1982
Agriculture, forestry, power, water and mining		7,381	7,509	7,730	7,842	7,920
Manufacturing industries		96,558	97,434	98,783	95,229	90,257
Construction		16,047	16,218	16,025	15,498	14,517
Distributive trades		47,134	47,217	46,831	45,480	44,638

Transport and communication	20,572	21,833	22,852	23,043	22,792
Finance and insurance	18,734	19,094	19,660	19,702	19,686
Service activities	58,816	60,474	62,485	63,428	63,929
Non-profit organisations and private households	7,435	7,541	7,671	7,892	8,066
Territorial authorities and social insurance	20,558	21,139	21,671	21,600	23,429
Total	313,275	293,235	298,459	303,708	299,814	295,234

Date: 30 June

a) No detailed data available for 1974.

Source: Statistisches Bundesamt 1980, 1981, 1982.

Unemployment in percentage

1983	:	11.2
March 1984	:	12.6

Source: BAFA 1983, 1984.

4.3 Transportation

Modal split

	1962			1975			1980		
Total trips (not including pedestrians and bicycles) Origin and destination from the hinterland to the city of Hannover and vice versa	PT	:	IT	PT	:	IT	PT	:	IT
	56	:	44	30	:	70	33	:	67
Total trips, origin and destination city of Hannover	-			33	:	67	39	:	61

188

	1980		
	PT	:	IT
Trips by commuters from the hinterland to the city	65	:	35
Trips by commuters from the hinterland to the city and inside the city	45	:	55
Trips during the day from the hinterland to the city and vice versa	38	:	62
Trips during the day inside the city	40	:	60

Source: Hannover Landeshauptstadt 1980, pp.10, 11.
        Grossraumverkehr Hannover 1981, p.9.
        ÜSTRA 1982a, p.6.

Public transportation

A kind of Verkehrsverbund since 1970, called Grossraumverkehr.
There are differences in its organisation structure and in its
financing to the existing Verkehrsverbünde.
The area consists of the city of Hannover and its Landkreis.
No classical S-Bahn system planned

Source: ÜSTRA 1983a, p.53.

Opening of the first light rail line   :   1975

Network (km., route length) 1984:   Number of routes/services

Light rail	:	93	6
Tram	:	63	6
Bus	:	450	36

Source: ÜSTRA, 1983a, p.17.

Total trips[a] in millions (Grossraumverkehr Hannover)

	1975	1976	1977	1978	1979	1980	1981	1982
Light rail and tram·	57.5	60.0	60.5	63.5	69.0	72.5	73.0	72.0
Bus	27.5	28.5	30.0	30.0	31.0	32.5	33.0	32.0
Train and others	28.0	27.5	29.5	30.0	30.5	30.5	31.5	31.5
Total	113.0	116.0	120.0	123.5	130.5	136.5	138.0	135.5

a) Calculated according to tickets sold.

189

Source: USTRA 1982b, 1983a.

Car ownership per 1,000 inhabitants

1970 : 209
1980 : 316
1981 : 322
1982 : 316

Source: Hannover Landeshauptstadt 1982.

4.4 Pedestrianisation in the City Centre (excluding Lister Meile)

Total length of pedestrianisation : about 3,500 m excluding
squares

Date of first inception : 1956
Further extension after : 1974

Pedestrian concept : area[a]
Future of pedestrianisation : no further extensions planned

Loading provision : front and rear

Parking provision in the city
centre[b]
Total parking space : about 19,150
Public parking space in multi-
storey car parks : 6,160
others (parking meters, streets) : 5,800
Private parking spaces : 7,130
New construction of another multi-
storey car park (Lützowstr) : about 450 spaces

a) See above under Bremen, pedestrianisation.
b) Definition of city centre not clear in the publication.
Own calculations.

Source: Hannover Landeshauptstadt 1980,p.17.
Monheim 1975, p.146.

5   KÖLN

5.1   Basic Data

Population	1970		1981
Population CBD[a]	22,499		21,471
Population city	994,705[b]	848,352[c]	971,403
Population density (city)	26.0/ha		26.0/ha
Population regional[d]	834,639[b]	539,232[c]	1,056,488

Area in hectares

Area CBD	243		243
Area city	49,684[b]	20,137[c]	40,512
Area region	330,787[b]	179,386[c]	371,500

a) Altstadt Nord
b) Population and area size at boundaries 1.7.1976.
c) Population and area size at boundaries in 1970.
d) Regional population consists of the Kreise: Erft Kreis,
   Rheinisch-Bergischer Kreis, Oberbergischer Kreis, Kreis
   Euskirchen. (Erftkreis was newly formed 1.1.1975.).

Source: LDSNW 1972, 1976, 1983.

5.2   Economic Data

Census of Population 1970	CBD	City
Total employment by residence	12,494	454,434
Employment in:		
Industry (excluding construction and mining)	3,836	203,670
Trade and transportation	3,098	101,784
Other tertiary activities	5,098	146,263

Employment	CBD	City
Total employment at workplace	77,097	528,710
Employment in:		
Industry (excluding construction and mining)	7,574	182,045
Trade and transportation	29,525	137,833
Other tertiary activities	37,263	164,828

Source: Köln Stadt, Statistisches Amt 1976.

Socially insured workers and employees

	1974[a]	1978	1979	1980	1981	1982
Agriculture, forestry, power, water and mining	16,601[b]	6,645	6,325	6,581	6,777	
Manufacturing industries		138,629	140,698	137,098	130,102	127,665
Construction		22,322	22,704	23,663	23,786	23,382
Distribution trades		68,149	69,244	70,776	70,694	68,436
Transport and communication		28,268	28,272	28,591	29,607	28,784
Finance and insurance		33,601	34,128	34,671	34,685	34,655
Service activities		84,034	86,266	89,318	91,483	93,235
Non-profit organisations and private households		9,871	10,194	10,616	10,720	10,688
Territorial authorities and social insurance		22,791	24,035	24,013	22,990	21,856
Total		408,856	424,367	422,339	425,071	420,648	415,478

Date: 30 June.

    a) No detailed data available for 1974.
    b) This figure is clearly an exaggeration as admitted by the
       Statistische Bundesamt.

Source: Statistisches Bundesamt Wiesbaden 1980, 1081, 1982.

Unemployment in percentage

1983	:	12.4
March 1984	:	13.0

Source: BAFA 1983, 1984.

5.3 Transportation

Modal split (excluding bicycles and pedestrians)

		1966	
		PT	: IT
Trips (origin and destination) in the city centre (Innenstadt)		47	: 53
Trips (origin and destination Köln)		30-40	: 60-70
Trips by employees, pupils etc. in Köln		35-50	: 50-65
Trips by employees, pupils etc. to inner city areas		55-75	: 25-45

Source: Wehner 1973 p.13 and Abb. 19.
(No other data on modal split available.)

Public transportation

No S-Bahn system, Verkehrverbund planned 1985 (interview).

Opening of the first light rail stretch, 1968 (Dom/Main Station to
Friesenplatz;) length   :   1.3 km.

Network (km., track length) 1982:   Number of routes/services

Light rail[a)]	:	35.2	-
Tram	:	121.6[b)]	14[c)]
Bus	:	343.8	33

76.5 per cent of all passengers are carried by train, light rail
and tram; 23.5 per cent by bus.

a) Not including Line 16, Köln-Bonn: track length calculated only to
   Köln-Marienburg.
b) Most of it has its own right of way.
c) Light rail lines consist in most cases of a mixture of pure light
   rail lines and upgraded trams, therefore the number of light rail
   lines is difficult to define.

Source: KVB and KBE 1980, p.1.

Total trips per year: see Table 7.2

Finance see Chapter 2

Car ownership per 1,000 inhabitants

1970 : 212
1982 : 394

Source: Köln Stadt Der Oberstadtdirektor 1982, n.p.
       Wehner 1983, p.11.

5.4 Pedestrianisation in the City Centre

Total length of pedestrianisation : over 3,000 m (not including the Dom area and other squares.

Date of first inception   : about 1930
First inception after the
Second World War   : 1966 (Schildergasse)
Date of second inception   : 1970
Date of third inception   : 1974

Pedestrian concept   : linear and areal[a]
Future of pedestrianisation   : increase of size planned by planning office

Loading provision   : mostly rear

Costs for the two main shopping
streets   : half of the costs were paid by adjoining property owners, 1,060,000 DM

Parking provision in proximity
of the two main shopping streets
multi-storey parking spaces   : 3,000
private spaces   : about 3,500

Parking space for enlarged
city centre
(Stadtbezirk 1 = 1,600 ha)
public   : 26,800
private   : 12,700
total   : 39,500

About 4,000 new parking facilities are planned in the city centre.

a) See above under Bremen, pedestrianisation.

Source: Köln Stadt 1979, Hermanns 1972, p.7.
        Köln Stadt 1982, pp.30, 33.

6 MÜNCHEN

6.1 Basic Data

Population	1970	1982[b]
Population CBD[a]	25,161	20,471
Population city	1,293,590	1,291,828
Population density (city)	42/ha	42/ha
Population regional	2,112,410	2,305,444
(Planning Region 14)		

Area in hectares

Area CBD	208	208
Area city	31,055	31,039
Area region	198,350	198,350

a) Stadtbezirk 1 + 12.
b) 1.1.1982

Source: München Landeshauptstadt, Statistisches Amt 1983.
        München Landeshauptstadt, Amt für Statistik und Datenanalyse der
        Landeshauptstadt München 1972.

6.2 Economic Data

Census of Population 1970	CBD	City
Total employment by residence	15,452	685,390
Employment in:		
Industry (excluding construction and mining)	4,957	282,320
Trade and transportation	3,493	145,383
Other tertiary activities	6,965	254,335

Source: München Landeshauptstadt, Amt für Statistik und Datenanalyse
        1972.

	CBD	City
Total employment at workplace	76,342	784,000

Employment in:

Industry (excluding construction and mining)	8,786	261,200
Trade and transportation	19,339	162,700
Other tertiary activities	44,999	257,600

	1977	
	CBD	City
Total employment at workplace	76,366	765,500
Employment in:		
Industry (excluding construction and mining)	7,424	237,800
Trade and transportation	21,802	168,000
Other tertiary activities	47,659	292,500

	1981[a]	
	CBD	City
Total employment at workplace	77,717	782,600
Employment in:		
Industry[b] (excluding construction and mining)	6,656	249,500
Trade and transportation	21,558	168,300
Other tertiary activities	47,659	301,400

a) Estimate by München - Stadtplanungsamt.
b) Estimate in employment in industry probably too high.

Source: Bayerisches Statistisches Landesamt 1971.
München Landeshaupstadt 1978.
München Landeshauptstadt 1984b.

Socially insured workers and employees

	1974	1978	1979	1980	1981	1982
Agriculture, forestry, power, water and mining	7,421	7,715	7,840	7,909	7,396	8,214
Manufacturing industries	212,913	197,906	201,698	204,147	200,953	193,263
Construction	54,063	44,939	47,088	46,619	45,134	43,074
Distributive trades	102,600	101,411	102,561	104,494	103,216	102,854

Transport and communication	40,969	37,951	39,648	40,821	41,225	40,685
Finance and insurance	50,061	48,874	50,196	51,069	50,272	51,174
Service activities	127,831	141,849	147,515	152,870	152,761	157,665
Non-profit organisations and private households	17,950	18,851	19,874	19,503	19,601	19,906
Territorial authorities and social insurance	34,409	33,967	33,145	32,977	33,778	34,287
Total	648,217	633,463	649,565	660,404	654,333	651,122

Date: 30 June

Source: Bayerisches Statistisches Landesamt 1974, 1978, 1979, 1980, 1981, 1982.

Unemployment in percentage

        1983   :   6.1
  March 1984   :   6.7

Source: BAFA 1983, 1984.

6.3 Transportation

Modal split (excluding bicycles and pedestrians)

	1977		1980[a]	
	PT : IT		PT : IT	
Trips (origin and destination) within München, about 1.9 million daily	45 : 55		46 : 54	
Trips in München, either origin or destination in München, about 2.5 million daily	43 : 57		44 : 56	

197

Trips in CBD, either origin or destination in CBD, about 0.4 million daily	67 : 33	70 : 30
Trips origin München, destination hinterland about 0.6 million daily	34 : 66	35 : 65
Commuting total origin and destination within München	44 : 56	46 : 54
Commuting to the CBD	73 : 27	75 : 25

a) Estimated by the Stadtplanungsamt

Source: München Landeshauptstadt 1984b, p.99.

Public transportation

Opening of the Underground and S-Bahn system	:	1972
Foundation of the Münchener Verkehrsverbund	:	1972

Network (km., track length):   Number of routes/services

		1972	1982	1984
U-Bahn	:	14	32	4
S-Bahn	:	396	412	12
Tram	:	112	101	14
Bus	:	922	2,624	-

Source: MVV 1984.

Trips per year, in millions (Verkehrsverbund) see Table 7.4

Finance: up to 1980

Since 1967 for U-Bahn construction: 1.195 Billion DM (Federal Government) and about   800 million (Land and City of München which totals to about 2 Billion DM (until 1980).

Since 1967 for S-Bahn construction: 0.680 Billion DM (Federal Government) and 0.450 Billion DM Land and City which totals to about 1.100 Billion DM.

Since 1972 the Federal Government spent 1.474 Billion DM for the Münchener Verkehrsbund.

Source: Federal Ministry of Transport 1983, internal information.

Car ownership per 1,000 inhabitants

1973	:	285
1982	:	366

Source: München Landeshauptstadt 1976, 1984a.

6.4 Pedestrianisation in the City Centre

Total length of pedestrianisation	: over 2,000 m not including the large squares

Date of first inception	: 1972
Date of second inception	: 1975
Date of third inception	: 1980

Pedestrian concept	: areal[b]
Future of pedestrianisation	: no extension currently planned

Loading provision	: 70 percent of stores have rear access

Parking provision in the city centre[a] (in the vicinity of the schemes)	: 7,000 (1970) about 5000 (1974)
Multi-storey garages	: 5,000
On street	: 3,250
Private parking spaces	: 5,000
	No possibility of extending parking facilities.

a) Stadtbezirk 1
b) See above under Bremen, pedestrianisation

Source: Monheim 1975.
        München Landeshauptstadt 1975, 1984a.

7 NÜRNBERG

7.1 Basic Data

	1970	1981	1982
Population			
Population CBD[a]	22,434	–	17,255
Population city	480,407	483,472	480,878
Population density (city)	27.50/ha	26.1/ha	25.8/ha
Population regional (Planungsregion 7)	1,022,752	1,077,503	1,163,556

Area in hectares

Area CBD[a]	286	286	286
Area city	13,718	12,576	18,576
Area region	-	293,500	293,500

a) Stadtbezirke; 01, 02, 03, 06.

Source: Nürnberg Stadt, Amt für Stadtforschung und Statistik 1972a, 1983.

7.2 Economic Data[a]

Census of Population 1970	CBD	City
Total employment by residence[a]	11,350	228,773
Employment in:		
Industry (including construction and mining)	4,702	116,297
Trade and transportation	2,632	54,432
Other tertiary activities	3,996	56,464

	CBD	City
Total employment[a] at workplace	62,189	314,064
Employment in:		
Industry (including construction and mining)	10,380	127,798
Trade and transportation	25,587	89,651
Other tertiary activities	26,221	93,507

a) Boundary changes in 1972.
   Data : 1970 boundaries.

Source: Nürnberg Stadt, Amt für Stadtforschung und Statistik 1972b.

Socially insured workers and employees

	1974	1978	1979	1980	1981	1982
Agriculture, forestry, power, water and mining	3,711	3,538	3,579	3,593	3,684	3,695
Manfacturing industries	119,598	108,057	108,937	107,701	104,923	100,245
Construction	22,728	17,004	17,701	18,348	17,592	16,396

Distributive trades	46,064	49,152	50,597	51,147	51,657	49,875
Transportation and communication	23,309	19,598	20,221	20,736	20,810	20,392
Finance and insurance	12,566	12,445	12,756	13,009	13,321	13,031
Service activities	30,295	31,609	33,781	35,902	34,994	37,995
Non-profit organisations and private households	3,740	3,651	3,899	3,967	4,196	4,218
Territorial authorities and social insurance	14,429	16,203	16,464	16,997	19,344	18,024
Total	276,443	261,263	267,925	271,400	270,521	263,871

Date: 30 June

Source: Nürnberg Stadt, Amt für Stadtforschung und Statistik 1977, 1980, 1982, 1983.

Unemployment in percentage

1983	:	9.6
March 1984	:	9.8

Source: BAFA 1983, 1984.

7.3   Transportation

Modal split

			1967			
Trips (not including pedestrians)	PT	:	IT	:	Bicycles	
Origin: Nürnberg	39.7	:	49.0	:	11.3	
Origin: Fürth	34.1	:	51.5	:	14.4	

Trips
Origin: CBD[a] (Nürnberg)   47.8 : 46.9 :   5.3

a) Definition of CBD = transport region 1 - definition not clear.

Source: Nürnberg Stadt 1972c, table 6

Public transportation

Verkehrsverbund planned 1985, no S-Bahn system. (Construction of
first S-Bahn line started.)
Opening of the first rapid rail line   :   1972

Network (km., track length) 1984:   Number of routes/services

Rapid rail	:	18	2
Tram	:	43	7
Bus	:	346	41

Source: Nürnberg VAG internal information.

Trips per year for trams and rapid rail (Version 1)

Year	Total trips in 1000	Tram	Rapid rail
1955	161,742	103,802	-
1956	167,826	134,349	-
1957	136,694	111,244	-
1958	129,026	105,246	-
1959	128,921	104,830	-
1960	130,287	104,803 (break in series 61-66)	
1967	113,881	82,644	-
1968	105,458	75,192	-
1969	112,511	79,860	-
1970	116,217	81,339	-
1971	122,433	83,944	-
1972	119,395	82,095	-
1973	124,062	81,423	6,674
1974	138,087	88,860	10,184
1975	144,170	89,315	13,251
1976	144,615	87,410	14,085
1977	137,213	81,257	11,140
1978	148,317	74,763	26,404
1979	154,152	74,050	30,686
1980	164,405	75,118	34,307
1981	169,548	65,261	41,827

After 1956, there is a clear decline in the number of passengers
which continued until 1969. Since 1970 there has been an increase

in the number of trips apart from 1972 and 1977. In 1981 more
trips were made on public transportation than in 1956.

Nürnberg can also show some increase in the number of trips between
1981 and 1982, in contrast to many other public transportation
systems.

Since 1973, there has been a change in the counting of trips; in
fact the statistics has somewhat become more realistic because the
calculation of season ticket holders had been too generous.

Version 1 gives trip figures on the old calculation basis, Version
2 shows the new calculations.

Total trips in 1,000 (Version 2)

Year	Total trips	Rapid rail
1973	120,081	6,646
1974	119,669	8,825
1975	117,169	10,769
1976	117,585	11,452
1977	109,622	8,900
1978	117,206	20,864
1979	121,344	24,156
1980	124,841	26,053
1981	128,445	31,688
1982	129,721	38,062

Source: Nürnberg VAG internal statistics

With the opening of the city centre underground stations in 1978,
the number of trips nearly trebled. The significant increase of
trips in 1981 has been the result of the opening of the underground
line to Fürth.

Car ownership per 1,000 inhabitants

1961	:	158
1970	:	283
1981	:	341
1982	:	346

Source: Nürnberg Stadt, Amt für Stadtforschung und Statistik 1972a, 1983.

7.4   Pedestrianisation in the City Centre

Total length of pedestrianisation : about 5,000 m. (excluding squares)

Date of first inception : 1966
Date of second inception : 1970
Date of third inception : 1972

Pedestrian concept : areal[a)]
Future of pedestrianisation : no further extension planned

Loading provision : front and rear access

Parking provision inside the
medieval city
Private parking spaces : about 5,000
Public parking spaces: : about 5,000
(Street and multi-storey garages)

a) See above under Bremen, pedestrianisation.

Source: Nürnberg Stadt 1979, internal information.

8   GLASGOW

8.1   Basic Data

Population	1971		1981
Population CBD[a)]	6,931		11,300[a)]
Population city[b)]	977,500	(897,500)	755,429
Population density (city)	57.26/ha		38.77/ha
Population regional (Strathclyde)	2,564,550		2,375,410

Area in hectares			
Area CBD	199		181.9
Area city	15,673		19,757
Area region (Strathclyde)	1,353,698		1,353,698

a) Conurbation centre figures for 1981 are from District Council.
b) Figure in brackets is the population figure in 1971, other figures are from the 1981 census.

8.2 Economic Data

Employment	CBD[a]	1971 City	Conurbation
Total employment by workplace	110,970	426,100	740,430
Employment in:			
Industry (excluding construction and mining)	21,450	134,100	283,460
Trade and transportation	42,640	110,520	162,280
Other tertiary activities	43,250	147,960	230,310

a) According to 1971 census - Central Clydeside Conurbation Centre.

Source: Census 1971, Scotland County Report; Census 1971, Workplace and transport tables.

	1981 City	Conurbation
Total employment by workplace	326,310	890,090
Employment in:		
Industry (excluding construction, energy and water)	83,900	250,660
Trade and transportation	99,760	228,680
Other tertiary activities	143,670	309,620

Source: Census 1981, Scotland, Vol.1.

Unemployment in percentage

1971	:	8.3
1981	:	16.6
March 1984	:	16.6

Source: Census 1971 and 1981; Department of Employment pp.532-33.

8.3 Transportation

Modal split

Rush hour (8-9am) to the Central Area:

one way	1976	1981
	(in per cent)	
Car	24	28
SPTE Bus	43)	25
SBG Bus	)	14
Underground	33)	4
Rail	)	29

Source: Glasgow District Council 1982 8.2 and Table 8.1.
Strathclyde Regional Council 1983, p.113.

	1976		
	PT	:	IT
24 hours (one way) to the central area	60	:	40
in the Glasgow District	28	:	72
Rush hour: to the central area	76	:	24
in the Glasgow District	39	:	61

Source: Glasgow District Council 1983, 6.2, Table 1.

Daily shopping trips:	1981	
	(in per cent)	
	Weekdays	Saturdays
Public transport	68	50
Private car[a]	32	50

a) Does not include uncontrolled and illegal parking (Strathclyde
Regional Council 1981, p.113.

Public transportation (Strathclyde PTE)

Opening of the underground system in 1980, closed in 1977 for
modernisation, originally opened in 1896. Electrification of Ayr
and Ardossan line planned.

Network (in km track length) 1984:   Number of routes/services

Light Rapid rail	:	10.45	1
Bus	:	1,713[a]	120[a]
Rail	:	322	-

a) Strathclyde PTE services.

Total trips per year (in million) SPTE

Year[a]	SPTE		Glasgow	in 000s
	Total Trips	Bus	Underground	Strathclyde SBG[b]	Strathclyde BG
1960	1,173.8	510.8	28.0	635.0	-
1961	1,172.2	490.7	27.1	625.0	29.4
1962	1,121.7	479.8	26.9	615.0	-
1963	1,129.5	454.4	26.0	600.0	49.1
1964	1,107.4	434.7	26.1	598.1	48.5
1965	-	384.4	22.9	-	52.6
1966	-	369.6	22.1	-	-
1967	-	353.4	21.3	-	-

1968	-	324.2	19.2	-	57.7
1969	-	307.8	17.7	-	57.6
1970	-	293.3	16.6	-	54.3
1971	641.10	277.2	15.3	293.2	55.4
1972	592.60	255.3	13.9	272.2	51.2
1973	-	230.8	13.2	-	50.9
1974	-	217.6	12.1	-	46.2
1975	-	193.6	9.7	-	51.4
1976	465.0	210.1	7.1	199.9	47.9
1977	437.7	199.5	0.3	193.8	44.1
1978	413.5	179.1	-	190.0	44.4
1979	418.3	185.7	-	189.1	43.5
1980	408.7	167.7	9.8	182.9	48.3
1981	388.8	150.7	10.6	181.1	46.4
1982	364.6	137.1	11.8	175.6	40.1
1983	365.7	133.5	12.4	179.1	40.7

a) 1960/61 Strathclyde PTE, (1984) internal information.
b) SBG = Scottish Bus Group

Finance	1980/81	1981/82
Expenditure (Total direct operating costs)	50.018	52.269
Income (fares)	33.014	35.795
Private hire/contract	232	287
Other revenue	268	224
Total income	33,514	36,306
Concessionary fares	5,263	6,741
Total subsidies	16,504	15,963
Total subsidies in per cent	33	31

Source: Strathclyde PTA and PTE 1982, p.27.

Car ownership per 1,000 inhabitants

		1971	1981
Glasgow	:	95	142
Clydeside	:	130	198
Strathclyde	:	147	184

In 1976 only 17 per cent of households in inner city areas had access to car.

Source: Glasgow District Council 1982, Table 8.2.

8.4 Pedestrianisation in the City Centre

Total length of pedestrianisation : 895 m

Date of first inception : 1972

Pedestrian concept : linear[a]

Future of pedestrianisation : some further pedestrianisation or footpath widening planned for sections of Buchanan St., Trongate, Dixon St., Royal Exchange Square, Gordon St., Sanchiehall St., and Union St.

Loading provision : mainly rear access, except Buchanan Street.

Parking provision in the city
centre (1982) : about 14,000
Total public parking spaces : 9,855
Multi-storey car parks : 4,249
Private parking space : 4,000

According to the Glasgow Parking Study, the total number of parking spaces in the Central Area was in July 1982 about 20,000 including, 7,792 private non-residential parking and 2,399 uncontrolled parking.

a) See above under Bremen, pedestrianisation.

Source: Glasgow District Council 1982, Section 6.30 - 6.31.
   Glasgow District Council 1983, Section 6.41.
   Strathclyde Regional Council 1983, p.111.
   Strathclyde Regional Council 1984.
   Strathclyde Regional Council 1982, pp.3-4.
   Roberts 1981.
   GLC 1972.
   Acton 1979.
   Price 1982.

9 LEEDS

9.1 Basic Data

Population	1971		1981
Population CBD[a]	12,927		-
Population city[b]	738,931	(496,009)	704,885
Population density (city)	30.18/ha		12.5/ha
Population regional[b]	2,067,642		2,037,165
(West Yorkshire)			

Area in hectares

Area CBD[a]	395	-
Area city	16,434	56,215
Area regional[b]	203,912	203,912
(West Yorkshire)		

a) CBD is defined to be the City ward.
b) Population in brackets, actual population figure in 1971 census, regional population according to 1981 census.

9.2 Economic Data

Employment	1971 City	Conurbation
Total employment by workplace	255,700	810,970
Employment in:		
Industry (excluding construction and mining)	94,620	362,360
Trade and transportation	55,580	149,230
Other tertiary activities	87,250	237,460

	1981 City	Conurbation
Total employment by workplace	317,640	856,300
Employment in:		
Industry (excluding construction, energy and water)	87,210	-
Trade and transportation	87,540	-
Other tertiary activities	105,420	-

Source: Census 1971, Economic Activity Leaflet.
Census 1981, Workplace and transport to work.

Unemployment in percentage

```
      1971   :    4.1
      1981   :    9.4
March 1984   :   11.8
```

Source: Census 1971 and 1981, Department of Employment 1984, pp.532-33.

9.3   Transportation

Modal split   see Table 7.3.

Public transporation

Creation of West Yorkshire PTE : 1972

Total trips per year : see Table 7.2.

Finance see Chapter 2.

9.4   Pedestrianisation in the City Centre

Total length of pedestrianisation : 1,677 m (including bus only
                                          streets)
Pedestrian Streets   : 877 m

Date of first inception   : 1970
Date of last inception   : 1972

Pedestrian concept   : linear and areal[a]
Future of pedestrianisation   : extensions planned

Method of finance   : 100% by city
Capital cost of scheme   : £120,000
Essential running costs   : £50,000 annually

Loading provision   : front

Environment:
Noise in dBA before   : 65-75 dBA
Noise in dBA after   : 60-65 dBA

Parking provision in the city
centre (1981)
a) public
   free   :   570
   long stay   :   5,210
   short stay   :   4,410

```
    b) private                              6,920
       total off street parking        :   17,110
       on street parking meters            2,010
       uncontrolled                    :      640
    Total on street parking            :    2,650
    Total parking provision            :   19,760
```

a) See above under Bremen, pedestrianisation.

Source: West Yorkshire County Council 1984, internal information.
        GLC 1972, pp.163-164, own calculations.

10   LIVERPOOL

10.1   Basic Data

	1971		1981
Population			
Population CBD[a]	6,525	(7,321)	-
Population city	599,453		503,722
Population density (city)	54.21/ha		45.17/ha
Population regional[b]	1,642,963		1,503,120
(Merseyside)			

	1971		1981
Area in hectares			
Area CBD[1]	248	(380)	-
Area city	11,254		11,291
Area region (Merseyside)	-		65,202

a) CBD of Liverpool is defined in this study to be the Central ward
   figure for conurbation centre according to 1971 census in
   brackets; population regional and city population according to
   1981 census.

Source: Census 1971 and 1981, County Report,

10.2   Economic Data

		1971	
Employment	CBD[a]	City	Conurbation
Total employment by workplace (by workplace)	91,900	325,200	562,190
Employment in:			
Industry (excluding construction and mining)	13,940	99,420	188,100
Trade and transportation	36,610	95,290	145,110
Other tertiary activities	38,220	110,280	183,230

a) Employment in City Centre according to 1971 census

	CBD	1981 City	Conurbation
Total employment by workplace	-	258,770	599,260
Employment in:			
Industry (excluding construction)	-	55,690	-
Energy and water	-	80,590	-
Other tertiary activities	-	104,400	-

Source: Census 1971, Economic Activity County Leaflet.
Census 1981, Workplace and Transport to work.

Unemployment in percentage

```
    1971   :   8.0
    1981   :  18.2
March 1984 :  19.2
```

Source: Census 1971 and 1981; Department of Employment 1984, pp.532-33.

10.3 Transportation

Modal split see Table 7.3.

Journey to work for those who work in the conurbation centre but
live elsewhere, in per cent (1971 Census).

```
Train  :  16.7      PT   :   IT
Bus    :  47.5     64.2  :  26.8
Car    :  26.8
Other  :   9.0
```

Public transportation (Merseyside PTE)

Opening of the first rapid rail line   : 1977
Creation of Merseyside PTE   : 1969

Network (km., track length) 1982:   Number of routes/services

```
Rapid rail  :         4.2                        2
Buses       :    not known               about 200a)
Rail        :         137                        7
```

Total trips per year: see Table 7.2.

a) Merseyside PTE services.

10.4 Pedestrianisation in the City Centre

Total length of pedestrianisation : 2,000 m (including bus only streets).
Bus only streets   : about 700 m
Pedestrian streets   : 1,300 m

Date of first inception   : 1968
Date of last inception   : 1974

Pedestrianisation concept   : area[a]
Future pedestrianisation   : not known

Loading provision   : some with frontage un-
                                    restricted hours and some with
                                    frontage restricted hours, and
                                    back service access.

Parking provision in the city
centre (1981)   :
off street   : 19,200
on street   : 4,900
total   : 24,100

a) See above under Bremen, pedestrianisation.

Source: Roberts 1981, Liverpool City 1981 and internal information.

11 MANCHESTER

11.1 Basic Data

	1971		1981
Population			
Population CBD[a]	3,740	(2,776)	–
Population city	543,650		437,663
Population density (city)	60.0/ha		46.0/ha
Population regional	2,721,815		2,575,407
(Greater Manchester)			

213

Area in hectares

Area CBD	340 (317)	-
Area city	11,029	11,621
Area region	-	128,674
(Greater Manchester)		

a) CBD of Manchester is defined in this study to be the ward St. Peters, CBD of South East Lancashire Conurbation in brackets.

Source: Census 1971, 1981, County Report.

11.2 Economic Data

Employment	CDB	1971 City	Conurbation
Total employment by workplace	122,870	335,540	1,123,140
Employment in:			
Industry (excluding construction and mining)	24,960	108,580	483,820
Trade and transportation	37,950	83,480	230,700
Other tertiary activities	54,700	122,000	324,980

	1981 City	Conurbation
Total employment by workplace	295,090	1,113,580
Employment in:		
Industry (excluding construction, energy and water)	67,850	-
Trade and transportation	84,850	-
Other tertiary activities	119,850	-

Source: Census 1971, Economic Activity Leaflet.
Census 1981, Workplace and transport to work.

Unemployment in percentage

1971	:	6.0
1981	:	14.9
March 1984	:	13.5

Source: Census 1971 and 1981; Department of Employment 1984, pp.532-33.

214

11.3 Transportation

Modal split see Table 7.3.

To the city centre (1976) more than 50 per cent of work trips and
more than 60 per cent of shopping trips are made by bus.

1978 less than 30 per cent of households in the inner area had no
access to a car.

	PT	:	IT
Work trips	50	:	50
Shopping trips	60	:	40

Source: Manchester City 1980, p.67.

Public transportation (Greater Manchester PTE)

No light rail system; plans for a surface light rail system in the
city centre, basically from Piccadilly to Victoria Station - see
Chapter 4.

Creation of Greater Manchester PTE : 1969

Network (km., track length) 1984:   Number of routes/services

Bus	:	2,364	about 700[a]
Rail	:	263	16

a) Greater Manchester PTE services.

Source: Greater Manchester PTE, internal information.

Total trips per year see Table 7.2.

Finance

| | 1979/1980 | | 1980/1981 | |
	Total	Rail	Total	Rail
Total revenue:	84,172	9,832	93,689	11,322
Total grants:[a]	33,680	9,980	42,846	12,711
	117,852	19,812	136,535	24,033

a) Including bus and rail support, concessionary travel, total
   revenue grant and capital grants (53 per cent).

About 46 per cent of fares were subsidised in 1980/81 of which rail
is subsidised over 50 per cent.

Source: GMC, GMPTE 1980, 1981.

Car ownership per 1,000 inhabitants

		1971	1981
Manchester	:	130	180
Greater Manchester	:	170	250

Source: Greater Manchester County Council 1982.

11.4 Pedestrianisation in the City Centre

Total length of pedestrianisation	:	2,150 m (including bus only streets).
Pedestrian streets	:	1,200 m (Market Street, St. Ann's Square and King Street).
Bus only streets	:	950 m (Oldham Street, part of Mosley Street, Piccadilly and Market Street).
Date of first inception	:	1976 (King Street)
Date of second inception	:	1983 (Market Street)
Date of third inception	:	1983 (St. Ann's Square)
Pedestrian concept	:	linear and areal[a]
Future of pedestrianisation	:	more pedestrianisation planned mainly in the form of widening the existing footpaths.
Loading provision	:	partly frontage restricted hours, and partly rear access.
Parking in the city centre	:	short stay : 6,869
	:	long stay : 9,430
		total : 16,299

Source: Manchester 1980, Roberts 1981, interviews.

12 NEWCASTLE UPON TYNE

12.1 Basic Data

Population	1971		1981
Population CBD[a]	7,921	(2,774)	-
Population city[b]	300,729		272,914
Population density (city)	49.5/ha		24.83/ha
Population regional[b] (Tyne and Wear)	1,209,959		1,135,492

Area in hectares

Area CBD[a]	285 (399)	-
Area city	4,489	11,187
Area region[b] (Tyne & Wear)	54,006	54,006

a) CBD of Newcastle is defined in this study to be the ward of St Niclas and half of Westgate in 1971, figure for conurbation centre according to 1971 census in brackets.
b) Population of city and region according to the 1981 census.

Source: Census 1971, and 1981, County Report,

12.2 Economic Data

Employment	CBD[a]	1971 City	Conurbation
Total employment by workplace	66,840	152,710	378,720
Employment in:			
Industry (excluding construction and mining)	9,490	42,770	138,790
Trade and transportation	23,050	36,750	75,800
Other tertiary activities	30,820	61,910	127,390

a) Employment in city centre according to 1971 census.

	1981 City	Conurbation
Total employment by workplace	168,750	482,520
Employment in:		
Industry (excluding construction energy and water)	33,010	-
Trade and transportation	43,020	-
Other tertiary activities	76,250	-

Unemployment in percentage

1971	:	6.4
1981	:	12.7
March 1984	:	17.2 (Tyne and Wear)

Source: Census 1971 and 1981;, Department of Employment 1984 pp.532-33. Gazette - no figures available for Newcastle in 1984.

12.3 Transportation

Modal split

	Inner Tyneside PT	:	IT	:	Walk Cycle/others	Tyne & Wear PT	:	IT	:	Walk Cycle/others
1966	54	:	23	:	23	53	:	23	:	25
1971	48	:	29	:	23	45	:	30	:	25
1975	48	:	-	:	-	34	:	43	:	23

Source: Tyne & Wear County Council 1979b, p.170.

Public transportation (Tyne and Wear PTE)

Opening of the first light rail line in 1980, last stretch of Metro opened in 1984.

Creation of the Tyneside PTE : 1969

Network (km., track length) 1983:   Number of routes/services

Light rail	:	56
Bus	:	555
Rail	:	13[a)

(Number of routes/services)
- Light rail: 4
- Bus: -
- Rail: 1

a) Including line to Wylam.

Total trips per year: see Table 7.2.

Finance

Finance account 1980/81

Total expenditure	:	77,733 million
Total income	:	53,003 million (including concessionary travel contribution)
Subsidies	:	24,730 million
Subsidies in per cent	:	31.8 (without concessionary travel contribution)
Operating expenses	:	74,754
Traffic revenue	:	39,146
Total subsidies	:	35,608

Source: Tyne and Wear County Council, Tyne and Wear PTE 1981.

218

Car ownership per 1,000 inhabitants

```
                    1971    1981
Newcastle     :      -       -
Tyne & Wear   :     134     194
```

Source: Tyne and Wear County Council 1982.

12.4 Pedestrianisation in the City Centre

Total length of pedestrianisation : about 1,300 m. (bus only streets)

Pedestrianised streets : none

Date of inception : 1971 (most schemes)
Date of second inception : 1975 (Clayton Street)

Pedestrian concept : linear[a]
The main pedestrian Street is Northumberland St; between 11.30 - 15.30 only buses are allowed to enter.
Clayton Street and Blackett Street have no restricted period.

Future of pedestrianisation : more pedestrianisation planned.
Future plans are to pedestrianise lower Northumberland Street, and extend round the area of the Grey Monument, in order to provide a link between Northumberland Street and Grainger Street.

Service access : front and rear access.

Car parking provision in the city centre : 12,860

a) See above under Bremen, pedestrianisation.

Source: Tyne and Wear County Council, 1982, p.155.
        Newcastle upon Tyne, 1983, interview.

13   SHEFFIELD

13.1   Basic Data

Population	1971	1981
Population CBD[a]	16,643	-
Population city[a]	520,327	530,843
Population density (city)	28.35/ha	14.44/ha
Population regional[a] (South Yorkshire)	1,313,957	1,292,029

Area in hectares		
Area CBD[a]	277,3	-
Area city	18,353	36,756
Area regional[a] (South Yorkshire)	156,049	156,049

a) CBD of Sheffield is defined in this study to be half of the
wards; Netherthopse, Sharrow and Castle in 1971, population in
city and region according to 1981 census.

Source: Census 1971, 1981 County Reports.

13.2   Economic Data

Employment	1971	1981
Total employment by workplace	266,300	253,860
Employment in:		
Industry (excluding construction and mining)	123,460	90,040[a]
Trade and transportation	48,040	61,860
Other tertiary activities	74,080	81,520

a) 1981 excludes construction, energy and water.

Source: Census 1971, Economic Activity Leaflet, Census 1981, Workplace
and transport to work.

Unemployment in percentage

1971	:	3.5
1981	:	10.0
March 1984	:	13.8

Source: Census 1971 and 1981, Department of Employment 1984, pp.523-33.

13.3 Transportation

Modal split

Person in employment by normal mode of travel to work

Sheffield	Central area destination		all destinations	
	1971	1977/78	1971	1977/78
Car, van or motor:	30	34	30	43
Bus:	61	58	41	34
Others:	9	8	29	23

Source: Goodwin Bailey et al. 1983, p.114.

Public transportation (South Yorkshire PTE)

No light rail system, plans for a surface light rail system.
Creation of the South Yorkshire PTE: 1972.

Network (km, track length) 1983:	Number of routes/services
Bus : 1,225 (total operating service of South Yorkshire buses)	-
Rail : about 90	4

Source: South Yorkshire Transport 1983b, p.16.

Total trips per year (in millions) South Yorkshire PTE

1975	1976	1977	1978	1979	1980	1981	1982
242	249	249	249	251	261	259	261

Source: South Yorkshire County Council, South Yorkshire PTE, annual
reports

Finance

	1980/81	1981/82	1982/83
Expenditure	50.793	62.514	69.619
Income (fares)	14.944	15.013	15.111
Other (advertising etc)	181	195	206
Total income	15.125	15.208	15.317
Concessionary fares	13.931	17.359	18.921
Support for fares & service level	21.737	29.731	35.133
Subsidies from other local authorities		216	248
Total subsidies	35.668	47.306	54.302

Total subsidies in
per cent   70.2   75.7   78

Source: South Yorkshire County Council, South Yorkshire PTE 1981, 1982,
1983.

Car ownership per 1,000 inhabitants

                          1971   1981
Sheffield   :   160   230
South Yorkshire :   -   -

Source: Goodwin Bailey et al. 1983, p.58.

13.4 Pedestrianisation in the City Centre

Total length of pedestrianisation : 1,700 m. (bus only streets)
Pedestrian streets   : 955 m.

Date of first inception   : 1971
Date of second inception   : 1979 (The Moor)

Pedestrian concept   : linear[a]
Future of pedestrianisation   : no further pedestrianisation
                                     planned, (widening of side-
                                     walks on some streets in the
                                     city centre).

Loading provision   : rear servicing possible for
                                     most streets but also front
                                     servicing (restricted and un-
                                     restricted hours for two
                                     streets).

Pedestrian flows/per day:
Some streets in the central area : less than 100, in others more
                                     than 50,000
Over 15,000 per week day are
counted in   : The Moor - pedestrian street
                                     Pinstone Street - traffic -
                                     even through traffic
                                     Leopold Street - traffic -
                                     even through traffic
                                     Fargate - pedestrian street
                                     Surrey Street - traffic

```
Parking provision in the city
centre                           :  19,000 car parking spaces in
                                    the central area
Short stay parking               :  2,000
Long stay parking                :  17,000
```

a) See above under Bremen, pedestrianisation.

Source: Sheffield District 1983, p.9

References

Acton, P. (1979), Strathclyde Strategy for Transport Transformation: Glasgow's "Clockwork Orange", **The Surveyor**, March, pp 15-21.

Anon (1983), Table of existing and planned Rapid Transit Systems and Light Rail Systems in the Federal Republic of Germany including Berlin (West), **V & T**, 36, p.68.

Anon (1984a), Stadtbahn-Zeitalter begann im Mai 1983. **Dortmunder Bürgerbrief**, 1, March.

Anon (1984b), Stadtbahn zwingt zu neuem Umsteigen. **Dortmunder Zeitung**, 57, 7 March.

Anon (1984c), Bringing back the High Technology Trolley, **Town and Country Planning**, 53, pp. 179-180.

Apel D.K. (1984), **Umverteilung des städtischen Personenverkehrs**, Stadtverkehrsplanung, Teil 3, Difu, Berlin.

ASF (Arbeitsgemeinschaft Stadtverkehrsforschung) (1982) **Schnellbahn und Siedlungsstruktur** - Fallstudie München - Forschungsauftrag des Bundesministers für Raumordnung, Bauwesen und Städtebau (not published) München.

BAFA (Bundesanstalt für Arbeit) (1983), **Amtliche Nachrichten der BAFA, Arbeitsstatistik**, 1983 Jahresheft, Nürnberg.

BAFA (Bundesanstalt für Arbeit) (1984), **Amtliche Nachrichten de BAFA**, Heft 5, 1984, Nürnberg.

BAG (Bundesarbeitsgemeinschaft der Mittel- und Grossbetriebe) (1981), **Untersuchung Kundenverkehr Oktober 1980** (not published), Köln.

Balchin, J. (1980), **First New Town: An Autobiography of the Stevenage Development Corporation 1946-80**, Stevenage Development Corporation, Stevenage.

Bayerisches Statistisches Landesamt (1971), **Arbeitsstättenzählung**, 1970, München.

Bayerisches Statistisches Landesamt (1974), 1978, 1979, 1980, 1981, 1982, 1983), **Ergebnisse der Beschäftigtenstatistik der BAFA**, München.

Bollhöfer, D. (1983), Zum Beispiel Stadtbahn Köln - der Erfolg einer Idee, **V + T**, 36, pp. 8-10.

Bennison, D. J., Davies, R. L. (1980), The Impact of Town Centre Shopping Schemes in Britain, **Progress in Planning**, 14, Part I, pp. 1-104.

BMBau (Bundesminister für Raumordnung, Bauwesen und Städtebau) (ed.) (1969, 1971, 1973, 1975, 1979, 1983), **Raumordnungsbericht 1968, 1970 (etc)**, BMBau, Bonn-Bad Godesberg.

BMBau (Bundesminister für Raumordnung, Bauwesen und Städtebau) (1978a), **Schnellbahn und Siedlungsstruktur** (by Bremer, H., Eckstein, W. et al), BMBau, Bonn-Bad Godesberg.

BMBau (Bundesminister für Raumordnung, Bauwesen und Städtebau) (1978b) **Siedlungsstrukturelle Folgen der Einrichtung von verkehrsberuhigten Zonen** (by H. Monheim), BMBau, Bonn-Bad Godesberg.

BOStrab (1983), **Begründung zur Verordnung über den Bau und Betrieb der Strassenbahnen** (5.4.1983), Entwurf, Bonn-Bad Godesberg.

Braitsch, H. (1983), Im Stadtbahnnetz Köln besteht zu 59% Kreuzungsfreiheit oder absoluter Vorrang der Bahn, **V + T**, 36, pp.31-34.

Bremen, Handelskammer (1982), **Konzept Innenstadt**, Bremen.

Bremen Land, Statistisches Landesamt (1972), **AZ 1970**, Bremen.

Bremen Land, Statistisches Landesamt (1981, 1982), **Statistische Berichte 1981, 1982: Die Ortsteile in Bremen**, Bremen.

Bremen Land, Statistisches Landesamt (1981), **Statistisches Handbuch 1975-1980**, Bremen.

Bremen Stadt, Der Senator für das Bauwesen, Senatsvorlage (1982), **Konzept für den ruhenden Verkehr in der engeren Innenstadt**, Bremen, 20.1.1982, Internal paper (not published), Bremen.

Bremen Stadt, Der Senator für das Bauwesen (1984), **ÖPNV-Konzept**, (not published), Bremen.

Bremen Strassenbahn AG (1959, 1983) **Internal Statistics**, (not published), Bremen.

Bremische Bürgerschaft (1975), **Orientierungsrahmen für die Verkehrsplanung 1975-1985**, Drucksache 8/952S, Bremen.

Buchanan, C. D. (1958), **Mixed Blessing: The Motor in Britain**, Leonard Hill, London.

Bundesminister für Verkehr, (1982), **Kriterien der Bahnarten des öffentlichen Personennahverkehrs**, (not published), Bonn.

Cashmore, J. F. (1981), **Towards an Evaluation Method for Pedestrianisation Schemes**, Final Year Dissertion, Diploma in Town and Regional Planning, Leeds Polytechnic (not published), Leeds.

Census 1931, England and Wales, **County Report**, HMSO, London.

Census 1971, England and Wales, **County Report**, HMSO, London.

Census 1971, England and Wales, **Economic Activity County Leaflets**, HMSO, London.

Census 1971, England and Wales, **Workplace Tables**, HMSO, London.

Census 1981, England and Wales, **County Report**, HMSO, London.

Census 1981, England and Wales, **Workplace and Transport to Work**, HMSO, London.

Census 1931, Scotland, **Vol. II**, HMSO, Edinburgh.

Census 1951, Scotland, **Vol. I**, HMSO, Edinburgh.

Census 1971, Scotland, **County Report**, HMSO, Edinburgh.

Census 1971, Scotland, **Workplace Tables**, HMSO, Edinburgh.

Census 1981, Scotland, **Report for Strathclyde Region**, **Vol. I**, HMSO, Edinburgh.

Census 1981, Scotland, **Workplace and Transport Tables**, HMSO, Edinburgh.

Cherry, G. E. (1972), **Urban Change and Planning: A History of Urban Development in Britain since 1750**, Foulis, Henley on Thames.

Crampton, G. R. (1982), **The Subsidisation of Public Passenger Transportation in Greater London and the English Metropolitan Counties**, University of Reading, Department of Economics, Discussion Paper in Urban and Regional Economics, Series C, 15, Reading.

Davies, R. L. (ed.) (1979), **Retail Planning in the European Community**, Saxon House, Farnborough.

Davies, R. L. (1984), **Retail and Commercial Planning**, Croom Helm, London.

Debenham Tewson & Chinnocks (1982), **Office Rents and Rates 1973-1982**, London.

Debenham Tewson & Chinnocks (1983), **Shop Rents and Rates 1978-1983**, London.

Department of Employment (1984), **Employment Gazette**, 92, pp.532-533.

D.M.f.W.M.u.V.d.L.N.-W. (Der Minister für Wirtschaft, Mittelstand und Verkehr des Landes Nordrhein-Westfalen), (ed.) (1970), **Auswertungsbericht der Sachverständigen Kommission zum Generalverkehrsplan Nordrhein-Westfalen**, Düsseldorf.

D.M.f.W.M.u.V.d.L.N.-W. (Der Minister für Wirtschaft, Mittelstand und Verkehr des Landes Nordrhein-Westfalen) (ed.) (1976/77), **Stadtbahn an Rhein und Ruhr**, Köln.

Difu (Deutsches Institut für Urbanistik), Deutscher Städtetag (1980), **Kommunaler Investitionsbedarf bis 1990, Grundlagen-Probleme-Perspektiven**, Difu, Berlin-Köln.

Dorsch Consult (1977), **Untersuchungen zur Generalverkehrsplanung der Stadt Bremen**, Wiesbaden, Hamburg.

Dortmund Stadt (1975, 1977), **Generalverkehrsplan**, Part A (1975), Erhebungen; Part B (1977): **Verhaltensweisen und Entwicklungstendenzen**, Aachen.

Dortmund Stadt, Amt für Statistik und Wahlen (1978), **Dortmunder Statistik**, Heft 82/1, Dortmund.

Dortmund Stadt, Amt für Statistik und Wahlen (1982), **Dortmunder Statistik**, Sonderheft 76, Dortmund.

Dortmund Stadt, Amt für Statistik und Wahlen (1983), **Dortmunder Statistik**, Sonderheft 96, Dortmund.

Dübbel, R. (1983), 20 Jahre Kölner U-Bahn- und Stadtbahnbau, in **V + T**, 36, pp. 4 and 6.

Dyett, M., Dornbusch, D., et al (1979) **Land Use and Urban Development Impacts of Bart**: Final Report, National Technical Information Service, Springfield, Virginia.

Essen Stadt, Amt für Entwicklungsplanung (1980), **Die Essener Innenstadt, Analyse, Kritik, Probleme, Ziele, Ideen**, Essen.

Essen Stadt, Amt für Statistik und Wahlen (1972), **Ergebnisse der AZ 1970**, Heft 2, Essen.

Essen Stadt, Amt für Statistik und Wahlen (1980), **Handbuch der Essener Statistik 1975-1979**, Essen.

Essen Stadt, Amt für Statistik und Wahlen (1981), **Bevölkerungsentwicklung**, Sonderheft 2, Heft 2, Essen.

Essen Stadt, Amt für Statistik und Wahlen (1983), **Statistische Vierteljahresberichte 1983/1**, Essen.

Essen Stadt, IVV Aachen (1979), **Zukünftige Verkehrsnachfrage im Stadtgebiet**, Essen.

Essen Stadt, Stadtplanungsamt (1971), **Fussgängerstrassen in Essen**, Essen.

Essener Verkehrs AG, Stadtbahngesellschaft Rhein-Ruhr mbH (1977), **Betriebskonzept Essen für den Stadtbahnbetrieb B**, Essen.

Essener Verkehrs AG (1982), **Bericht über das Geschäftsjahr 1982**, Essen.

Farenholtz, C., Jürgensen, H., Strauf, H-G. et al (1977), **Stadt und Verkehr: Zur künftigen Entwicklung von Siedlungs- und Verkehrsstrukturen**, Schriftenreihe des Verbandes der Automobilindustrien e.v., 24, Frankfurt.

FfH (Forschungsstelle für den Handel) (1978), **Die Bedeutung der Fussgängerzonen für den Strukturwandel im Einzelhandel**, FfH, Berlin.

First, W.C. (1962), **Chaos oder Ordnung auf unseren Strassen**, Deutscher Städtetag, Köln.

Forschungsinstitut der Friedrich-Ebert-Stiftung (1981), Entwicklung des ÖPNV in Kooperationen unter besonderer Berücksichtigung der Fahrplan- und Tarifgestaltung sowie der Einnahmen und Kostenentwicklung. Teil III, Intensivuntersuchung Hannover, in: Grossraumverkehr Hannover (ed.) **Schriftenreihe zum Verbundverkehr Hannover**, Heft 1, Bonn, Hannover.

Galley, K. A. (1973), Newcastle upon Tyne, in: Holliday, J., **City Centre Redevelopment**, Charles Knight, London.

Geist, J. F. (1983), **Arcades: The History of a Building Type**, Harvard U.P., Cambridge, Mass. and London.

GfK (Gesellschaft für Konsumforschung) (1983), **Begutachtung der Entwicklungsmöglichkeiten des Einzelhandels in der Nürnberger Südstadt,** Stadt Nürnberg (ed.), Amt für Wirtschaft und Verkehr, Nürnberg.

GGPTE (Greater Glasgow Passenger Transport Executive) (1980), **Trans-Clyde: Strathclyde Region's Passenger Transport System,** Glasgow.

Girnau, G. (1983), Wo kann gespart werden im U- und Stadtbahnbau?, **Der Nahverkehr,** 1/83, pp. 8-16.

Glasgow District Council (1982), **Glasgow Central Area Local Plan,** Survey and Issues Report (Draft), Glasgow.

Glasgow District Council (1984), **Glasgow Central Area Local Plan, Written Statement** (Draft), Glasgow.

GLC (Greater London Council) (1972), **Study Tour of European and American Pedestrianised Streets,** London.

GMC (Greater Manchester Council), GMPTE (Greater Manchester Passenger Transport Executive), (1980, 1981), **Annual Report and Accounts 1979/1980, 1980/1981,** Manchester.

GMC (Greater Manchester Council) (1975), **The Picc-Vic Project,** Manchester.

GMC (Greater Manchester Council) (1982), **Census Digest,** Manchester.

Goodwin, P. B., Bailey, J. M., et al (1983), **Subsidised Public Transport and the Demand for Travel: The South Yorkshire Example,** Gower, Aldershot.

Grabe, W. (1967), **Öffentlicher Nahverkehr Bremen,** Teil 1: Textband, Hannover.

Gregory, T. (1973), Coventry, in: Holliday, J. C. (ed.), **City Centre Redevelopment: A Study of British City Centre Planning and Case Studies of five English City Centres,** pp.78-134, Charles Knight, London.

Grossraum Hannover (1977), **Strukturdaten,** Statistik und EDV, Nr. 9, Hannover.

Grossraum Hannover (1978), **Arbeitsstättenerhebung Grossraum Hannover 1976,** Hannover.

Grossraumverkehr Hannover (1981), **Grossraumverkehr Hannover 1970-1980,** Hannover.

Guhl, D. (1975), **Schnellverkehr in Ballungsräumen,** Alba, Düsseldorf.

Hall, P., Hay, D. (1980), **Growth Centres in the European Urban System**, Heinemann, London.

Hannover Landeshauptstadt (1980), **Verkehr in Hannover**, Hannover.

Hannover Landeshauptstadt (1982), **Statistische Vierteljahresberichte Hannover**, 81 JGG, 1982.

Hannover Landeshauptstadt, Referat für Stadtentwicklung (1973), **Stadtentwicklungsprogramm 1974-1985**, Diskussionsentwurf, Hannover.

Hass-Klau, C. (1982) 'New Transport Technologies in the Federal Republic of Germany, **Built Environment**, Vol. 8, No.3 pp.190-197.

Heinz, W., Hübner, H., Meinecke, B., Pfotenhauer, E. (1977), Sozioökonomische Aspekte der Einrichtung von Fussgängerbereichen, in: Peters, P. (ed.) **Fussgängerstadt**, pp. 130-145, Callwey, München.

Hermanns, H. (1972), Fussgängerbereiche in Kölner Einkaufsstrassen, **MIHK, Mitteilungen der Industrie- und Handelskammer zu Köln**, p.7.

Hollatz, J. W., Tamms, F. (eds.) (1965), **Die kommunalen Verkehrsprobleme in der Bundesrepublik Deutschland**, Vulkan, Essen.

Howard, D. F. (1980), **Integrated Public Transport in Tyne and Wear**, paper presented at Mass Transport in Asia conference, Hong Kong.

Ingeniergruppe Aachen (1975), **Zukünftige Verkehrsnachfrage im Stadtgebiet Essen**, Essen.

Jones, A. E. (1984), **Roads and Rails of West Yorkshire 1890-1950**, Ian Allan, London.

Joyce, J. (1962), **Tramway Twilight: The Story of British Tramways from 1945-1962**, Ian Allan, London.

Joyce, J. (1965), **Tramways of the World**, Ian Allan, London.

Joyce, J. (1982), **Roads and Rails of Manchester, 1900-1950**, Ian Allan, London.

Kalwitzki, K. P. (1981), **Stadtplanung und öffentlicher Nahverkehr**, Fernuniversität Gesamthochschule Hagen, Hagen.

Kreibich, V. (1978), Die Münchener S-Bahn als Instrument der Wachstumsentwicklung, in: Ruppert, E. (ed.) **Dortmunder Beiträge zur Raumplanung, 4, Raumplanung und Verkehr**, pp. 293-311, Universität Dortmund, Dortmund.

Köln Stadt (1982), **Entwicklungsprogramm Innenstadt**, Köln.

Köln Stadt, Der Oberstadtdirektor, Amt für Brücken - und U-Bahnbau in Verbindung mit der Kölner Verkehrs - Betriebs AG und dem Nachrichtenamt (ed.) (1980), **Kölner Informationen, Rheinbrücken im Kölner Stadtbahnnetz**, Köln.

Köln Stadt, Der Oberstadtdirektor, Amt Für Statistik und Einwohnerwesen, Presse und Informationsamt (1982), **Zahlen, Daten, Fakten**.

Köln Stadt, Kölner Verkehrsbetriebe (1983), **U-Bahn Deutz, 20 Jahre Stadtbahnbau in Köln**, Köln.

Köln Stadt, Stadtplanungsamt (1979), **Fussgängerzone Hohe Strasse, Schildergasse** (not published).

Köln Stadt, Statistisches Amt (1976), **Arbeitsstättenzählung** 1970, Köln.

Kölner Verkehrsbetriebe AG Köln-Bonner Eisenbahn AG, (1980), **Verkehrszählung 1979**, Köln.

KVB and KBE (1980), see Kölner Verkehrsbetriebe .....

LDSNW (Landesamt für Datenverarbeitung und Statistik in Nordrhein-Westfalen) (1976), **Sonderreihe Volkszählung 1970**, Heft 1, Düsseldorf.

LDSNW (Landesamt für Datenverarbeitung und Statistik in Nordrhein-Westfalen) (1972), **Volkszählung 1970**, Heft 16, Düsseldorf.

LDSNW (Landesamt für Datenverarbeitung und Statistik in Nordrhein-Westfalen) (1983), **Statistisches Jahrbuch 1982 des LDSNW**, Düsseldorf.

Leatherbarrow, J. (1984), Still Waiting for the Tube, **Town and Country Planning**, 53, pp. 278-281.

Linder, W., Maurer, U., Resch, H. (1975), **Erzungene Mobilität: Alternativen zur Raumordnung, Stadtentwicklung und Verkehrspolitik**, Europäische Verlagsanstalt, Köln.

Liverpool City (1981), **Liverpool City Centre Transportation Plan, Review of Parking Policy in Liverpool**, Liverpool.

Lloyd, D. (1965), **Save the City: A Conservation Study of the City of London**, Society for the Protection of Ancient Buildings, London.

MacDonald, K. (1979), Streetscape: Case Study Norwich, **Planning**, 329, pp. 11-13.

Manchester City, Planning Officer (1980), Report of Survey/Issues and Choices, Draft Consultation Document, **Manchester City Centre Local Planning**, Manchester.

Manchester City (1980), **City Centre Local Plan**, Manchester.

Martin & Voorhees Associates, Scottish Development Department, TRRL (Transport and Road Research Laboratory) (1982), **The Glasgow Rail Impact Study** (GRIS), Edinburgh.

McKay, D. H., Cox, A. W. (1979), **The Politics of Urban Change**, Croom Helm, London.

Mckay, J. P. (1976), **Tramways and Trolleys: The Rise of Urban Mass Transport in Europe**, Princeton University Press, Princeton.

McKean, C. (1974), Sheffield Minitram, **Architects Journal**, 23 October, pp.952-971.

Menke, R. (1982), Forderungen des ZGH zum Ausbau des Nahschnellverkehrs des DB, in: Grossraumverkehr Hannover, (ed.) **Informationen '82** p.5, Hannover.

Meyer, L. (1973), Neue Stadtbahnstrecke in Bremen, **V + T**, 12, pp. 551-552.

Meyer, W. (1983), Wirtschaftliche Nutzung staatlicher Investitionszuschüsse im Kölner Mischsystem, **V + T**, 36, pp. 11-15.

Milton Keynes Development Corporation (1970), **The Plan for Milton Keynes**, MKDC, Wavendon.

Minister of Transport (1963), **Traffic in Towns: A Study of the Long Term Problems of Traffic in Urban Areas**, HMSO, London.

Ministry of War Transport (1946), **The Design and Layout of Roads in Built-up Areas**, HMSO, London.

Monheim, R. (1975), **Fussgängerbereiche**, Reihe E, DST-Beiträge zur Stadtentwicklung, Heft 4, Köln.

Monheim, H. (1977), Siedlungsstrukturelle Folgen der Einrichtung verkehrsberuhiger Zonen in Kernbereichen, in: Peters, P. (ed.), **Fussgängerstadt**, pp. 125-130, Callway, München.

Monheim, R. (1980), **Fussgängerbereiche und Fussgängerverkehr in Stadtzentren**, Bonner Geographische Abhandlungen, Bonn.

Monheim, H. (1984) Die städtebauliche Einbindung des öffentlichen Personennahverkehrs, 17-19.9.84, Konferenz: Verkehrsberuhigung (not published), Mainz.

MPTE (Merseyside Passenger Transport Executive) British Rail (1978), **The Story of Merseyrail**, Liverpool.

MPTE (Merseyside Passenger Transport Executive) (1983), **Corporate Action Plan**, Liverpool.

Mumford, L. (1961), **The City in History**, Secker and Warburg, London.

München Landeshauptstadt (1978), **Arbeitsstättenerhebung 1977**, München.

München Landeshauptstadt, Amt für Statistik und Datenanalyse (1972, 1976), **Statistisches Handbuch 1971, Statistisches Handbuch 1975**, München.

München Landeshauptstadt, Referat für Stadtforschung und Stadtentwicklung (1976), **Stadtentwicklungsplan 1975**, München.

München Landeshauptstadt (1980) **Fussgängerzonen in der Münchner Altstadt**, Planungsreferat, München, (not published).

München Landeshauptstadt, Referat für Stadtplanung und Bauordnung (1984a), **Stadtentwicklungsplan 1983**, München.

München Landeshauptstadt, Referat für Stadtplanung und Bauordnung (1984b), **Materialien zum Stadtentwicklungsplan 1983**, München.

München Landeshauptstadt, Statistisches Amt (1984a), **Münchener Statistik 1983**, Heft 12, München.

München Landeshauptstadt, Statistisches Amt (1984b), **Statistisches Jahrbuch München 1983**, München.

MVV (Münchener Verkehrs- und Tarifverbund) (1981), **Report 1980**, München.

MVV (Münchener Verkehrs- und Tarifverbund) (1982a, 1984), **Report 1981, 1983**, München.

MVV (Münchener Verkehrs- und Tarifverbund) (1982b), **The Integration of the various Transport Systems in the Munich Area: A Report after Ten Years' Experience**, München.

MVV (Münchener Verkehrs- und Tarifverbund) (1983), **Verbund-Fahrplan, Sommer 1983**, München.

Myatt, P. R. (1975), **Carnaby Street Study** (Greater London Council, Research Memorandum, RM 466), Greater London Council, London.

Newcastle upon Tyne, City (1983), **Newcastle City Centre Local Plan**, Newcastle upon Tyne.

Nicholas, R. (1945), **City of Manchester Plan**, Jarrolds, Norwich.

Niedersächsisches Landesverwaltungsamt, Abteilung Statistik (1982, 1983), **Statistische Berichte Niedersachsen, Bevölkerung der Gemeinden am 31. Dez. 1981, 1982**, Hannover.

Nordrhein-Westfalen Land (1962), **Beiträge zur Statistik, Der Einzelhandel in Nordrhein-Westfalen, Ergebnisse der Handels- und Gaststättenzählung 1960**, Heft 155, Düsseldorf.

Nordrhein-Westfalen Land (1970), **Beiträge zur Statistik, Der Einzelhandel in Nordrhein-Westfalen, Ergebnisse der Handels- und Gaststättenzählung am 30.9.68**, Heft 286, Düsseldorf.

Nürnberg Stadt (1979), **Fussgängerzonen in Nürnberg**, Nürnberg.

Nürnberg Stadt (1980), **U-Bahn Nürnberg, 7**, Nürnberg.

Nürnberg Stadt (1982), **U-Bahn Nürnberg-Fürth, 8**, Nürnberg.

Nürnberg Stadt, Amt für Stadtforschung und Statistik (ed.) (1972a, etc), **Statistische Jahrbücher der Stadt Nürnberg 1972, 1977, 1982, 1983**, Nürnberg.

Nürnberg Stadt, Amt für Stadtforschung und Statistik (ed.) (1972b), **Arbeitsstätten und Arbeitsplätze 1970, Sonderheft der Statistischen Nachrichten der Stadt Nürnberg**, Nürnberg.

Nürnberg Stadt, Arbeitsgruppe Nürnberg-Plan (ed.) (1972d), Reihe G: Verkehr, Versorgung, Wirtschaftsförderung Heft 1, **Generalverkehrsplan der Städte Nürnberg und Fürth, Teil Nürnberg, Öffentlicher Personennahverkehr**, Nürnberg.

Nürnberg Stadt, Städtische Werke GmbH, VAG (Verkehrsaktiengesellschaft) (1983), **Geschäftsbericht 1983**, Nürnberg.

Osborn, F. J., Whittick, A. (1963), **The New Towns: The Answer to Megalopolis**, Leonard Hill, London.

Ove Arup Partnership (1973), **Commercial Road Precinct, Portsmouth: Monitoring Study**, Ove Arup, London.

Pällmann, W. (1982), Zukunftssicherung des öffentlichen Personennahverkehrs durch Investionen, **Hochschullehrerforum des VÖV**, 7-8 May, Soltan.

Parker, J., Hoile, C. (1975), Central London's Pedestrian Streets and Ways, in: **Greater London Intelligence Quarterly,** 33, December 1975, pp.16-27.

Perrett, K. E. (1982), **Results from the Tyne and Wear Public Transport Impact Study,** Symposium 17.11.82, Crowthorne.

Price, J. H. (1982), Glasgow's New Underground, **Modern Tramway,** 45, 2-9, pp. 53-59.

RDM (Ring Deutscher Makler), **Preisspiegel** 1972-1983, Frankfurt.

Reschke, O. (1979), Fussgängerzone in Essen, in: Stadt Dortmund, (ed.) Stadtplanung, **Forum Nr. 4, Verkehrsberuhigung,** Dortmund.

Roberts, J. (1981), **Pedestrian Precincts in Britain,** Transport and Environmental Studies, London.

Scheelhaase, K. (1980), The Status of German Light-Rail Systems, **Journal of Advanced Transportation,** 14, pp. 197-212.

Schreck, K., Meyer, H., Strumpf., R. (1979), **S-Bahnen in Deutschland: Planung, Bau, Betrieb,** Alba, Düsseldorf.

Schwarz, R. (1950), Das Neue Köln - Ein Vorentwurf, in: Stadt Köln (ed.), **Das Neue Köln,** pp. 1-64, Köln.

Schwartz, G. G. (1981), **Advanced Industrialization and the Inner Cities,** Lexington Books, Lexington.

SELNEC (South East Lancashire and North East Cheshire Passenger Transport Authority) (1973), **Public Transport Plan for the Future,** Manchester.

Sharp, T. (1932), **Town and Countryside: Some Aspects of Urban and Rural Development,** Oxford University Press, London.

Sharp, T. (1940), **Town Planning,** Penguin, Harmondsworth.

Sharp, T. (1946), **Exeter Phoenix: A Plan for Rebuilding,** Architectural Press, London.

Sharp, T. (1948), **Oxford Replanned,** Architectural Press, London.

Sheffield District (1983), **City Centre Plan,** Sheffield.

Starkie, D. N. M. (1982), **The Motorway Age,** Pergamon, Oxford.

Statistisches Bundesamt (1980, 1981, 1982), **Ergebnisse der Beschäftigtenstatistik der BAFA,** Kohlhammer, Wiesbaden.

Statistisches Bundesamt (1951, 1961, 1974, 1976, 1982), **Statistische Jahrbücher für die Bundesrepublick Deutschland 1951, etc.,** Kohlhammer, Wiesbaden.

Stein, C. (1951), **Toward New Towns for America,** Liverpool University Press, Liverpool.

Strathclyde Regional Council (1983), **Transport Policies and Programmes 6, 1983-1988,** Glasgow.

Strathclyde Regional Council (1984), **Arrangement for Servicing Vehicles** (internal report), Glasgow.

Strathclyde PTA (Passenger Transport Authority) and PTE (Passenger Transport Executive) (1982), **Annual Report and Accounts 1981-1982,** Glasgow.

Strathclyde Regional Council, Department of Roads (1982), **Review of Planning Policy in Glasgow Central Area** (internal report), Glasgow.

SYCC (South Yorkshire County Council) and SYPTE (South Yorkshire Passenger Transport Executive) (1981, 1982, 1983), **South Yorkshire Transport, Annual Report and Accounts 1980-1981, 1981-1982, 1982-1983,** Sheffield.

SYCC (South Yorkshire County Council), Joint Officer Working Group, Sheffield City Council (1983), **Central Area District Plan Development Principles and Strategy,** Sheffield.

SYPTE (South Yorkshire Passenger Transport Executive) (1978), **Transport Development Plan,** Sheffield.

SYPTE (South Yorkshire Passenger Transport Executive) (1983a), **Transport Act 1983, The Three Year Plan - 1984/1985 to 1986/1987,** Sheffield.

SYPTE (South Yorkshire Passenger Transport Executive) (1983b), **South Yorkshire Transport, Facts and Figures,** Sheffield.

Tetlow, J., Goss, A. (1965), **Homes, Towns and Traffic,** Faber and Faber, London.

TEST (Transport and Environmental Studies) (1981), **Buses and Pedestrian Areas,** London Transport, London.

Tripp, H. A. (1942), **Town Planning and Road Traffic,** Edward Arnold, London.

TRRL (Transport and Road Resarch Laboratory), Access and Mobility Division (1982), **Public Transport Impact Studies,** Crowthorne.

Tyne and Wear County Council (1979a), **Structure Plan,** Newcastle upon Tyne.

Tyne and Wear County Council (1979b), **Report of Survey,** Newcastle upon Tyne.

Tyne and Wear County Council (1984), **Tyne and Wear Metro Commemoration,** Newcastle upon Tyne.

Tyne and Wear County Council, Tyne and Wear PTE (Passenger Transport Executive) (1981), **Annual Report and Accounts 1980/81,** Newcastle upon Tyne.

Tyne and Wear County Council (1982), **Structure Plan,** Newcastle upon Tyne.

Tyne and Wear PTE (Passenger Transport Executive) (1983), **Tyne & Wear Public Transport Plan 1984/1985,** Newcastle upon Tyne.

Tyne and Wear PTE (Passenger Transport Executive), Howard, D. T. (1984), **Tyne and Wear Metro: A Light Rapid Transit System,** Newcastle upon Tyne.

Tyneside Passenger Transport Authority (1973), **Public Transport on Tyneside - A Plan for the People,** Newcastle upon Tyne.

ÜSTRA (1982a), **Stadtbahnsystem Hannover,** Hannover.

ÜSTRA (1982b), **Geschäftsbericht '81,** Hannover.

ÜSTRA (1983a), **Geschäftsbericht '82,** Hannover.

ÜSTRA (1983b), **Folgewirkungen von Investition im öffentlichen Personennahverkehr, insbesondere Sekundärinvestitionen und Struktureffekte, dargestellt am Beispiel der Stadtbahnstrecke A in Hannover** (Pilotstudie), Schlussbericht, Materialband zum Schlussbericht, Hannover.

van den Berg, L., Drewett, R., Klaaseen, L. H., Rossi, A., Vivverberg, C.H.T. (1982), **A Study of Urban Growth and Decline** (Urban Europe, Volume 1), Pergamon, Oxford.

VÖV (Verband öffentlicher Verkehrsbetriebe) (1964, 1966, 1967, 1969, 1971

VRR (Verkehrsverbund Rhein-Ruhr) (1977), **Verbund in der Entscheidung,** Gelsenkirchen.

VRR (Verkehrsverbund Rhein-Ruhr) (n.d.), **Info 10,** Gelsenkirchen.

VRR (Verkehrsverbund Rhein-Ruhr) (1981), **Erster Verbundbericht,** Gelsenkirchen.

VRR (Verkehrsverbund Rhein-Ruhr) (1981), **Info 2**, Gelsenkirchen.

VRR (Verkehrsverbund Rhein-Ruhr) (1982a), **Info 4**, Gelsenkirchen.

VRR (Verkehrsverbund Rhein-Ruhr) (1982b), **Verbundbericht 81**, Gelsenkirchen.

VRR (Verkehrsverbund Rhein-Ruhr) (1982c), **Info 7**, Gelsenkirchen.

VRR (Verkehrsverbund Rhein-Ruhr) (1983a), **Verbundbericht 82**, Gelsenkirchen

VRR (Verkehrsverbund Rhein-Ruhr) (1983b), **Info 8**, Gelsenkirchen.

Wehner, B. (1973), **Stadt Köln, zusammenfassende Darstellung der Ergebnisse zum Generalverkehrsplan**, Köln.

Wentzel, E. (1982), U-Bahn Nürnberg-Fürth, **Modern Tramway and Light Rail Transit**, 531, pp. 90-97, 532, pp. 134-141.

Wyborn, J. H. (1973), Pedestrianisation in Leeds - an Assessment, **Journal of the Institution of Municipal Engineers**, 100, pp. 253-258.

Young, A. P., Berry, J. C. (1984), **Light Rail Transit in Greater Manchester**, (not published), Manchester.

Index